I0016174

COMPUTER PROGRAMMING FOR BEGINNERS A STEP-BY-STEP GUIDE

THIS BOOK INCLUDES:

KALI LINUX, PYTHON FOR BEGINNERS, LEARN SQL, COMPUTER PROGRAMMING JAVASCRIPT

ADAM HARRIS

Table of Contents

Kali linux:

Python for beginners:

Learn sql:

Computer programming Javascript:

KALI LINUX:

Introduction

Hacking is like cooking. You need to get ready with all the ingredients (i.e. programs) and know in detail about the properties of that ingredients (or programs) and use them together to produce a culinary material. What if the food doesn't taste good? That is if you are unable to get the better results after all the hacking process? There is only one way you can do i.e.; to try again.

There are five important areas you need to learn in detail to master hacking.

1) Information Gathering

2) Automatic Vulnerability Scanning

3) Exploiting

4) Password Attacks

5) Sniffing and wireless attacks

1) Information gathering

Information gathering is always considered a pivotal job hacker should do before attacking a target. It roughly sums up that by using information gathering tools we can acquire a lot of information about the target hosts, which can help us create exploits that would help us create a backdoor for further exploitation. We can even use tons of publicly available information about the target to get a good idea on what strategy we should use to make this attack successful.

2) Automatic Vulnerability scanning

Vulnerability Scanner is a program that automatically finds and discovers security vulnerabilities in computers, network applications, web applications and software. It detects the target system through the network, generates data to the target system, and matches the feedback data with the built-in vulnerability signature database to enumerate the security vulnerabilities existing on the target system. Vulnerability scanning is an indispensable means to ensure system and network security. In the face of Internet intrusion, if users can detect security vulnerabilities through network scanning as soon as possible according to the specific application environment, and timely take appropriate measures to repair, it can effectively prevent the occurrence of intrusion events. Because the work is relatively boring, we can implement it with some convenient tools, such as Nessus and OpenVAS.

3) Exploiting

Exploiting is an important way to gain control of the system. The user finds a vulnerable vulnerability from the target system and then uses the vulnerability to obtain permissions to control the target system. In order to facilitate the user's practice, this chapter will introduce Metasploitable 2 released by Metasploit. Users can use it as a Linux operating system for practice. This chapter will use the vulnerabilities on the Metasploitable system to introduce various penetration attacks, such as MySQL database, PostgreSQL database and Tomcat service.

Privilege escalation is to maximize the minimum privilege a user has. Often, the users we gain access to may have the lowest permissions. However, if you want to perform a penetration attack, you may need the administrator account permissions, so you need to increase the permissions. Permission elevation can be achieved by using fake tokens, local privilege escalation, and social engineering.

4) Password Attacks

A password attack is to recover the password plaintext without knowing the key. Password attacks are an important part of all penetration testing. If you are a penetration tester and don't understand passwords and password cracking, it's hard to imagine. So, no matter what you do or how far our technical capabilities are, passwords still seem to be the most common way to protect data and restrict access to the system. This chapter describes various password attack methods, such as password online attacks, router password attacks, and creating password dictionaries.

5) Sniffing and wireless attacks

This is where people use wireless network tools along with a network adapter to capture packets and crack password or acquire sensitive information from the target. Sniffing tools like Wireshark are famous and can be used for a lot of attacks and finding out the packets.

Information Gathering

Information gathering is an important pre attack phase where the hackers collect a lot of information that is available in public about the target he is going to attack. Many hackers use social engineering techniques to get a solid bunch of information about target and the technology it is using along with the operating system and version it uses. Every hacker uses different set of methodologies to create a good information about the host before targeting.

There are three important phases in information gathering as explained below

1) Gathering information from search engines

Use search engines like Google to get good information about the host you are trying to attack. You will be surprised with the fact that how much you can find information that is public.

2) Social engineering techniques

Social engineering techniques are crazy because you can just psychologically trick an employee or the target you are chasing with a simple thing like phishing email to create a backdoor via your exploit. All great hackers rely on social engineering instead of doing things in a more complex way.

3) Port Scanning

If you are curious to know about what a port scan is associated with follow the next few paragraphs carefully. There are various services provided by the server, such as publishing a home page and sending and receiving e-mails.

Services that perform network communication include a window called "port" for communication, which is managed by numbers. For example, well-known services are basically pre-assigned port numbers, such as 80 for HTTP services that publish their home pages on the Internet and 587 for sending emails.

The act of investigating from the outside (attacker point of view) that what kind of port the server is opening is called "port scan".

How a port scan be done?

Port scanning is the process of sending specific data from the outside and examining the corresponding responses in order to investigate the running services on servers connected to the network. By analyzing the response obtained, you can identify the version of the service running on the server, the OS, etc.

Nmap

Nmap is one of the famous hacking tools and is widely known for its popularity among penetration testers. People often mistake that Nmap is only popular for its information gathering abilities but often doesn't understand that Nmap can also be used as a vulnerability detector that can be automated. It can be used in various operating systems that are open source and in Windows.

Nmap is a powerful tool that can be used for port discovery, host discovery, service discovery, detection of operating system and its version. Nmap can be used in both command line and with graphical user interface (GUI). But remember that good hackers use the Command line.

How Nmap works?

Nmap is programmed in a way such that it can perform scanning using different technologies like TCP and FTP protocol scans. All these scans are prone to their strengths and weaknesses and hackers can understand it vividly when they are trying to attack hosts with Nmap.

In hacking terminology, we call the target technically as the target host. When using Nmap we need to first understand the complexity of target to decide which scan to use either simple easy scan or a complex scan that would take a lot more time. We need to polish our skills to use some very complex and intuitive techniques to get past from intrusion detection systems to get good results.

Below are some strategies that will help you appreciate various operations Nmap can perform:

1) You can scan a single host with the following command

nmap www.hackingtools.com

nmap 192.232.2.1

2) You can scan an entire subnet with the following command

nmap 192.232.2.1/24

3) Nmap can also be used to scan multiple targets with the following command

#nmap 192.232.2.1 192.232.2.4

4) There is also an option in Nmap that will let you scan a range of targets as follows

#nmap 192.232.2.1-100 (This in precise scans every host that is in between the IP addresses 192.232.2.1 and 192.232.2.100)

5) Nmap has an option where you can store all the Ip addresses you have in a text file that is in .txt format and place in the same directory of Nmap so that it can scan every IP address present in the text file without manually entering each one of them.

#nmap -iL sampleip.txt

6) If you want to see a list of all the hosts you need to scan you can enter the following command

#nmap -sL 192.232.2.1/24

7) Nmap provides an option where we can exclude a single IP address from scanning with subnet hosts

#nmap 192.232.2.1/24 -exclude 192.232.2.4

   And if you want to exclude more than one IP, you can include all of them in a text file so that they can be excluded while doing the subnet scan like shown below.

#nmap 192.232.2.1/24 -exclude excludeIp.txt

Before learning about the scanning procedures Nmap offers let us know about scanning ports on a specific host. You can scan individual ports in a host using the following command.

#nmap -p78,56,23 192.232.2.1

Scanning technology in Nmap

There are different types of scanning strategies that Nmap follows to do the work. In this section, we will describe about these procedures in detail along with few commands that will give you a good overview.

1) sS scan (Tcp SYN)

This is a typical scan that Nmap uses if nothing is specified by the hacker to the software. In this scan usually, Nmap will not give a full handshake to the target system. It will just send an SYN packet to the target host, which will then check for any open ports, but not creating any sessions that may be used after logging. This is one of the greatest strengths of this scanning strategy. To use this scan the hacking tool should be given root access otherwise it will show an error. Below we give the command line for this scan.

hacking@kali #nmap -sS 262.232.2.1

2) sT scan (TCP connect)

If the sS scan is not used due to the reason that it is not feasible for the current attack situation people normally use sT scan as their next savior. It gives three handshakes with open ports and calls a method called connect () which makes the software to find TCP ports. sT scan when preferred can also be used to find UDP ports although people use it rarely.

  Below is the command for -sT scan:

hacking @kali #nmap -sT 292.232.2.1

3) sU scan (UDP scan)

This scanning is also in the penetration-testing checklist after the importance of -sS scan. There is no need to send SYN packets like in TCP scan because this will just find UDP ports that are open. When the hackers start using the scan A UDP packet reaches the target host and waits for a positive response. If at all a response is received an open port is found. If it sends an error message with an Echo command then the port is closed.

Below is the command line for -sU scan

hacking @ kali #nmap -sU 292.232.2.1

4) sF scan (FIN scan)

This is a special type of scan that is used because some targets may have installed intrusion detection systems and firewalls that stop SYN packets that are sent using a TCP scan. For this sole reason, Fin scan is used if there is any extra detection scan happening on the other side. Fin scan does not save any log information to be detected so there is a great chance of the Fin packet to find out few open ports by sneaking into the target systems.

Here is the command for -sF scan

hacking@kali #nmap -sF 292.232.2.1

5) sP scan (Ping scan)

Ping is a famous network protocol method that checks whether a host is live or not by trying to connect to the target host. Ping scanning in Nmap also is used for the same purpose and is not used to check open ports. Ping scan asks for root access to start a scan. If you are not ready to provide the administrative privileges you can just use the connect method to start a ping sweep from Nmap.

Here is the command for -sP scan

hacking @ kali #nmap -sP 292.232.2.1

6) sV scan (version detection scan)

A version detection scan is one of the obsessive usages of Nmap for hackers. To attack a target system, you need to know about the technology and operating system the host is using so you create your exploits and backdoor strategies to break into the system. However, unlike TCP scans version detection scan takes a lot of time because when we start a sV scan in the background TCP scan gets started and searches for the open ports. After the hunt for open ports gets finished sV scan automatically analyzes them and determines the information about the target host. Due to this complex procedure, it may take a lot of time.

Here is the command for -sV scan

hacking @ kali #nmap -sV 292.232.2.1

7) sL scan (Idle scan)

This is one of the craziest features of Nmap because it just acts like a proxy server while doing attacks.

When using idle scan you can send packets using another host Ip. This anonymity can help hackers to stay in the dark if something goes wrong or severe. Protecting himself from the investigation is what every hacker strives for especially in these modern times.

Here is the command for -sL scan

hacking @ kali #nmap -sL 292.432.2.6 292.432.2.1

Things Nmap can detect:

Nmap can detect the Device type of the host that is (router, workgroup, etc.), running operating system, operating system details i.e. version and network distance (approximate distance between the target and the attacker).

While using Nmap always use ping scan only when necessary because some firewalls in the target hosts can detect that an attack is going to happen and will block the attacker's addresses to make any connection.

By using the below command you are saying to the software that doesn't ping the remote host:

hacking @ kali # nmap -O -PN 292.428.5.6/ 12

Using the-PN parameter can bypass the Ping Command, but it does not affect the discovery of the host system. NMAP operating system detection is based on open and closed ports. If Os scan cannot detect at least one open or closed port, it will return the following error.

The error code is below:

Warning: we cannot find any open or closed ports to get information on the target system

It is difficult to accurately detect the remote operating system with NMAP, so we need to use NMAP's guess function, osscan-guess operation guesses which operating system type is closest to the target.

#nmap -O -osscan -guess 192.232.2.1

Before going to talk about Nessus let us have a simple exercise. Please try to do this Exercise for better understanding of the Information Gathering.

Exercise:

Start kali Linux terminal and enter into Nmap using the commands. Find the subnet masks for www.nmap.com and find the operating system and version that it uses. Complete different scans and create a detailed report on all the ports that are available.

Chapter 1 How to Setup and Install Kali Linux a USB Key

Kali Linux is the best hacking tool out there. It is super secure, and it is made by seasoned professionals who know what they are doing. What's so great about this system is that you can run it from a USB key and not have to worry about compromising or altering your current operating system. When you carry this OS on a USB key, it can be taken to any computer or compatible device and made to work. It only temporarily overrides the current operating system on that device.

Once you take out your USB key, you remove Kali Linux from the device. It doesn't leave behind any trace, and it doesn't change the settings or operating system of the device you used it on. It is compatible with any operating system because it works around them.

This is considered a non-destructive way to use Kali Linux. It lets everything go back to normal on whatever device you use it on, making no changes to the host's system. It's also portable, so you can take it from one workstation to the next and from one device to the next and do what you need to do. It starts up very fast, usually in just a few minutes, on whatever system you put it into.

You can also customize your bootable drive, using a Kali Linux ISO image that you rolled yourself. It is also potentially persistent. This means that, once you perform the proper configurations, your Kali Linux Live drive will keep the data it has collected no matter how many times you reboot it.

Installing onto Your Bootable USB Key

For Windows users, you will have to first download the Win32 Disk Imager utility. You'll find that here.

https://launchpad.net/win32-image-writer

If you are using a Linux or an OS X, just use the dd command. This has already been installed on both of th§ose platforms.

We recommend using a 4GB USB thumb drive or larger. If you want to use an SD card, then that's fine, since the procedure is the same for both. Just make sure the devices you are going to be using it on are compatible with your storage device.

The method for doing this will differ depending on what OS you have. We'll break it down on both of the major ones for you.

For Windows

Start by plugging your USB drive into a USB port on a PC operating Windows. Pay attention to the drive designator that it uses when it starts to mount. That designator will look like "F:\". Then launch the Win32 Disk Imager software. Once you open that software, pick out the Kali Linux ISO file you downloaded. Then click "Write" to copy it onto the USB drive, be sure you pick the right drive for this operation.

When the imaging process is finished, you can take out your USB. On most Windows OS, you will need to click on the small arrow near the bottom right corner of your screen to open a tab that shows connected devices. Be sure to click on your USB drive there to safely eject it and ensure that no information is lost when you disconnect it.

Once all that is done, you can boot Kali Linux from your USB device.

For Linux

Doing the same thing on a Linux is equally easy. Start with the verified ISO image and copy it over to the drive using the dd command. You have to be running as a root for this to work. Alternatively, you can execute the dd command using sudo. The instructions we're going to give you assume that you have a Linux Mint 17.1 desktop. Other versions are going to vary slightly, but the basic operations required for this task should all be about the same.

Just a word of warning before we get into the actual instruction: if you aren't sure what you are doing with dd command or you just aren't careful, you can accidently overwrite something you aren't meaning to. Be sure to double check everything you are doing so you don't make any mistakes.

Start by identifying the device path you are going to use to write the image onto the USB drive. Before the drive is inserted, perform the command "sudo fdisk -1"

You have to be using elevated privileges with fdisk, otherwise there won't be any output. Enter the above command in a terminal window at a command prompt. If you did it properly, you should see a single drive. That will probably look like this "/dev/sda". That drive will be separated into three partitions. These are /dev/sda1, /dev/sda2, and /dev/sda5.

From there, plug in the USB drive, then run the original command again. That's sudo fdisk -1. Once you do that, you will see another device that wasn't there initially. It could look something like this: "/dev/sdb".

Then take the ISO file and image it onto the USB device. It may take 10-15 minutes to image the USB device, so be patient. In order to perform this process, you need to execute the command below:

dd   if=kali-linux-1.0.9a-amd32.iso   of=/dev/sdb bs=512k

Let's dissect this command for a second. In the example we are using here, the ISO image that you want to write onto the drive is named "kali-linux-1.0.9a-amd32.iso". Yours may look slightly different. Note the "32" in the name. This refers to the size of the image. We use the blocksize value "bs=512k" because it is safe and reliable. You can make it bigger if you want, but that can cause some problems, so it isn't recommended.

Once the command is completed, then it will provide feedback and not before then. Your drive could have an access indicator. If it does, then it will blink every so often. How long this whole process takes will depend on a few factors- how fast your system is, what kind of USB drive you are using and how well your USB port works. The output, once the imaging is complete, will tell you how many bytes are copied and give you numbers for records in and out, which should be the same number.

Now your USB is ready to boot into a Kali Live environment.

Chapter 1 Darknet Markets

Just how safe is a Darknet in light of the vulnerabilities discussed? The short answer is, *as safe as you make it.*

You are the weak link. The last link in the security chain. And although you need Tor to access Onion sites, the term can apply to any anonymous network - networks like I2P or Freenet or anything else that cloaks the source of data transmit, and by extension, your identity.

Which brings us to the *Darknet Marketplace*.

The complete list of such marketplaces on the deep web are numerous, and the risk of getting scammed is quite high. It's one reason why you may not have heard about them. They are often taken down quickly by either a venomous reputation or a law enforcement bust. Sometimes they piss off the wrong people and then spammers ddos the site. But there are numerous places one can go if you're curious about what is sold by whom.

When I say *sold*, what I mean is, anything you want that cannot be gained through the usual legal channels. And remember that what is legal in one country may be illegal in another. In Canada, lolicon comics are illegal and can get you in big trouble if you cross the border. But not in America. In the USA you can pretty much write any story you want. In Canada? TEXT stories involving minors are verboten.

The other difference is that there are safety nets in buying almost anything in a first world country on the open market. Think BestBuy. Mom and Pop stores. Florist shops. If customers get injured, what happens? Customers sue via the legal safety net and make a lot of lawyers a lot of money.

But the Darknet Marketplace laughs at any such safety nets. In fact, you're likely to get scammed at least a few times before finding a reputable dealer for whatever goods you seek. And it really doesn't matter what it is, either - Teleportation devices? Pets? Exotic trees? It's all the same that goes around. Whatever is in demand will attract unsavory types and not just on the buyer's end.

Therefore, research any darknet market with Tor, being careful to visit forums and check updated information to see if any sites have been flagged as suspicious or compromised. Some other advice:

- Always use PGP to communicate.

- Never store crypto-currency at any such marketplace.

- Assume a den of thieves unless proven otherwise by *them*. The responsibility is theirs just as it is offline, to prove they are an honest business. If you open your own, keep this in mind: customers owe you nothing. You can only betray them once.

Now for some examples of Phishers and Scammers and other Con men. By their fruits, ye shall know them.

1.) SILK ROAD 2.0 *(e5wvymnx6bx5euvy...)* Lots of scams with this one. Much like Facebook and Google emails, you can tell a fake sometimes by the address. Paste the first few letters into a shortcut next to the name. If it doesn't match, steer clear.

2.) **Green Notes Counter**
(67yjqewxrd2ewbtp...)
They promised counterfeit money to their customers but refuse escrow. A dead giveaway.

3.) *iPhones for half off: (IPHONEAVZHWKQMAP...)*

Now here is a prime example of a scam. Any website which sells electronic gadgets on the deep web is ripe for scamming customers. Whereas in the Far East you will merely get counterfeit phones with cheap, Chinese made parts that break within a month, on the Deep Web they will simply take your money and say adios. Actually, they won't even bother saying that.

So then, how does one tell a scam?

Because many new darknet vendors will arise out of thin air, with rare products that will make customers swoon and send them money - without doing any research on their name or previous sales. A real hit and run operation. Hit quick and fast and dirty. Seduce as many as they can before the herd catches on to the wolf in disguise. Many are suckered, thinking "it's only a little money, but a little money from a lot of Tor users goes a long way in encouraging other scammers to set up shop.

When you ask them why they do not offer escrow, they say "We think it is unreliable/suspicious/unstable" amid other BS excuses. It is better to hold on to your small change than leave a trail to your treasure chest. And make no mistake some of these scammers are like bloodhounds where identity theft is concerned.

Do your research! Check forums and especially the dates of reviews they have. Do you notice patterns? Are good reviews scattered over a long period of time or is it rather all of a sudden--the way some Amazon affiliate marketers do with paid reviews that glow? Not many reviews from said customers?

If you've seen the movie "Heat," with Al Pacino and Robert de Niro, you know when it is time to Walk Away. In the middle of a nighttime heist, Niro goes outside for a smoke. He hears a distant cough. Somewhere. Now, this is middle of the night in an unpopulated part of the city that comes from across the street - a parking lot full of what he thought were empty trailers. Hmm, he thinks maybe this isn't such a great night for a hot score. Not so empty (it was a cop in a trailer full of other hotshot cops). He walks back into the bank and tells his partner to abort.

The other aspect is time. Some fake sites will set a short ship time and count on you not bothering to see the sale as finalized before you can whistle Dixie out of your ass. After finalization, you're screwed since the money is in their wallet before you can even mount a protest.

Fraud Prevention

One is Google believe it or not, at

http://www.google.com/imghp.

Dating sites like Cherry Blossoms and Cupid sometimes use reverse image search to catch fakers and Nigerian scammers masquerading as poor lonely singles to deprive men of their coinage. If they can catch them, so can you. If the image belongs to some other legit site, chances are it is fake. **Foto Forensics** also does the same, and reports metadata so that it becomes even harder to get away with Photoshop trickery.

When it is Okay to FE (Finalize Early)

FE means 'Finalize Early'. It's use online can usually be found in black marketplaces like Silk Road and Sheep's Marketplace. It simply means that money in escrow is released before you receive your product. Every customer I've ever spoken with advises against this unless you've had great experience with that business.

But... quite a few vendors are now making it a *standard practice* to pay funds up front before you have anything in your hands.

On more than one Marketplace forum, there's been heated exchange as to when this is proper. You might hear, "Is this guy legit? What about this Chinese outfit over here? He seems shady," and others: "A friend said this guy is okay but then I got ripped off!". You get the idea.

Here is my experience on the matter.

1.) It is okay when you are content with not getting what you paid for. This may seem counterproductive, but think how many gamblers go into a Las Vegas casino and never ask themselves "How much can I afford to lose?"

The answer, sadly, is not many. Vegas was not built on the backs of losers. Some merchants do not like escrow at all. Some do. So don't spend more than you can afford to lose. Look at it the way a gambler looks at making money.

2.) It is okay when you are guaranteed shipment. There are FE scammers out there that will give you an angelic smile and lie right into your eyes as they swindle you. Do not depend solely on reviews. A guy on SR can be the best merchant this side of Tatooine and yet you will wake up one day and find yourself robbed. He's split with a million in BTC and you're left not even holding a bag. Most won't do this to you. But a few will.

When it is NOT Okay to FE

When losing your funds will result in you being evicted or a relationship severed. Never borrow money from friends and especially not family unless you want said family to come after you with a double-bladed ax. If you get ripped off, you lose not only the cash but the respect and trustworthiness of your family. Word spreads. You don't pay your debts. What's that saying in Game of Thrones?

Right. A Lannister always pays his debts. So should you.

MultiSigna

Sounds like something from Battlestar Galactica to pass from ship to ship. A badge of honor perhaps some hotshot flyboy wears on his fighter jacket that bypassed a lot of red tape.

While not exactly mandatory, it makes for interesting reading, and is something Tor users might want to know about if they wish to make purchases anonymously. Here's what happens:

When a purchase is enacted, the seller deposits money (in this case, Bitcoins) in a multi-signature address. After this, the customer gets notification to make the transaction ($,€) to the seller's account.

Then after the seller relays to MultiSigna that the transaction was a success, MultiSigna creates a transaction from the multi-signature address that requires both buyer and seller so that it may be sent to the network. The buyer gets the Bitcoins and ends the sale. Confused yet? I was too at first. You'll get used to it.

Critical

MultiSigna only exists as a verifier/cosigner of the entire transaction. If there is disagreement between seller and buyer, NO EXCHANGE occurs. Remember the scene in Wargames when two nuclear silo operators have to turn their keys simultaneously in order to launch? Yeah, that.

MultiSigna will of course favor one or the other, but not both if they cannot mutually agree. The upside is that is if the market or purchaser or vendor loses a key, two out of three is still available. A single key cannot spend the money in 2/3 MultiSig address.

Is it Safe? Is it Secret?

I don't recommend enacting a million dollar exchange for a yacht, or even a thousand dollar one as they both carry risk, but ultimately it is up to you.

Just remember that trust is always an issue on darknets, and you're generally safer making several transfers with a seller/buyer who has a good history of payment. In other words, reputation as always, is everything.

Alas, there are a few trustworthy markets that have good histories of doing things properly, thank heavens.

Blackbank is one. **Agora** is another. Take a look at the Multi-Sig Escrow Onion page here with Tor:

http://u5z75duioy7kpwun.onion/wiki/index.php/Multi-Sig_Escrow

Security

What the effect would be if a hacker gained entry to the server? What mischief might he make? What chaos could he brew if he can mimic running a withdrawal in the same manner that the server does?

If a hacker were to gain access and attempt to withdraw money, a single-signature would be applied and passed to the second sig signer for co-signature. Then the security protocol would kick in where these policies would be enforced:

1.) Rate limits: the rate of stolen funds slows

2.) Callbacks to the spender's server: Signing service verifies with the original spender that they initiated and intended to make the spend. The callback could go to a separated machine, which could only contain access to isolated approved withdrawal information.

3.) IP limiting: The signing service only signs transactions coming from a certain list of IPs, preventing the case where the hacker or insider stole the private key.

4.) Destination Whitelists: Certain very high security wallets can be set such that the signing service would only accept if the destination were previously known. The hacker would have to compromise both the original sending server as well as the signing service.

Let me repeat that MultiSigna are *never in possession* of your bitcoins. They use 2 of 3 signatures (seller, buyer & MultiSigma) to sign a transaction. Normal transactions are signed by the seller and then by the buyer.

Purchaser Steps for MultiSig Escrow

1.) Deposit your Bitcoins. Purchase ability is granted after 6 confirmations

2.) Make a private & public key (Brainwallet.org is a JavaScript Client-Side Bitcoin Address Generator)

3.) Buy item, input public-key & a refund BTC address

4.) Retrieve purchased item

5.) Input the private key and close

Chapter 2 Web Security

In this chapter, we will briefly talk about web security and about some attacks that you need to have in mind. I'm absolutely sure you've heard a lot of times on TV, radio or from other sources of the company's X site being broken, the organization's Y site being down and hackers replacing the main site with a fake page.

Well, I want to tell you that at large (Less Experienced Hackers) they all look for many vulnerabilities well known to their sites 1 to 2 that they can take advantage of. There are many tools that help them locate these vulnerabilities relatively easily, and then help them exploit them.

Some of these vulnerabilities (web-level) are extremely well presented and documented in the Open Web Application Security Project (*OWASP*). OWASP is a nonprofit organization dedicated to improving the security of software and web applications.

They have a *top 10* with the most commonly reported security incidents in previous years on websites and web applications. OWASP organizes even local events (you can research on Google or Facebook for such events), creating a community of passionate cyber security people.

If you hear at some point of such an event and you have the opportunity to go, I recommend you to take this step because you will see that it is worthwhile first and secondly that you learn a lot of things from many people.

As you can see for the most part, it's about the same type of vulnerabilities, with the top changing very little over a three-year period. We will only take some of these attacks and explain to you what each person represents and how you can do them on your own site.

Here are the attacks, we will discuss further:

- SQL injection

- **XSS**
- Security Misconfiguration

Now let's start talking about web attacks with the first attack / vulnerability (and most common) from the list above:

1) SQL Injection

When we talk about SQL injection, we are talking primarily about databases, and secondly about the attack (a vulnerability) at their level. Let's first look at what SQL is. *SQL* (*S*tructured *Q*uery *L*anguage) is a query language with databases. It is used to communicate directly with the database through various commands addressed to it. There are several types / forms of SQL, but the basics are the same.

Where are the SQL injection attacks? Most often these occur when the attacker finds a "box" in which he can enter data. For example, think about a search box in which anyone can write anything.

If the back code (most often PHP) is not written properly, then the hacker can enter SQL commands that interact directly with the database, so they can extract different information.

Now I want you to think that when you interact with an "input form" (a box where you can write and send something to the server), this happens:

```
███████████████████████████████████████
```

That is, PHP language will generate such an order to interact (and search) with the database. In the place where '%' appears, it will be replaced with what you enter in that input form.

Here's an example of a SQL code that can be entered in this field (ATTENTION: it will not work for any site. I suggest using the bWAPP application and testing it):

```
 OR 1=1;--
```

You can try on **this site** (https://sqlzoo.net/hack/) to enter the SQL statement above instead of the username and password.

SQLmap (http://sqlmap.org/) is a great tool you can use to *test database vulnerabilities* on a site. SQLmap will do all these queries that automatically automate SQL injection for you (and even try to break the hash of the passwords you will find in the database).

Another reason why WordPress is so used is due to the number of existing plugins that can be used to improve the site, user experience, etc. So the person who manages a site / blog using such a CMS does NOT need programming skills because the plugins deal (mostly) with everything that's needed. There are over 50,000 free plugins available in the WordPress marketplace, and besides these, the paid ones that have been developed by different companies.

Another very interesting aspect related to WordPress is that he is Open Source. This means it is developed by a community of programmers to whom anyone can take part.

As running technologies, WordPress needs *LAMP* (*Linux, Apache, MySQL, PHP*). Each of these components is critical in running a site. If you are not familiar with LAMP I will briefly explain what each component is:

> 1. *Linux* - The OS on which the site will work, the reason being simple: a flexible,

stable OS and more secure than Windows

2. *Apache* - The web server used to host the site, most widespread in the Internet

3. *MySQL* - The database used by WordPress to store the information site (articles,

users, comments and any other type of content that requires storage)

4. *PHP* - The programming language that interacts with each component (base data, web server and OS). PHP is a web programming language used on the backhand side (what we do not see when we access a site)

If you want to install WordPress for your own use, you will need a web hosting server. I recommend you USE THIS ONE (BLUEHOST) - http://bit.ly/2HvO3je- (which provides you with 1-click install so you can start immediately using your WordPress site.

Now, after installing WordPress, I suggest we move on to a security scanning tool for your website.

WPScan

WPScan is a scan tool (and of course a crack) of a WordPress-based site. It is open source, so it can be used by anyone who wants to test their site for vulnerabilities. This tool can give you a lot of information about your site:

- The WordPress version used (a very good indicator)
- Plugins installed
- Potential vulnerabilities existing on the site, which can then be exploited
- Finding existing users on the site
- Making Brute Force attacks by using a password finder

Often, scanning can be perceived as actively testing your system to see what you can find through it. You can compare this concept to the one in which someone (stranger) wants to "see" what you have in the house. Enter the door (without you being home) and start looking through your things, but do not take anything in order to use that information later.

Makes a non-intrusive scan ():

 # wpscan --url www.example.com

Enumerates (lists) the installed plugins:

 # wpscan --url www.example.com --enumerate p

Runs all enumeration tools in order to learn as much information as possible:

 # wpscan --url www.example.com -- enumerate

List the existing users on the site:

 # wpscan --url www.example.com -- enumerate u

These are some ways to use the WPScan tool. In below, I placed my first order on a WordPress-based site (whose identity I will not publish) to see what information we can find out about it. I mention that I was authorized to do such a scan on this site.
And from a simple scan of how many vulnerabilities I found on this site (he definitely needs an update). As you see, there are many vulnerabilities that can be exploited using different methods. Moreover, there are also these **CVE**S (*Common Vulnerability and Exposures*) https://www.cvedetails.com/browse-by-date.php that describe the vulnerability and how it can be exploited.

Because we're talking about WordPress and *vulnerabilities* after all, **HERE** (https://wpvulndb.com/) you can see a database that contains all the *vulnerabilities known* and made *public* for each version. In addition to this, I want to tell you that all the attacks, we have talked about in this chapter also apply to the WordPress case. Unfortunately, *SQLi, XSS, Traversal Directory* are only a few (of many) attacks that can be done relatively easily on this platform. With WPScan all you do is find them much faster.

It's important *to be aware* of them, to frequently scan your website (yourself or a client), discover new vulnerabilities, and do them to resolve them as quickly as possible.

5) Google Hacking

I think you had a slightly different reaction when you saw the title of this topic: "Wow! can I hack up Google?" or "can I hack with Google?" I can tell you yes, in the 2nd situation (although the first is not excluded: D). You can use Google to discover different sites that have certain *pages indexed* in the search engine. Thus, using a few specific search keywords, Google can give you exactly what you are looking for (*sites* that contain exactly the *URL* you are looking for with a vulnerable plug-in, a database information page like that be the user, the password and the name of the database, etc.).

Yes, site administrators are not mindful (probably not even aware) of their site being able to *leak valuable information on Google*, making it extremely exposed to Internet attacks.

Again, I give you this information because you can use it for ethical purposes (to research and test your site or that of a customer). Do not forget that unauthorized access to a system will be penalized and you may take a few years in prison for this (I know a few people who have suffered this ...).

Now that you have remembered this, here are some examples where you can do a research. With this search, Google will display sites that have a WordFence plugin (a site security plug-in - firewall, virus scanner, etc.)

inurl:"/wp-content/plugins/wordfence/"
This was just one example (in). Of course you can replace search content by "*inurl:*" with whatever you want, depending on your current interest.

By following the order in Google Search, you will be able to see different sites depending on the version of WordPress they use. Then you can use WPScan and find out more about the vulnerabilities that exist on it, then you can try to take advantage of it (ethically). You will see that there are many very old, extremely vulnerable versions of WordPress. What I recommend you is to get in touch with the site admin, to make him aware that he is exposed to a massive risk and to ask him to let you prove it (that is, attacking his site) : D).

inurl:"wordpress readme.html"

Chapter 3 Information Gathering Tools

The beginning of any attacks initiates from the stage of information gathering. When you gather as much information about the target, the attack becomes an easy process. Having information about the target also results in a higher success rate of the attack. A hacker finds all kinds of information to be helpful.

The process of information gathering includes:

1. Gathering information that will help in social engineering and ultimately in the attack
2. Understanding the range of the network and computers that will be the targets of the attack
3. Identifying and understanding all the complete surface of the attack i.e. processes and systems that are exposed
4. Identifying the services of a system that are exposed, and collecting as much information about them as possible
5. **Querying specific service that will help fetch useful data such as usernames**

We will now go through Information Gathering tools available in Kali Linux one by one.

Nmap and Zenman

Ethical hacking is a phase in Kali Linux for which the tools NMap and ZenMap are used. NMap and ZenMap are basically the same tool. ZenMap is a Graphical Interface for the NMap tool which works on the command line.

The NMap tool which is for security auditing and discovery of network is a free tool. Apart from penetration testers, it is also used by system administrators and network administrators for daily tasks such as monitoring the uptime of the server or a service and managing schedules for service upgrades.

NMap identifies available hosts on a network by using IP packets which are raw. This also helps NMap identify the service being hosted on the host which includes the name of the application and the version. Basically, the most important application it helps identify on a network is the filter or the firewall set up on a host.

Stealth Scan

The Stealth scan is also popularly known as the hal open scan or SYN. It is called the half open scan because it refrains from completing the usual three-way handshake of TCP. So how it works is a SYN packet is sent by an attacker to the target host. The target host will acknowledge the SYN and sent a SYN/ACK in return. If a SYN/ACK is received, it can be safely assumed that the connection to the target host will complete and the port is open and listening on the target host. If the response received is RST instead, it is safe to assume that the port is close or not active on the target host.

acccheck

The acccheck tool was developed has an attack tool consisting of a password dictionary to target Windows Authentication processes which use the SMB protocol. The accccheck is basically a wrapper script which is injected in the binary of 'smbclient' and therefore depends on the smbclient binary for execution.

Server Message Block (SMB) protocol is an implementation of Microsoft for file sharing over a network and is popularly known as the Microsoft SMB Protocol.

It was then extended to the SMB "Inter-Process Communication" (IPC) system which implements named pipes and was one of the first inter process services that programmers got access to and which served as a means of inheritance for multiple services for authentication as they would all use the same credentials as that which were keyed in for the very first connection to the SMB server.

Amap

Amap is a scanning too of the next generation that allows a good number of options and flags in its command line syntax making it possible to identify applications and processes even if the ports that they are running on are different.

For example, a web server by default accepts connections on port 80. But most companies may change this port to something else such as 1253 to make the server secure. This change would be easily discovered by Amap.

Furthermore, if the services or applications are not based on ASCII, Amap is still able to discover them. Amap also has a set of interesting tools, which have the ability to send customized packets which will generate specific responses from the target host.

Amap, unlike other network tools is not just a simple scanner, which was developed with the intention of just pinging a network to detect active hosts on the network. Amap is equipped with amapcrap, which is a module that sends bogus and completely random data to a port. The target port can be UDP, TCP, SSL, etc. The motive is to force the target port to generate a response.

CaseFile

A huge number of Maltegousers were using Maltego to try and build graphical data from offline investigations and that is how CaseFile was born. Since there was no need of the transform provided by Maltego and the real need was just the graphing capability of Maltego in and more flexible way, CaseFile was developed.

CaseFile, being an application of visual intelligence, helps to determine the relationships, connections and links in the real world between information of different types. CaseFile lets you understand the connections between data that may apart from each other by multiple degrees of separation by plotting the relationships between them graphically. Additionally, CaseFile comes bundled with many more entities that are useful in investigations making it a tool that is efficient. You can also add your custom entities to CaseFile, which allows you to extend this tool to your own custom data sets.

braa

Braa is a tool that is used for scanning mass Simple Network Management Protocol (SNMP). The tool lets you make SNMP queries, but unlike other tools which make single queries at a time to the SNMP service, braa has the capability to make queries to multiple hosts simultaneously, using one single process. The advantage of braa is that it scans multiple hosts very fast and that too by using very limited system resources.

Unlike other SNMP tools, which require libraries from SNMP to function, braa implements and maintains its own stack of SNMP. The implementation is very complex and dirty. Supports limited data types, and cannot be called up to standard in any case. However braa was developed to be a fast tool and it is fast indeed.

dnsmap

dnsmap is a tool that came into existence originally in 2006 after being inspired from the fictional story "The Thief No One Saw" by Paul Craig.

A tool used by penetration testers in the information gathering stage, dnsmap helps discover the IP of the target company, domain names, netblocks, phone numbers, etc.

Dnsmap also helps on subdomain brute forcing which helps in cases where zone transfers of DNS do not work. Zone transfers are not allowed publicly anymore nowadays which makes dnsmap the need of the hour.

DotDotPwn

The dotdotpwn tool can be defined simply to call it a fuzzer. What is a fuzzer? A fuzzer is a testing tool that targets software for vulnerabilities by debugging and penetrating through it. It scans the code and looks for flaws and loopholes, bad data, validation errors, parameters that may be incorrect and other anomalies of programming.

Whenever an anomaly is encountered by the software, the software may become unresponsive, making way for the flaws to give an open door to an attack. For example, if you are an attacker whose target is a company's web server, with the help of dotdotpwn, you will be able to find a loophole in the code of the web server. Perhaps there has been a latest HTTP update on the server overnight. Using a fuzzer on the web server shows you there is an exploit with respect to data validation which leaves an open door for a DoS attack. You can now exploit this vulnerability, which will make the server crash and server access will be denied to genuine employees of the company. There are many such errors that can be discovered using a fuzzer and it is very common for technology to have error when it releases something new in the market and it takes time to identify the error and fix it.

Another example would be an attack with respect to SQL called SQLi where 'i' stands for injection. SQL injection attacks are achieved by injecting SQL database queries through web forms that are available on a website. The conclusion is that software will always be vulnerable allowing attackers to find a way to break their way into the system.

Fierce

Fierce is a Kali tool which is used to scan ports and map networks. Discovery of hostnames across multiple networks and scanning of IP spaces that are non-contiguous can be achieved by using Fierce. It is a tool much like Nmap but in case of Fierce, it is used specifically for networks within a corporate.

Once the target network has been defined by a penetration tester, Fierce runs a whole lot of tests on the domains in the target network and retrieves information that is valuable and which can be analyzed and exploited by the attacker.

Fierce has the following features.

- Capabilities for a brute-force attack through custom and built-in test list

- Discovery of nameservers

- Zone transfer attacks

- Scan through IP ranges both internal and external

- Ability to modify the DNS server for reverse host lookups

Wireshark

Wireshark is a kali too that is an open source analyzer for network and works on multiple platforms such as Linux, BSD, OS X and Windows.

It helps one understand about the functioning of a network thus making it of use in government infrastructure, education industries and other corporates.

It is similar to the tcpdump tool, but WIreshark is a notch above as it has a graphical interface through which you can filter and organize the data that has been captured, which means that it takes less time to analyze the data further. There is also an only text based version known as tshark, which has almost the same amount of features.

Wireshark has the following features.

- The interface has a user-friendly GUI

- Live capture of packets and offline analysis

- Support for Gzip compression and extraction

- Inspection of full protocol

- Complete VOiP analysis

- Supports decryption for IPsec, Kerberos, SSL/TLS, WPA/WPA2

URLCrazy

URLCrazy is a Kali tool that can that tests and generates typos and variations in domains to target and perform URL hijacking, typo squatting and corporate espionage. It has a database that can generate variants of up to 15 types for domains, and misspellings of up to 8000 common spellings. URLCrazy supports a variety of keyboard layouts, checks if a particular domain is in use and figures how popular a typo is.

The Harvester

The Harvester is a Kali tool that is not your regular hacking tool. Whenever there is a mention of hacking tools that are implemented using the command line, one usually thinks of tools like Nmap, Reaver, Metasploit and other utilities for wireless password cracking. However, the harvester refrains from using algorithms that are advanced to break into firewalls, or crack passwords, or capture the data of the local network.

Instead, the Harvester simply gathers publicly available information such as employee names, email addresses, banners, subdomains and other information in the same range. You may wonder as to why it collects this data. Because this data is very useful in the primary stage of information gathering. All this data helps study and understand the target system which makes attacking easier for the hacker or the penetration tester.

Furthermore, it helps the attacker understand as to how big and Internet footprint the target has. It also helps organizations to know how much publicly available information their employees have across the Internet. The latest version of the Harvester has updates which lets it keep intervals between the requests it makes to pages on the Internet, improves search sources, plotting of graphs and statistics, etc.

The Harvester crawls through the Internet as your surrogate, looking for information on your behalf as long as the criteria provided by you matches the information on the Internet. Given that you can also gather email addresses using the Harvester, this tool can be very useful to a hacker who is trying to penetrate an online login by gaining access to the email account of an individual.

Metagoofil

Metagoofil is a kali tool that is aimed at fetching publicly available such as pdf, xls, doc, ppt, etc. documents of a company on the Internet.

The tool makes a Google search to scan through documents and download them to the local machine. It then extracts the metadata of the documents using libraries such as pdfminer, hachoir, etc. It then feeds the information gathering process with the results of its report which contains usernames, server or machine names and software version which helps penetration testers with their investigation.

Miranda

Miranda is a Kali tool that is actively or passively used to detect UPnP hosts, its services, its devices and actions, all through on single command. The Service state parameters and their associated actions are correlated automatically and are then processed as input/output variables for every action. Miranda uses a single data structure to store information of all the hosts and allows you access to that data structure and all its contents.

Let's discuss what exactly ÚPnP is. Universal Plug and Play or UPnP is a protocol for networking that allows devices on the network such as computers, printers, routers mobile devices, etc. to discover each other seamlessly over a network and established services between them for sharing of data, entertainment and other communication. It is ideally for networks inside a private residence as opposed to corporate infrastructure.

Ghost Phisher

Ghost Phisher is a Kali tool, which is used as an attack software program and also for security auditing of wired and wireless networks. It is developed using the Python programming language and the Python GUI library. The program basically emulates access points of a network therefore, deploying its own internal server into a network.

Fragroute

Fragroute is a Kali tool that is used for intercepting, modifying and rewriting traffic that is moving toward a specific host. Simply put, the packets from attacking system known as frag route packets are routed to the destination system. It is used for bypassing firewalls mostly by attackers and security personnel. Information gathering is a well-known use case for fragroute as well which used by penetration testers who use a remote host, which is highly secured.

Masscan

Masscan is a Kali tool, which is used by penetration testers all around the world and has been in the industry for a long time. It is a tool of reconnaissance which has the capability to transmit up to 10 million packets every second. The transmission used by masscan is asynchronous and it has custom stack of TCP/IP. Therefore, the threads used for sending and receiving packets are unique.

Masscan is used to simultaneously attack a large number of hosts and that too quickly. The tool developer claims that masscan can scan the entire Internet in 6 minutes. Given its super high transmission rate, it has a use case in the domain of stress testing as well.

However, to achieve those high transmission rates, special drives and NICs are required. The communication of the tool with the users is very similar to that between the user and the Nmap tool.

Feature of masscan are as follows.

-       It can be used to enumerate the whole Internet

-       It can be used to enumerate a huge number of hosts

-       Various subnets within an organization can be enumerated

-       It can be used for random scanning and fun on the Internet

Chapter 4 Advanced Kali Linux Concepts

Using abusive services

Services are the most important mechanisms that Linux operates for a better functioning of the operating system. Even windows have services that run-in background. Basically, services are processes that run in the background until you use it. For example, consider a proxy server like Burp suite that will intercept every information that goes on in the browser and if you click No it stops the service and nothing goes there. In windows, which is quite well dominated by graphical user, interfaces services are easily closed down by a click. Whereas in Linux we need to start using command line to start, stop and restart services.

Why services matter to hackers?

Hackers should be well learnt about services because when you are trying to exploit a system you need to stop services that can interrupt what you are doing. Clever administrators use services to make hackers confuse. So, you need to understand the services that are making your exploitation difficult and stop them as soon as possible. Some advanced hackers install their own services after exploiting the system in a way that they will receive valuable information from the host regularly. In the below section we will explain with command line examples that will help us understand dealing with services.

1) Starting a Service

To start burp suite as a service go to Linux terminal as a root user and just use the following command.

root @ kali:service burpsuite start

This will start the service and you can check it using the ps command.

2) Stopping a Service

Stopping a service will completely abort everything that service is dealing with. So always, be careful while stopping a service as any unsaved data will be lost. Now use the following command to stop the service.

root @ kali:service burpsuite stop

You can check using ps command where you will not see anything related to burpsuit service.

3) Restarting a Service

Restarting a service just reboots everything about a particular service. Data will be lost and new service arises all on its own.

root @ kali:service burpsuit restart

This can be used when any service is struck or stops abruptly.

Now in this below section we will use the Apache web server and MySQL to explain how services can be useful for a hacker. This is a very basic and introductory level of abusing services. If you are an efficient hacker, you will understand hundreds of services and will try to learn about them in time and time to be a professional. Now let us start exploring these below services.

1) Apache Web server:

Apache is a famous web server that is being used by several hosting companies for deploying their web services. It is a well known open source web server that is well structured and of good security. We will use this apache web server to learn a few things that can help us as a hacker.

Step 1: Starting Apache

Apache webserver can be started using the following command. Normally in windows and Hosting environment there will be a GUI that lets us start the Apache web server. But in Linux we need to enter the following command as a root user.

root @ kali: service apache start

This will start the web server in the background, which can be accessed from the localhost. You can check if everything is going well or not using ps command.

Step 2: Accessing the local host

Now after starting the server you can go to your local host address that is http://127.0.0.1 using your browser to access apache. You will be welcomed with an apache page that asks your permission to show the default page.

Step 3: Modify the webpage

Now for a practical example, modify html file to your desired and save it using any text editor. After few seconds come back to localhost and refresh. Boom! You can see the modified webpage. This confirms that service is being run on the background.

How an apache web server can help hackers?

Programmers to create a local host website during development phase usually use Apache web server. This can be linked with WAMP to further expand it with Php or MySQL servers. However, hackers can use it to learn about loopholes in websites without being blocked or banned. Hackers can also use Apache web server applications like Vulnerable App to expand their hacking skills. Almost every Hackathon program use the Apache web server for making their Hacking boxes.

Logging system

Being a hacker, you will certainly visit networks with high-level protection and maintained by hardworking security engineers. And if with all your skills you have exploited the system. After the attack, obviously a forensic investigation will take place and will try to find how an attack has been planned and executed. Everything of this investigation will be based on logfiles that you have left while exploiting the system.

Linux unlike windows is not vulnerable to exploits and attacking's because it has good logging system that records everything the user does. But some smart hackers use different techniques to make themselves undetectable by reading logfiles. We will explain in detail about how hackers need to develop skills to manipulate the logging system.

rsyslog

rsyslog is a definite daemon program that takes care of log files to be created in the UNIX or Linux system. Every Linux distribution uses different techniques to deploy log files. Arch Linux uses a different process unlike Debian rsyslog function. As we are discussing about kali Linux that is a Debian system we will continue with rsyslog explanation along with few examples.

kern.*   -var/log/kern.log

This is where log instructions are given to the Linux kernel. When we look at it thoroughly, we will find a basic command that log functionality uses. It is as the command shown below.

facility.priority action

We need to describe these three things in detail to get a thorough overview about the concept.

1) Facility

Facility is something, which is being logged. For example, mail designates about the mail system. There are few that comes under this category as explained below.

a) mail

This explains about the mailing system that is present in kali Linux. This precisely says that mail usage is being logged

b) user

All user related instructions or functions comes under this category.

c) kern

All messages that deals with the kernel comes under this category

d) lpr

All messages that deals with the inbuilt printing system comes under this.

2) Priority

If the facility describes which messages to log, priority decides on what to log. There are different types of messages that can be used to a better logging system. We will describe some of them below.

a) debug

This is used to log the things that happen as it is.

b) warning

This is used to log things that work but can go wrong.

c) info

This is used to log about normal information that exists. This can also be used to log date and time.

d) error

This can be used if something badly goes wrong while doing a work in Linux.

3) Action

This is quite simple to understand than the rest. It just means that the logs should be sent into this particular category. We may manually assign folder but it's better to leave them, as it is to go to var folder for better management. We will give some example destinations that logs are sent normally

a) Kernel files:

These are normally sent to /var/log/kernel . You can just go to the directory and open the log file using leafpad to analyze them.

Now as we have learned everything we will just look at an example that deals with all of this.

mail.warning /var/log/warning

This precisely means that mail system warning message logs will be sent to /var/log/warning path.

Automatically clean logs

Log files can make up a lot of mess if you use them extensively. We need to make a strategy to keep how many logs depending on the time interval. However, we can use logrotate function in kali Linux to configure few functions that can help us clean log files.

Open logrotate.conf file and modify the text file to create your own log system according to your own necessity.

How to spoof log files?

You might wonder being a hacker how people get rid of tracking when they attack any target host. Luckily, Linux provides few functions, which can help us to spoof log files that is to modify them in a way such that network administrators cannot detect what happened during the attack. This process is called shred. We will explain about this process in detail in the below section.

Step 1:

Shred function just fills the log data with randomly generated UTF-8 code in the logged data again and again to make it as unusable data. To check shred function just click the below command in the Linux terminal as a root user.

root @ kali: shred

Step 2:

To make any file into unusable shred file you need to call the shred command with the file name. That's it. With a single click, all your data will be made into a difficult data that cannot be read or understood by anyone. The command is as below:

root @ kali: shred (insert file name here)

root @ kali: shred desktop/kalishred.txt

Step 3:

There is a special function in shred command that can help you shred the file as number of times you needed to be. But the only negative thing to worry about this is when you try to shred a file by 20 times the time taken will increase exponentially. So always listen to your senses when trying to shred a file multiple times. -n command describes the number of times function. Command is shown as below:

root @ kali : shred -n 20 /desktop/kalishred.txt

There is also another way to make logging stop. When you have control over system as a root user, you can simply disable the service by using the following command. We can use three commands start, stop and restart for this service.

a) start

This starts the logging function allover again.

root@kali: service rsyslog start

b) stop

This stops the logging function in a split of a second.

root@kali: service rsyslog stop

c) Restart

This will first stop the logging function and will start again as a new variable.

root@kali: service rsyslog restart

Automating tasks with job scheduling

As a hacker, the most important skill you need to learn is to automate things. Whenever you attack a system or exploit a system, you need to get ready with a ton of things that will automate things for you. An automated backup or automated deletion of logfiles everything needs to be done for a better productivity and results. In this section, we will discuss in detail about automating tasks using kali Linux.

crontab

Crontab is a function that is available in kali Linux that will let us schedule an event or job for a particular time. We can enter the data from minutes to years to start a crontab task.

root @ kali : crontab

Click -help to check the functions of the crontab in detail.

Scheduling a backup task

Backup is one of the essential thing to do whenever you are dealing with an important data. When data is backed up, it can be used as an alternative if there is any leakage or corrupt in data. So administrators always prefer backing up the data. But it is a difficult and boring task to backup manually every day. So we can create an automatic backup with the following command.

00 1 18,28 ** backup/desktop/backup.sh

Here first 00 stands for the top of the hour. And ** to any day of the month.

Crontab shortcuts

Below we will display a few shortcuts that are used in crontab automatic task scheduling.

1) @yearly

This will make the task to run once a year.

2) @ weekly

This will make a task to run once in a week

3) @ midnight

This will make a task to run at midnight every day.

Starting tasks at startup with rc

While startup certain scripts start their tasks automatically using rc scripts. This will help them prioritize in the process and will give good results. If you are willing to add a service to start automatically on a startup, you can use the following command.

root @ kali : update-
rc.d servicename   enable/disable

Protecting you with TOR and VPN

It is obvious that the most important thing for any hacker is his anonymity. Now days due to restrictions of Government and constant spying had made people to find alternate options to maintain anonymity like TOR and VPN. Before going to learn how to maintain your anonymity in Kali Linux, we will have a good explanation about all the options we have for securing ourselves in this matrix world that is all connected.

Why Anonymity matters?
Imagine if your country has blocked your internet access to social networking during riots and all of your people want to use it for better communication. You can do with a VPN or TOR bundle and not are detected. However, tracking can be done in any other way if they want to. But make sure to follow this for some better peace. In the below section we will learn about anonymity services that has different uses.

What is a proxy server?

Proxy is a middle man between you and server that you are trying to reach. Imagine if you want to deliver a package from New York (your place) to Colorado (Server place). Instead of going and giving the package all by your own, you will ask your friend to deliver it. Here your friend acts a proxy for you. This is how the proxy server works.

There are many proxy servers like Socks4, http, https and Socks5.

How a hacker can use proxy server?

When doing a password attack you will normally be blocked by the website due to too many requests. In these situations, you can use a bunch of free proxies to randomly occupy the proxy address and attack the login page. This is a famous technique called cracking that is used by novice hackers to get an access into the system.

What is a VPN?

A VPN is a quite common advertisement that you might have used while watching ads in YouTube. A virtual private network abbreviated as a VPN acts like a middle man but delivers your request in encrypted form to the server in such a way that the server can't identify you. And when the server sends you the response it again encrypts it and sends towards you. Imagine this example to get a better understanding of how a Vpn works. Imagine that you want to deliver a Love Letter to your classmate. But you don't want any other person to read it other than your best friend. So, you write a Letter in quite a different way that no one can understand and sends by your friend to your classmate. Remember that your friends know how to read it. He will decrypt it to her and she will send a response in the same way. This is basically how a VPN works.

In the next section, we will describe about how internet communication works and will give a practical example that will let us understand the fact that Anonymity is a must.

How the internet works?

Every internet connected device has an IP address that can be easily tracked using different techniques by the government. When u send an email or surf internet without any Anonymity services, you are just being a product to Tech giants like Google. They will collect a lot of information from you and will sell you as adds to the businesses. Apart from that, every movement of yours will be tracked and can help them create new products.

Normally when we click on an URL the packet that contains your request will also contain the IP addresses of both yours and the server that you are trying to reach. In the communication process, it will travel through different routers called hops before reaching its final destination. When a packet is travelling, it can be easily sniffed and can be used to acquire information about you.

For an example, use traceroute command to check how many hops that a particular website takes as below.

root @ kali: traceroute bing.com

You will get an output that shows the number of routers it needs to travel to reach the final destination. When the packet is travelling, anyone can sniff it and can attain sensitive information about you and your request.

Chapter 5 Bash Scripting and Python Scripting

What is bash Scripting? A shell script is basically a text file that contains containing a string of commands in sequence. When the script is run, it executes all the commands that are in the file. The "shell" in the phrase refers to the command-line user interface that is used to communicate with the Linux kernel. There are a few different shells currently in use, with the most common ones being the C shell or csh, the Korn shell or ksh, the Bourne shell or sh, and the Bourne-Again shell or bash.

There are a number of scenarios that will require you to script with the shell. You may for instance have to support existing scripts, or you may wish to automate the system setup procedure before installing Oracle. In this scenario, you may use a script to determine the state of the operating system and any system requirements that you will have to meet before the software can be installed.

Linux

The most commonly used shell under Linux is called "Bash". This name is derived from "Bourne Again Shell". Although there are many other types of shells available for Linux, most experts recommend that you stick to the Bash shell, since this will increase the portability of your scripts between different systems and operating systems.

UNIX

Under UNIX, the shell allows a programmer to string together and execute a number of UNIX commands without having to compile them first. This makes it a lot faster to get a script running. In addition, shell scripting under UNIX makes it easier for other programmers to read and understand your code. Such shell scripts are also usually easily portable across the entire UNIX world, as long as they conform to a set standard.

Scripting for Windows

The Windows operating system conveniently includes a basic command structure that can be used to create scripts that will essentially streamline various administrative tasks. Some of the more common scripting languages under the Windows platform are Windows shell scripting, Visual Basic Scripting or VBS, and JScript. Shell scripting on the Windows platform is commonly used to produce logon scripts, which are in turn used to configure the Windows environment for specific uses when they log on. Marketing personnel for instance may use such scripts to automatically map network drives to the marketing network folder, and so on.

Despite what assembly code and C coders might tell us, high-level languages do have their place in every programmer's toolbox, and some of them are much more than a computer-science curiosity. Out of the many high-level languages we can choose from today, Python seems to be the most interesting for those who want to learn something new and do real work at the same time. Its no-nonsense implementation of object-oriented programming and its clean and easy-to-understand syntax make it a language that is fun to learn and use, which is not something we can say about most other languages.

In Python Training, you will learn how to write applications that use command-line options, read and write to pipes, access environment variables, handle interrupts, read from and write to files, create temporary files and write to system logs. In other words, you will find recipes for writing real applications instead of the old boring Hello, World! stuff.

Getting Started

To begin, if you have not installed the Python interpreter on your system, now is the time. To make that step easier, install the latest Python distribution using packages compatible with your Linux distribution. rpm, deb and tgz are also available on your Linux CD-ROM or on-line. If you follow standard installation procedures, you should not have any problems.

I also recommend that you have the Python Library Reference handy; you might want it when the explanations given here do not meet your needs. You can find it in the same places as the Python Tutorial.

Creating scripts can be done using your favorite text editor as long as it saves text in plain ASCII format and does not automatically insert line breaks when the line is longer than the width of the editor's window.

Always begin your scripts with either

```
#! /usr/local/bin/python
```

or

```
#! /usr/bin/python
```

If the access path to the python binary on your system is different, change that line, leaving the first two characters (#!) intact. Be sure this line is truly the first line in your script, not just the first non-blank line-it will save you a lot of frustration.

Use chmod to set the file permissions on your script to make it executable. If the script is for you alone, type chmod 0700 scriptfilename.py; if you want to share it with others in your group but not let them edit it, use 0750 as the chmod value; if you want to give access to everyone else, use the value 0755. For help with the chmod command, type man chmod.

Reading Command-Line Options and Arguments

Command-line options and arguments come in handy when we want to tell our scripts how to behave or pass some arguments (file names, directory names, user names, etc.) to them. All programs can read these options and arguments if they want, and your Python scripts are no different.

Bash script can be utilized for different purposes, for example, executing a shell order, running various directions together, tweaking managerial errands, performing task robotization and so on. So information of slam programming nuts and bolts is significant for each Linux client. This section will assist you with getting the fundamental thought on slam programming. A large portion of the regular activities of slam scripting are clarified with extremely basic models here.

Bash script can be utilized for different purposes, for example, executing a shell direction, running various directions together, modifying managerial errands, performing task robotization and so on. So learning of slam programming nuts and bolts is significant for each Linux client. This part will assist you with getting the essential thought on slam programming.

A typical example of bash scripting is sh-bang #!/bin/bash -e and an example of python scripting is magic 8-ball and port scanner in phyth

Chapter 6 Wireless Hacking

The proliferation of readily available Wi-Fi networks has made Wi-Fi one of the most common network mediums. Wi-Fi is in many ways superior to traditional copper wire physically connected networks. Aside from the convenience of connectivity and the flexibility of network configurations that wireless networks afford the users, the lack of physical infrastructure needed to complete the network makes it much cheaper and easier to implement than Ethernet. With this convenience, however, comes certain security concerns that are not associated with traditional hardwired networks. With a copper or fiber-based network, a physical connection is needed for a new machine to join the network. A hacker would normally have difficulty accessing the physical space of a target network and would likely arouse suspicion attempting to connect their own hardware to network cabling. Although the range of Wi-Fi is limited, it is omnidirectional and the radiofrequency signals admitted by the server and the various nodes on a wireless network traverse walls and other barriers and can be intercepted by anyone in range. This gives the hacker much more freedom to conduct a network intrusion without being detected.

Hacking Wi-Fi

Most Wi-Fi networks consist of a wireless router, or a group of wireless routers, that are connected to a modem which is delivering internet access to some physical location. The routers broadcast and receive radio signals on specific channels that carry the appropriate TCP/IP packets to and from other machines and devices that have similar wireless connectivity. All nodes communicating at any given time on the channels associated with the router or routers that are connected to the modem at that location comprise a Wi-Fi network. By nature, Wi-Fi networks are very dynamic and fluid. Especially in commercial settings, like coffee shops or office buildings that provide wireless access, the number and nature of the nodes on that particular network are in constant flux. In these public settings, it is easy for a hacker to hide in plain sight and attempt to intrude into any of the nodes on the network. Once the hacker is successfully on the network itself, they can scan the network for all connected machines and probe for vulnerabilities. Many networks have both wireless and wired subnetworks that are interconnected. When a hacker gains access to a wireless network they can conceivably use that to leverage access to all of the nodes on the wired portion of the network. This makes Wi-Fi hacking a very popular goal for modern hackers.

Wi-Fi Encryption Protocols

Since Wi-Fi signals are broadcast into the air as opposed to being confined within wires, it is important for the information contained in the signals to be encrypted. Otherwise, anyone could passively receive and view any information being sent between the nodes on the network. The encryption protocols used in Wi-Fi have necessarily evolved since wireless networks began gaining popularity. Moreover, as technology has improved and resulted in increased bandwidth and data rates, a great density of information can be broadcast from a wireless network in a very short period of time, making it especially important for it to be encrypted and kept out of the hands of malicious hackers.

The oldest and most common Wi-Fi encryption protocol is Wired Equivalent Privacy (WEP). The goal of the WEP standard, as the name implies, was to give network users the same amount of security that they would have on a physically connected network. Unfortunately, over time WEP has become the least secure of all of the existing encryption protocols and it is quite easily hacked by even the most inexperienced hackers. WEP is so insecure in fact, that many Wi-Fi router manufacturers no longer provide that type of encryption as an option on their hardware. Most security professionals recommend that router owners do not use WEP when other options are available. Step-by-step instructions and coding examples for attacking WEP protected Wi-Fi networks are freely and readily available on the internet. Although the level of encryption has increased from 64 bit to 128 bit to 256 bit, the underlying flaws in WEP remain easily exploitable by even the most green of neophyte hackers. The biggest problem with WEP is that a password can be quickly and easily deciphered simply through the passive "sniffing" (receiving and viewing network packets) of network traffic.

A significant step up from WEP Wi-Fi encryption is the Wi-Fi Protected Access (WPA) standard of encryption. This new protocol fixed many of the problems in WEP, but remained vulnerable to attack because it was still based on some of the same underlying encryption algorithms. Furthermore, WPA-protected routers were deployed with a feature that was designed to make it more convenient for home users to connect new devices to their network. This feature proved to be an additional vulnerability in systems that employed WPA.

It wasn't long before an update to WPA was needed to keep Wi-Fi networks more secure. A new encryption standard being used in other secure applications, the Advanced Encryption Standard (AES), became mandatory in the new Wi-Fi encryption protocol which became known as WPA-2. WPA-2 with AES encryption has become the recommended setting for wireless routers on which it is available because of its significant improvement in security over its preceding standards. Cracking WPA and WPA-2 requires more intrusive hacking techniques than the simple passive sniffing that can be used to attack WEP-protected networks.

Wi-Fi Attacks

In order to conduct a Wi-Fi attack a hacker needs, at a minimum, a computer (normally a laptop) that can run scripts which are used to decipher the Wi-Fi password. They also must acquire a special Wi-Fi adapter that can be purchased relatively cheaply. A list of suitable Wi-Fi adapters can be found on hacker resource websites, but in general the adapter must have a feature known as "monitor mode" in order to be able to execute a Wi-Fi attack. It is important to note that not all Wi-Fi adapters that can be found at retail computer supply stores have this feature, and most internal laptop adapters are not appropriate. In general, hackers prefer to use some sort of Linux distribution, usually Kali, to conduct a Wi-Fi attack because most of the readily available tools were written for the Linux OS and come preinstalled on Kali. It is also possible with some configuration to run Linux on a virtual machine within another OS to mount a successful attack. Although attacks from other operating systems are possible, it is much easier for the beginner to conduct them from either a native Linux distribution or a virtual machine. A hacker-friendly distribution like Kali is recommended.

The detailed procedures and recommended programs for conducting Wi-Fi attacks against the various encryption protocols changes over time, although the general principles are the same. For the simplest attack, which is against WEP encryption, the general steps are as follows:

1) monitor and view all Wi-Fi traffic in the range of the adapter while in "monitor mode" (set by a program called *airmon-ng*) using a program called *airodump-ng.*

Live W-Fi Traffic on Several Routers (aircrack-ng.org)

2) choose a target Wi-Fi network that is using WEP encryption and make a note of the name (ESSID) and network address (BSSID in the form XX:XX:XX:XX:XX:XX)
3) restart *airodump-ng* to begin capturing network traffic from the specific network that you are targeting
4) wait for a sufficient number of packets to be captured (this may take longer on networks with less traffic)

5) use a program called *aircrack-ng* to piece together the captured network packets into a coherent password

A Successfully Decrypted Wi-Fi Key (aircrack-ng.org)

If network traffic is too slow to capture a sufficient number of packets for decrypting the password in a reasonable period of time, some hackers choose to use a program called *aireplay-ng* to inject artificial packets into the network and create the necessary traffic to crack it more quickly. However, this activity requires the hacker's machine to actually broadcast signals from its Wi-Fi adapter, making it more conspicuous.

WPA encryption cannot be cracked passively and requires the additional step of packet injection. Cracking WPA can

take longer and is a more invasive procedure, but it is not much more difficult than cracking WEP. A program called *reaver*, normally available on the Kali distribution is typically used by hackers to crack

WPA. WPA-2 hacking is a much more advanced concept for more experienced practitioners. (Note: the software tools above are pre-installed on Kali Linux, or can be downloaded from www.aircrack-ng.org)

Chapter 7 Your First Hack

The neophyte hacker shouldn't even think about attempting an attack on a real target as their first foray into hacking. Sufficient tools and technologies exist which are easily obtained and with which various methods can be rehearsed in a virtual environment. This type of practice is essential for the hacker and is more valuable than all of the reading and study one could accomplish. To build confidence and gain appreciation for the nuances and practical pitfalls, the beginning hacker should aspire to accomplish the simple attacks suggested in this chapter. The details of the attacks will vary and currently applicable instructions should be researched by the reader, but the general principles of the setup and execution should be fairly universal.

Hacking Your Own Wi-Fi

The purpose of this practice attack is to successfully obtain the password of a WEP-encrypted Wi-Fi network. To minimize risk, the network and any connected devices should be owned or controlled by you, or by someone who has given you explicit permission to perform penetration testing.

What you need:

1) A computer
2) A wireless network adapter that supports "monitor mode"
3) Access to a Wi-Fi router with WEP encryption (does not have to have internet access)
4) The latest version of Kali Linux (installed as the primary OS or in a virtual machine)

Setting up:

1) Ensure that the router is set to WEP and give it a password of your choice
2) Turn off the internal Wi-Fi adapter on your laptop if you have one
3) Connect the "monitor mode" adapter to your attack machine and install any necessary drivers
4) Be sure the attack computer is in wireless range of the target network

Procedure:

1) Follow the "Wi-Fi Hacking" steps
2) Confirm that the cracked password matches the one you set for the network
3) Repeat the hack using aireplay-ng for packet injection and compare execution times
4) Change the length or complexity of the password and repeat the hack, comparing execution times

A Virtual Windows Vulnerability Assessment
Operating systems contain multiple software vulnerabilities that hackers are ready and willing to exploit. When a hacker discovers an un-patched version of an OS, there are a number of commonly available exploits with which to gain access. The first step in deploying those exploits is to analyze the OS for the most glaring vulnerabilities. Kali Linux features natively installed tools that will scan a system and provide a list of vulnerabilities. This exercise will require two virtual machines running within the same system (regardless of the host OS). It will also require an installation image for an older, unsupported, and un-patched version of Microsoft Windows (Windows '95 or '98 are good choices). These images can be obtained online (usgcb.nist.gov) or from an old CD.

What you need:

1) A computer with any OS
2) Virtualization software
3) The latest version of Kali Linux
4) An unsupported, un-patched version of Microsoft Windows

Setting up:

1) Install Kali Linux on a virtual machine
2) Install the target Windows distribution on a virtual machine (on the same host system as Kali)

Procedure:

1) Execute a network scan from the Kali virtual machine using a program called *nmap*
2) Practice changing various settings in *nmap* so that OS vulnerabilities will be detected and displayed
3) Make note of the listed Windows vulnerabilities and begin researching exploits!

Chapter 8 Scanning Ports

The reason you are going to want to scan ports is so that you can find an open one. With ports, you are going to be able to get into someone's system and leave a door open so that you can get in again later on. Port scans use host scans which can take up a lot of time if you have a wide range of IP addresses that have to be scanned and most of them end up being vacant.

Ports That Are Open

A network scanner is going to be used when you are connected to either of these ports and as soon as the port accepts the connection from the scanner, it is going to be best for you to assume that the program that is bound is running as it should be.

TCP ports are going to work with SYN packets that are sent back and forth between the servers, and the clients use them. Whenever the packet is sent to the server, it is going to send a SYN/ACK packet back resulting in the client sending the ACK packet back. After the SYN packet is received once more by the client, the port is going to be opened. In the off chance that an RST packet is sent instead, then the port is going to be closed. If the server does not send anything, then there is probably a firewall that is blocking it from the port or the port is not running on that IP address.

When you are scanning UDP ports, you are going to most likely run into problems because there are no handshakes exchanged and the programs are going to get rid of any packets that they are not going to be able to process. UDP packets are going to be sent to a port without a program that is bound to it. ICMP error packets are going to be what is returned. From there you are most likely going to consider the port to be closed. No answer is going to mean that a firewall is filtering out the packets or the port is opened. Too many people end up leaving their UDP scans because these scanners have difficulty telling the difference between when a port is opened and when it is filtering the packets.

Ports That Are More Common

To save yourself some time, Nmap is going to scan around 1667 ports that are going to be the default ports. But, you are going to get more results if you thoroughly scan all the ports; and there are 65536 ports. So, if you have the time, scan them all!

Port Specifications

When you are using the -p command, you are going to be able to tell the Nmap program exactly which ports you want it to scan so that you can save time on your scanning.

Target Specifications

Just like you can tell Nmap to scan specific ports, you can also tell it to go after a specific host or set of hosts. This host is going to be verified only by putting in the IP address for that host or by using the domain name. Should you wish to scan several different ports, you are going to want to set up the range for the IP addresses.

Scan Types

TCP SYN

A TCP SYN scan is going to be the default scan done by Nmap. When you use the -sS command, the program will only do that scan. As the administrator, you are going to be allowed to start the scan. If a user starts the scan, then a connect scan is going to be performed.

TCP connect

There is a command that you can use to make sure that Nmap has a full connection and that is the -sT command. This scan is not going to be as good as the TCP SYN scan because there is more that has to be sent back and forth between the client and the server. This scan is going to be executed with user privileges or whenever an IPv6 address is being scanned.

TCP null

When you use the -sN option, the program is going to send back all packets that do not have anything to do with SYN, ACK, or RST flags. If it comes back that the port is closed, the RST packet is going to be the one returned. If the port is opened or has a firewall filtering its packets, then there is not going to be a response sent back. Doing a null scan is going to be the best way to attempt to get passed the stateless firewall however if the firewall is stateful then it is not going to do anything.

UDP empty packet

When you use the -sU function, Nmap is going to send out UDP packets that contain no data. If an error message is returned, then you are going to assume that the port is closed. However, when there is no response, you will assume the port is opened or filtered. This scan cannot tell the difference between a filtered port or an open port which is going to leave some severe limitation in your scan.

UDP application

You are going to use -SU or -SV options to tell the program that you want data from an application or for the application to be identified. Since this has several different options put together, you are going to experience a slow scan.

Scanning Speed

Like most things, if things are sent at a speed that is faster than the system can deal with, then the packets are going to be dropped, and they are not going to be used in the scan thus you are going to get results that are not accurate. If there is an intrusion detection or an intrusion prevention that is in place on the target's network, then the faster that the scan is going through, the more likely that it is that you are going to be detected by the target.

There are a lot of devices as well as firewalls that work with IPS that are meant to respond to SYN packets that are sent in from the cookies created by these packets so that every port appears open even if they are not. When you are running a scan at full speed, then you are going to risk wreaking havoc on the network devices that are stateful.

With Nmap, there will be five templates that you can use to adjust the speed in case it does not adjust itself properly. With the -T0 option, you are going to force the program to wait about five minutes in between sending packets. -T1 waits for fifteen seconds, -T2 for 0.4 seconds, and -T3 which is going to be the default setting where the timing goes unchanged. Lastly, when -T4 is used, the timeouts are reduced, but the retransmission speed is upped ever so slightly. -T5 is similar to -T4but things are going to be sped up even more. A modern IPS or IDS device is going to figure out the scans that are using -T1 and detect that device so that the hacker is discovered. As the user of Nmap, you can also decide to make a new template with new parameters if you are not happy with the ones that are provided.

Identifying Applications

If you decide to use the -SV option, then Nmap is going to have to figure out which version of the application is currently being run.

Identifying the Operating System

If you want to discover which operating system is being used by the target, you will use the -O option in Nmap. There are packets that are specially crafted to be sent to the target to all of the ports so that the responses can be analyzed in the database that you are using on your operating system.

Save

When you want to save the output that you get returned to you, you will use the -oX<filename> option so that it is saved in an XML format.

Chapter 9 Attacking With Frameworks

Social Engineering

Due to the increase in the use of technology for almost all of our activities, companies and organizations have invested a huge amount of money in ensuring that the technologies they use are properly secured from hackers. These companies have developed and implemented extensive firewalls to protect against any possible security breach. Most internet users are not security conscious despite the ease with which information can be obtained over an internet connection. This is coupled with the fact that most malicious hackers concentrate their efforts on computer servers and client application flaws. Over the years, these hackers have become more creative in how they gather information and structure their attacks on websites and web apps. With the enormous amount of money invested in online security, we would expect that malicious information theft or control would have been eliminated. However, this has not happened.

This is where we use social engineering to achieve our goal. It is a non-technical approach circumvents a company's security measures. No matter how secure a company's online applications are, they are still susceptible to hacking. Hackers have been able to achieve this using social engineering and tools based on social engineering. Social engineering is a hands-on approach to hacking. It involves targeting individuals and manipulating them into giving out vital information that can lead to a breach in the security system. These individuals, who may be employees of the organization or even a close relative of the top person at the target organization, are approached and coerced into trusting the hacker. They begin to gather information that could be of use in the hacking process. This is usually an approach taken when the company's firewalls are effective at thwarting outside penetration. When the hackers have obtained the necessary information (for instance, the login information of the social engineering target), they can hack the company from the inside out.

It is believed that human beings are the weakest link in any information security chain. The physical approach toward social engineering can occur in so many ways that it is impossible to cover all of them in this chapter. However, popular means include approaching and becoming friends with (or even a significant other of) employees at the company. Sometimes the employees are given a flash drive containing movies or other files in which they may be interested. The employees plug in the drive and launch a file that executes scripts in the background, granting the hackers access to the respective machines. The social engineer attack can also occur when a person calls an employee of a firm, impersonates a call center representative and tells the employee that he or she needs information to rectify a service that is important. The hacker would have gathered details about the employee from the employee's social media account or through personal conversations with the person. Once the hacker has received the information (which may include the victim's social security number or login details), the hacker hijacks the account and performs fraudulent transactions on it, or uses it for additional attacks. Social engineering makes it easy to build a username and password list that helps with logging into the target's accounts.

Hackers use the information they have gathered in combination with tools that ensure an easy hack of the company's system. Most of these tools are used in the client-side attack and are enhanced with the information gathered through social engineering. This information is used in conjunction with phishing and spoofing tools to attack a client if a direct social engineering attack fails. Social engineering is the information gathering procedure in this approach when it comes to attacking clients. Hacking has become a business venture. Hackers gain access to information simply to sell it for money, or to use it to transfer money. The motivation now is monetary. Usually, the target is selected, and the hacker uses information available to the public about the client to develop the attack. Typically, information obtained online is sufficient to build an attack. However, with an increase in employee education regarding hackers and social engineering, employees have begun to limit the personal information they share on social media and other public platforms.

The success of a social-engineering-based attack depends solely on the quality of information gathered. The attacker must be sociable and persuasive when interacting with the victim, such that the victim becomes open and begins to trust the hacker. Some hackers outsource this aspect to an individual who is skilled in getting people to tell them secrets.

Social Engineering Toolkit (SET)

The Social Engineering Toolkit is a very important tool used in a computer-aided social engineering attack. It comes pre-installed with the Kali Linux distro. It is written in the Python language and is also an open source toolkit. The Social Engineering Toolkit, or SET, was created by David Kennedy to exploit the human aspect of web security. However, it is important to make sure that the Social Engineering Toolkit is up to date. Once the tool has been updated, the configuration file can be set. The default configuration file is sufficient to make the SET run without any problems. Advanced users may want to edit and tweak certain settings. However, if you are a beginner, it is better to leave it the way it is until you become more familiar with the Social Engineering Toolkit. To access the configuration file, open the terminal and then change the directory to the SET. Open the config folder and you will find the set_config file, which you can open and edit with a text editor to change the parameters.

The Social Engineering Toolkit can be accessed by clicking on the Application icon, then clicking on the Kali Linux desktop. Next, click on BackTrack and then on the Exploitation Tools option. Click on Social Engineering Tools and select the Social Engineering Toolkit by clicking on SET. The SET will open in a terminal window. Alternatively, the SET can be opened directly from the terminal by typing "setoolkit" without the quotes.

The Social Engineering Toolkit opens in the terminal as a menu-based option. The menu contains different options based on the type of social engineering attack you need to use. The option at number 1 is for spear-phishing vectors which enable the user to execute a phishing attack. The phishing attack is an email attack. It is like casting a net by sending emails to random potential victims. Spear-phishing, on the other hand, targets one individual and the email is more personalized.

The second option on the SET menu is the website attack vector, which uses different web-attack methods against its target victim. The website attack vector option is by far the most popular and perhaps most used option in the Social Engineering Toolkit. Clicking on the website attack vector option opens menus containing the Java applet attack vector, the Metasploit browser exploits, the credential harvester attack used in cloning websites, the tabnabbing attack, the man-in-the-middle attack, the web jacking attack and the multi-attack web method.

The third option on the Social Engineering Toolkit menu is the infectious media generator tool. This is a very easy tool to use and is targeted at individuals who can give a hacker access to the organization network, thus enabling the hacker to hack from inside the network. This tool allows the hacker to create a USB disk or DVD containing a malicious script that gives the hacker access to the target shell. Choosing this option opens a menu with a prompt to choose from between a file-format exploit or a standard Metasploit executable. Choosing the file-format option opens a list of payloads from which to select. The default is a PDF file embedded in an executable script. This is then sent to the drive where the autorun.inf is created with the PDF file. When an employee opens the file on the drive, the file is executed in the background and the hacker gains shell access to the victim's computer.

The fourth option is the generate-a-payload-with-listener option. This option allows the hacker to create a malicious script as a payload and therefore generate a listener. This script is a .exe file. The key is getting the intended victim to click and download this script. Once the victim downloads the .exe file and executes it, the listener alerts the hacker, who can access the victim's shell.

The fifth option in the Social Engineering Toolkit is the mass mailer option. Clicking this option brings up a menu with two options: single email address attack and the mass mailer email attack. The single email address attack allows the user to send an email to a single email address while the mass mailer email attack allows the user to send an email to multiple email addresses. Choosing this option prompts the user to select a list containing multiple email addresses to which the email is then sent.

Sixth on the list is the Arduino-based attack. With this option, you are given the means to compromise Arduino-based devices. The seventh option, on the other hand, is the SMS spoofing option, which enables the hacker to send SMS to a person. This SMS spoofing option opens a menu with an option to perform an SMS spoofing form of attack or create a social-engineering template. Selecting the first option will send to a single number or a mass SMS attack. Selecting just a single number prompts the user to enter the recipient's phone number. Then you are asked to either use a predefined template or craft your own message. Typing 1 chooses the first option while typing 2 chooses the second option depending on your preference for the SMS. Then you enter the source number, which is the number you want the recipient to see as the sender of the SMS. Next, you type the message you want the recipient to see. You can embed links to a phishing site or to a page that will cause the user to download a malicious .exe file. After the message has been crafted, the options for services used in SMS spoofing appear on the screen. Some are paid options and others are free.

Option eight in the SET is the wireless AP attack vector. This option is used to create a fake wireless AP to which unsuspecting users of public Wi-Fi can connect and the hacker can sniff their traffic. This option uses other applications in achieving this goal. AirBase-NG, AirMon-NG, DNSSpoof and dhcpd3 are the required applications that work hand in hand with the wireless AP attack vector.

Option nine in the menu is the QR code attack vector. Today, QR codes are used everywhere, from the identification of items to obtaining more details about products on sale. Now QR codes are even used to make payments. Some websites use QR codes for logins or as web apps. This login method is used because it is perceived as a more secure way of gaining access due to hackers' being able to steal cookies, execute a man-in-the-middle attack and even use a brute-force password to gain unauthorized access. However, this increase in the use of QR codes has given hackers more avenues for exploiting their victims. The QR code attack vector helps the hacker create a malicious QR code. Then the hacker creates or clones a website like Facebook using the credential harvester option and embeds this malicious QR code with the link to the cloned website. The hacker then sends a phishing email or spoofed SMS to a victim, which prompts that person to scan the code with a mobile device. This reveal's the victim's GPS location and other information when the victim visits the website and enters their login details.

The tenth option in the menu is the PowerShell attack vector. This option allows the hacker to deploy payloads in the PowerShell of an operating system. The PowerShell is a more powerful option than the command prompt in the Windows operating system. It allows access to different areas of the operating system. It was developed by Microsoft to ease the automation of tasks and configuration of files and has come with the Windows operating system since the release of Windows Vista. The PowerShell attack vector enables the attacker to create a script that is then executed in the victim's PowerShell. The selection of this option brings out four menu options: PowerShell alphanumeric injector, PowerShell SAM database, PowerShell reverse and PowerShell bind shells. Any of these options creates a targeted PowerShell program and is exported to the PowerShell folder. Tricking the target to access, download and execute this program creates access for the attacker.

By now, you should realize how powerful the SET is in executing computer-aided social engineering attacks. This tool is very valuable for a penetration tester, as it provides a robust and diverse means of checking the various vulnerabilities that may exist in an organization's network.

BeEF

BeEF stands for Browser Exploitation Framework. This tool comes with most of the security-based Linux distro, like the Parrot OS and Kali Linux. BeEF started as a server that was accessed through the attacker's browser. It was created to target vulnerabilities in web browsers that would give access to the target systems for executing commands. BeEF was written in the Ruby language on the Rails platform by a team headed by Wade Alcorn. As stated before, passwords, cookies, login credentials and browsing history are all typically stored on the browser, so a BeEF attack on a client can be very nasty.

On Kali Linux, however, BeEF has been included in the distro. The BeEF framework can be started by going into applications, clicking on exploitation tools and then clicking on the BeEF XSS framework. This brings up a terminal that shows the BeEF framework server has been started. Once the server has been started, we open our browser of choice and visit the localhost at port 3000. This is written in the URL space of the browser as localhost:3000/ui/authentication or 127.0.0.1:3000/ui/authentication. This would bring us to the authentication page of the BeEF framework, requiring a login username and password. By default, the username is beef ; the password is also beef.

Once you are in the BeEF framework, it will open a "Get Started" tab. Here you are introduced to the framework and learn how to use it. Of particular importance is hooking a browser. Hooking a browser involves clicking a JavaScript payload that gives the BeEF framework access to the client's browser. There are various ways by which we can deploy this payload, but the simplest way is to create a page with the payload, prompt the target to visit that page and execute the JavaScript payload. You can be very creative about this aspect. On the other hand, there is a link on the Get Started page that redirects you to The Butcher page. Below this page are buttons containing the JavaScript payload. Clicking on this button will execute the script and, in turn, hook your browser. When your browser is hooked, you will see a hook icon beside your browser icon on the left side of the BeEF control panel with the title "Hooked browser" along with folders for online and offline browsers.

Once a browser is hooked, whether it's online or offline, we can control it from our BeEF control panel. Clicking on the details menu in the control panel will provide information like the victim's browser version and the plugins that are installed. The window size of the browser also can be used to determine the victim's screen size, the browser platform (which is also the operating system on the PC), and a lot more information. For executing commands on the browser, we click on the command menu in the control panel. This brings up a different command we can execute on the victim's browser. This command would create a pop-up message on the victim's browser, so it can be renamed creatively before execution to avoid raising any suspicion. Some of the commands that can be executed in this menu include the Get all Cookie command (which starts harvesting the victim's browser cookies), the Screenshot command, the Webcam command for taking pictures of the victim, the Get visited URL command and so on. There are a lot of commands in this menu.

The BeEF framework JavaScript payload can also hook mobile phone browsers. Checking the details tab after hooking will give that particular information if we end up hooking a phone browser. Clicking on the module and searching the PhoneGap command allows us to execute phone targeted commands like geolocating the device and starting an audio recording on the victim's device. Clicking on the Ipec menu also displays a terminal we can use to send shell commands to the victim's system.

Once the BeEF framework hooks a browser, the possibilities are endless. We can do virtually anything. Therefore, it is important to be careful when clicking links and pop-up or flash messages.

METASPLOIT

The Metasploit framework is perhaps the larget, most complete penetration testing and security auditing tool today. This tool is an open source tool that is regularly updated with new modules for monitoring even the most recent vulnerabilities. Metasploit comes with the Kali Linux distro. It is written in Ruby, although when it was created it was written in Perl. This tool was developed by HD Moore in 2003 and was then sold to an IT company called Rapid7 in 2009.

Metasploit is an immensely powerful tool that has great versatility. To fully utilize Metasploit, you must be comfortable using the terminal, which is a console type window. However, there is an option that allows for the use of Metasploit in a GUI window. Armitage, an opensource tool, makes this possible, although it does not have the capacity to fully utilize all aspects of the Metasploit framework in an attack. The meterpreter in the Metasploit framework is a module that is dumped in the victim's system, making it easy for the hacker to control that PC and maintain access for future hacks in that system. Getting started with Metasploit on Kali Linux is as good as opening the terminal and typing "msfconsole" without the quotes.

Metasploit contains modules that can be used during a hack. Some of these modules are written by developers or contributors from the open source community. An important set of modules includes the payloads. The payloads are very important when it comes to performing attacks within the Metasploit framework. These payloads are codes that have been written so that the hacker can gain a foothold in the victim's computer. Perhaps the most popular among these payloads is the meterpreter. This particular payload is very powerful, as it leaves no trace of a hack on the system's drive. It exists solely on the victim's system memory.

Then there is the Exploits module. These exploits are codes that have been written and packed for specific flaws in a victim's operating system. Different exploits exist for different operating system flaws, so flaws that are targeted for one vulnerability would fail when used for another.

The encoders are modules that encode the different payloads deployed into the target system to avoid detection by the victim's antivirus, anti-spyware or other security tools.

Other modules available on the Metasploit framework are the Post modules (which allow the hacker to gather passwords, tokens and hashes), the Nops modules (most of which allow for 100 percent execution of the payload or exploit) and the Auxiliary modules (which do not fit into other categories).

This framework is quite robust, as many kinds of hacking procedures can be carried out. Several procedures are executed by combining the modules and making them work in different ways. A good way for a beginner to learn more about the Metasploit framework is to type "help" without the quotes in the Metasploit framework console.

Chapter 10 Strategies To Combat Cyber Terrorist Threats

Implement strategic plans to counter cyber terrorist efforts will ensure that your organization has the means to combat any threats it may face. There are a number of strategies which a business can employee or in order to stay ahead and heighten their security capabilities in the face of a threat. These are:

Prosecuting Perpetrators

Many attacks can behind the wall of anonymity with many smaller organizations failing to pursue and prosecute the hackers responsible. While this can be a costly activity, there are some advantages in identifying and taking the attackers to court. This can be a shock to the cyber terrorist community and set the standard for which other organizations should conduct themselves in the wake of an attack. If the case is particularly high profile, the organization can benefit from the hard-line response with the prosecuted hackers being an example to the rest of the criminal organizations that are determined to wreak havoc on your business. This example set can send waves throughout the rest of the community and can lead to improvements in the investigation and prosecution process of criminal cyber terrorists. Therefore, is always in the best interest of the parties that have been affected by an attack to seek justice.

Develop New Security Practices

Take a Proactive Approach

It is important for both corporations and the general public to take a proactive approach as the threat from cyber terrorism becomes more sophisticated and targeted. This involves keeping up to date with the latest information within the cyber security sphere such as threats, vulnerabilities and noteworthy incidents as they will allow security professionals to gain a deeper insight into how these components could affect their organizations. From there they are able to develop and implement stronger security measures thereby reducing the opportunities for hackers to exploit for cyber-attacks.

Organizations should constantly be on the forefront of cyber security having a multi-level security infrastructure in order to protect valuable data and user's private information. All activities that are critical in nature should have security audits frequently to ensure all policies and procedures relating to security are adhered to. Security should be treated as an ongoing and continuous process rather than an aftermath of the consequences of an attack.

Deploy Vital Security Applications

There are many tools available for security professionals to protect their networks and they can provide a significant benefit to the job at hand. These applications involve firewalls, IDS, as well as anti-virus software that can ensure better protections against potential hackers. Using these security systems, security personnel are able to record, monitor and report any suspicious activities that can indicate the system is at risk. The applications are able to streamline the process, making the job far more efficient and effective. Utilizing these types of tools ensures that security personnel are assisted with the latest in prevention technology and have a greater probability of combating attackers.

Establish Business Disaster Recovery Plans

In the event that an attack does occur, all businesses should have a worst-case scenario contingency plan in place to ensure that processes and operations are brought back to normally as soon as possible. Without such plans, the consequences can be disastrous leading to a loss in revenue and reputation on behalf of the business. Once these plans have been devised, they should be rehearsed regularly in order to test their effectiveness and also provide staff with training in the event of an attack.

These plans should be comprised of two main components, these being, repair and restoration. From the perspective of repair, the attacking force should be neutralised as soon as possible with the objective to return operations to normalcy and have all functions up and running. The restoration element is geared towards having pre-specified arrangements with hardware, software as well as a network comprised of service vendors, emergency services and public utilities on hand to assist in the restoration process.

Cooperation with Other Firms

Your organization would not be alone in dealing with the aftermath of a cyber-attack. Many organizations exist in order to deal with cyber terrorism threats both public and private. These groups can go a long way in helping with issues relating to cyber terrorism such as improving the security within your organization, helping devise and implement disaster recovery plans and further discuss how you can deal with threats in the future and what this means for the wider community. Having this extended network available to you will enhance your efforts in resisting cyber-attacks as well as having a role in discussing other emerging threats and protecting organizations facing these same threats.

Increasing Security Awareness

It is important not to become complacent in times where security threats are prevalent and this requires an increase in awareness with all issues relating to cyber security. Having your organization become an authority in raising awareness within the community will help educate other organizations in how they can defend themselves against attacks and strengthen their own security which in turn will damage the cyberterrorist community as they face a stronger resistance. You can also raise awareness within your own organization through security training programs which will help all employees equip themselves with the right skillset to combat threats that could arise through their own negligence and will also help them be more alert in times when threats could be present.

Chapter 11 Tails

Edward Snowden. The name rings a bell for most people around the globe. In tech circles he is a visionary. As for the non-techies, a few labels come to mind: Whistleblower. Hero. Traitor. Regardless of what you pin him with, one thing is certain: He hates censorship and loves anonymity, the kind of anonymity that calls for untrackable execution. Before discussing anything, he insisted liaisons use not only *PGP* (pretty good privacy) but the end-all-be-all of anonymity tools: *Tails*-- a thief-simple tool that frustrates even those in the upper echelon of the NSA. And for good reason, since even they do not know the wizard who designed it.

Where Tor is the worm of the anonymous fisherman, Tails is the fishing box. The fish at the other end have no idea who is inside the boat, watching, listening. It's a hacker's tool but also a patriot weapon. Using it is a breeze: install it on a USB stick, CD, whatever, boot from said stick and find yourself cloaked and shielded from the NSA, provided that you don't out yourself. And if you're using Tails, you're smarter than that anyway.

Built upon the shell of Linux, it acts as an operating system and comes with an assortment of nukes to launch under Big Brother's nose: Tor browser, chat client, email, office suite and image/sound editor, among others.

Snowden preferred Tails on account of its no-write rule: no direct data writing. A breach from a remote adversary? Not going to happen. Forensics investigation? Nope. No trace is going to be left on the DVD/USB. Obviously this is a no brainer to use if you're an NSA employee looking to spill the beans on unconstitutional spying, as well as a must-have for political dissidents and journalists. It is armored with plausible deniability, the same as Truecrypt.

Tor runs like warm butter when you boot with Tails. There's not much of a learning curve, and no excessive tweaking required. You can use it in the same PC you use at work. Boot from USB or DVD. Do your thing then reboot back into your normal PC with no record or footprint of your Tailing. For all intents, you're a ghost on the internet. And speaking of ghosts, the creators of Tails are anonymous themselves. No one knows their identities. But what we do know is that they will not bow to governments trying to muscle a backdoor into the code.

Linus Torvalds, creator of Linux, said in 2013, "The NSA has been pressuring free software projects and developers in various ways," implying that they had made the effort, and all with taxpayer funds. A bit like the cat saying to the mouse, "Transparency is good for you. Sleep out in the open and not the damp and dark, flea-infested mousehole." They don't like secrets.

You might be asking, how do we *know* that Tails does not already *have* a backdoor? How do we know that the NSA has not already greased their hands? The evidence is twofold: the code is open-source (anyone can audit it), and the mere fact that the NSA made an effort to sideline end-users says they fear such a powerful package. They cannot peer inside to see what the mice are doing. Snowden claimed that the NSA, while he was with them, was a major thorn in the side of that organization.

At the time of Tails conception five years ago, the interest had already started to build up in the Tor community for a more cohesive toolbox. "At that time some of us were already Tor enthusiasts and had been involved in free software communities for years," they said. "But we felt that something was missing to the panorama: a toolbox that would bring all the essential privacy enhancing technologies together and made them ready to use and accessible to a larger public."

PGP is also included in package. You owe it to yourself and peace of mind to learn it. Spend a Sunday with it and you'll be a competent user. Spend a week and you'll be an enthusiast. As well, *KeePassX* can be useful if you want to store different info (usernames, pass phrases, sites, comments) into one database. These two are like a good set of gauntlets no aspiring black knight would do without. And don't think the blacksmiths have just smelted down some cheap metal, either. The designers have gone to a lot of trouble to modify the privacy and security settings. The more they do, the less you have to.

But the true Achilles heel is the *metadata*. Tails is really lousy at hiding it. It doesn't try to. It doesn't clear any of it nor does it encrypt the headers of your encrypted emails. Are you an ebook author? Be careful about PDFs and .mobi files, as depending on which software you use, it can store the author's name and creation date of your work. But this is not really the fault of Tails. Rather, it is the wishes of the development team to stay compatible with the SMTP protocol.

The other problem with metadata is pictures: JPEGs, TIFF, BITMAPS and so on, which again, depending on the software, can store EXIF data--data that stores the date the picture was taken as well as the GPS coordinates of the image. Newer cameras and mobile phones like Samsung Galaxy are notorious for this, and even keep a thumbnail of the EXIF data intact for nose parkers with nothing to do all day but to sniff through other people's property. A *fake GPS spoofer* may be useful but even that won't eliminate the exif data. You'll need a separate *app* for this. You might even go so far as to only use formats that don't store any metadata at all. Plain-text is one option, though even that can be watermarked.

You might think, "Can I hide Tails activity?" The short answer is: maybe. It depends on the resources of the adversary. And just who is the adversary? The government? The private detective? The employer? The fingerprint Tails leaves is far less visible than what Tor leaves. And yes, it is possible for an administrator to see you are using Tor, as well as your ISP. They cannot tell what you're doing on Tor, mind you, but there are Tor Browser Bundle users, and Tails users. It all comes down to the sites you visit.

We've seen how they can build a profile on you from your resolution, window metrics, addons and extensions and time zones and fonts, but to alleviate this the Tails developers have tried to make everyone look the same, as if they were all wearing white Stormtrooper armor. Some fall through the cracks, making themselves easier for a correlation attack by installing too many addons and thus marking themselves in the herd: A purple-colored stormtrooper, if you will. Such and such user has a nice font enhancer while no other user does. This alone does not break anonymity, but with a hundred other factors and sufficient resources, it might be the one detail that breaks the house of cards. Death by a thousand stings.

You might find Tor *bridges* (alternative entry points on Tor) to be a good investment in reading, as they can better hide you from your ISP. In fact, using a bridge makes it considerably harder for your ISP to even know you are using Tor. If you decide this route (and you should if merely using Tor can get you arrested-- a case in which you should NOT use the default Tor configuration), the bridge address must be known.

Be mindful of the fact that a few bridges can be obtained on the Tor website. If you know about it, others do too--even adversaries like the NSA, but it is still stronger for anonymity purposes than the default Tor config. Like Freenet, it would be optimal if you personally know someone in a country outside the USA who runs a private obfuscated bridge that has the option *PublishServerDescriptor 0*. As always, luck favors the prepared.

Chapter 12 The Final Report

It is time now to send the client a final report with your feedback on all accomplished tasks.

It is important to stress how fundamental this part is. We need to present in a clear and complete manner all the information we gathered as well as each suggestion that could help to correct the weaknesses we spotted.

In addition to the list of vulnerabilities found and exploits used, we should include a part related to the so-called "remediation".

This part is meant to show the customer all the possible remedies for the risks we discovered.

It would be better to start the report with a general overview of the actions taken and then gradually enter into detail.

In this way, the report becomes easier to read for members of the management board and non-technicians, who will be able to understand exactly what is been reported.

Although we can also include other parts, a well-structured report usually consists of the following sections:

- Executive summary.
- Methodology used.

- Detailed analysis of the results.

Executive Summary

The executive summary is the report that can be understood even by non-technical staff, for example by managers.

First of all, we should define the scope and the estimated duration of this task.

By defining the scope of this task, we want to know exactly what type of penetration test we should perform and even more importantly what are the IP addresses or websites that we should include.

We must point out the evidences found and their level of criticality. We also need to prepare a graph showing the risk distribution according to the different variables:

Methodology

The methodology used integrates all the phases from the definition of the test scope to the final report.

We can summarize the procedure as follows:

- Definition of the test scope.
- Information gathering.
- Network scanning.
- Vulnerability assessment.
- Exploitation.
- Post exploitation.

- Other optional tests.
- Drafting of the report also through the use of automatic tools, for example with Dradis. (https://dradisframework.com/ce/).

As a side note, the report must also contain all the results you achieved that were related to the Web, including the **SQL Injection and XSS Cross Site Scripting**, which were not explained in this book.

You might also want to include the social engineering techniques you eventually used.

Detailed Analysis of The Results

The first task to complete in this sub-phase is defining the risk level of the various vulnerabilities you detected:

Then you can enlist all the vulnerabilities:

You can then conclude your report by mentioning the solutions and the suggestions that could help to block these risks and eradicate these problems.

Chapter 13 Banner Grabbing

This information will be useful to us in the next phase where we will look for vulnerabilities. In particular, the outdated version of a service could be exploited by a potential hacker.

We will start from the services normally associated with standard ports, and then move on the ones linked to unconventional ports.

Also, in this case we rely on a wizard that will lead us to define a specific service, make it active and try to grab the banner.

Installing The Web Server Microsoft Iis

We proceed with the installation of the IIS Web server directly from a **Windows Server 2012**.

You can refer to the following link for the installation steps: https://docs.microsoft.com/en-us/iis/get-started/whats- new-in-iis-8/8-installing-iis-on-windows-server-2012

At the end of the installation process, you can open your browser and type: *"http://127.0.0.1"*. If everything went well, this is what should appear on your screen:

We can see that IIS is listening by executing the "netstat" command and listening on port 80.

With the and filtering by port 80, we can see how the latter is listening:

Banner Visualization In Microsoft Iis

At this point, we must be able to grab the banner of our web server so that we can detect its type and version.

First of all, let's connect to the Web server using "*telnet*":

Once the channel has been set up, we can enter two commands that allow us to interact with the web server:

- GET / HTTP/1.1
- HOST: 127.0.0.1

This is what will appear on your screen:

We have captured the banner of our IIS web server. We can now identify the type of service and its version. This information will be useful during the vulnerability assessment phase.

Banner Configuration On Kfsensor

We should now use KFSensor to simulate a Microsoft IIS type web server.

Once the configuration is complete, we can use the Nmap feature called "**service detection**", which will attempt to grab the banner of the listening service and inform us of what version it is.

Nmap has correctly grabbed the banner and detected the exact version of the simulated service.

Installing A Ftp Server

We have previously installed a Microsoft web server. Now, instead, we will have to install an FTP server. You can find the installation steps at the following link:
https://social.technet.microsoft.com/wiki/contents/articles/12364.windows-server-2012-ftp-installation.aspx

Once the installation is complete, we can proceed with the creation of a new **FTP** site:

We are now listening port 21 without using SSL:

Ftp Banner Grabbing With Nmap

We can now capture the *FTP banner* using the Nmap service detection feature:

As you can see from the screenshot above, we have correctly detected the version of the FTP service running on the target machine.

Note that some system administrators may decide to obfuscate the banner for a certain service. We can also do this on the FTP server defined above:

Now we will no longer be able to detect the version of the service with Nmap:

Nmap was able to understand that port 21 is open. However, it does not provide any information about the version of the service running.

Ftp Banner Grabbing Wirh Metasploit

It is a tool that is used in the exploitation phase of a system. However, there are a number of additional modules that allow you to perform other activities, such as banner grabbing.

We start Metasploit by launching the *"msf"* command from terminal. Then we type the following command:

In *"rhost"*, we need to enter the IP address of the victim machine, that is where the listening FTP service is located.

Once this part is completed, we can run the **"exploit"** command and then start the scanner:

The scan is quickly completed, and the result obtained informs us of the presence of a *Microsoft FTP server*. We grabbed the banner once again.

Ftp Banner Grabbing With Netcat

NETCAT is another useful tool used for grabbing banners. You can click here to learn more: https://en.wikipedia.org/wiki/Netcat.

Below is the command used to grab the banner:

Ftp Banner Grabbing With Telnet

We have already seen how the Telnet command works. Let's use it now to grab a banner:

Even in this case, we are able to correctly detect and grab the banner.

Operating System Detection

In addition to detecting a certain running service, it is also important to know the operating system present on a given machine.

We can follow two different procedures:

- Active mode.
- Passive mode.

In the active mode, we interact directly with the target. Nmap is a tool commonly used in active mode.

On the other hand, the passive mode listens to network traffic. Based on the characteristics of each operating system, we can obtain fairly precise information. A tool that works in this mode is "**P0f**" (https://it.wikipedia.org/wiki/P0f).

Os Detection With Nmap

Let's see how to detect the operating system of a certain machine using Nmap. The option to use is "-o", so this command will be the command we need to execute:

By running this command, we will examine only the first 100 doors and try to detect the operating system.

The result is the following:

Nmap was able to identify that the operating system in use is probably Windows and specifically version 7, 2012 or 8.1.

For more details, you might have to use other tools as well.

Os Detection With Xprobe

XPROBE is another tool useful for detecting the operating system. This is the command we should execute:

We should see the following results:

We are dealing with a Linux operating system, probably with 2.6.11 kernel.

Os Detection With POf

As anticipated, this tool allows to perform a passive operating system detection. In this case, we do not need to interact directly with the target machine.

We need to capture some network traffic, so that **POf** can complete the detection process. This is the command we should execute:

We press "*send*" and place the tool on hold:

We generate random traffic using, for example, the netcat:

This is the screen we will see if the traffic generated is enough for P0f:

As you can see, P0f informs us of what operating system version is currently used on the machine.

Chapter 14 Enumeration

Enumeration is an important phase of the penetration test process. It consists in exploiting the characteristics of a certain service in order to obtain as much information as possible.

There are services that work well with this type of investigation, such as

- SMTP, TCP port 25.
- DNS, UDP port 53.
- SNMP, UDP port 161.
- NETBIOS, UDP port 137,138; TCP port 139.

In this chapter, we will examine enumeration related to the following services:

- NETBIOS enumeration.
- DNS enumeration.
- Enumeration through DEFAULT PASSWORD.

Enumeration With Netbios

Netbios is a protocol that operates at the session layer of the **ISO/OSI model**. This protocol allows us to explore the network resources of computers, printers or files.

We can use Netbios to extract several information, including the following:

- *Hostname.*
- *Username.*

- *Domain.*
- *Printers.*
- Available network folders.

First of all, we should use Nmap to confirm that the TCP ports 139 and 445 are actually open:

nmap -v -p 139,445 192.169.1.120

After completing this step, we can use a special command, the **NBTSCAN**, to investigate systems with **open ports 139,445.**

We have a whole range of extracted **NETBIOS** information.

We can refer to another Windows command - "net view" - to continue our investigation on a specific host:

net view 192.168.1.10

It gives us the list of shared resources on our target. The "*net use*" command allows us to access these resources.

Nmap contains many scripts that can be used to enumerate NETBIOS. You can find them on the following path: /usr/share/nmap/scripts.

These are the scripts we need to verify any NETBIOS vulnerabilities:

- *smb-vuln-conficker.*
- *smb-vuln-cve2009-3103.*
- *smb-vuln-ms06-025.*

- *smb-vuln-ms07-029.*
- *smb-vuln-regsvc-dos.*
- *smb-vuln-ms08-067.*

Enumeration With Dns

With a single command we can extract different DNS records, which are the following ones:

- *SOA.*
- *A.*
- *MX.*
- *NS.*
- *CNAME.*
- *PTR.*
- *HINFO.*
- *TXT.*

We need to run this command:

dnsenum domain.com

Enumeration With Default Password

Network devices – such as routers and switches – very often have a default password. These passwords are defined directly by the device manufacturer. I would obviously suggest you change them as soon as possible.

DefaultPassword is one of the many sites where default device passwords are stored (https://default-password.info/).

This website is very easy to use. You just need to select the device model and manufacturer:

Chapter 15 Vulnerability Assessment

Thanks to network scanning, banner grabbing, and enumeration, we should have at this point a pretty good understanding of the types of services running on our network.

Now it's time to look for any vulnerabilities and we will use specific tools to carry out this activity.

A part of this research should be carried out manually, while we can use some tools to automate other parts of this process.

At this link, you can find a detailed report written by **SANS** that lists all the steps we should take to perform a *vulnerability Assessment:* https://www.sans.org/reading-room/whitepapers/basics/vulnerability-assessment-421.

I also want to clarify that, unlike vulnerability assessment, a penetration test has the additional purpose of exploiting the vulnerabilities found.

Below is the list of tools we will use:

- *Nessus.* https://www.tenable.com/products/nessus-vulnerability-scanner.

- *Nexpose.* https://www.rapid7.com/products/nexpose/.
- *OpenVAS.* http://www.openvas.org/.

Installing Nessus

There are two available versions of **Nessus**: a paid one and a free one. We will obviously refer to the second one.

We start by going to https://www.tenable.com/products/nessus-vulnerability-scanner and downloading this software.

At this stage we need to obtain an activation code that validates the license we are using. Just click on "Get an Activation Code" as you can see from the screenshot here below:

You will receive an e-mail with the activation code within a short period of time. Once the installation is complete, a browser window will open and point to: **http://127.0.0.1:8834.**

You will then need to enter the activation code that was provided to you:

If all went well, we should now be able to start using this software.

Scanning With Nessus

Nessus has a set of pre-compiled scans that you just need to execute:

We can use KFSensor to test the vulnerabilities of our victim machine.

Once scanned, this is the first detected vulnerability:

More in detail:

To confirm this, we can verify that the service is simulated on KFSensor:

Below is an overview of the vulnerabilities found:

An interesting feature is the possibility to create an exportable report in .pdf format:

Installing Nexpose

At this step, we need to download the Nexpose software and type the free license key.

We can run this software by connecting to the following link: **https: // localhost: 3780.**

Once we open this software, we can perform various actions:

Scanning With Nexpose

The first action we need to take is to create a site:

We can specify the type of scan to be performed:

The scan results can be summarized as follows:

In the image below we can see a detailed list of the vulnerabilities found:

Nexpose offers us the possibility to create easy interactions with, for example, Metasploit.

We can also see enough details about each vulnerability:

We are also provided with suggestions regarding the remediation phase, which is meant to find a remedy to the vulnerabilities found:

Here too, we have the possibility to generate a customizable report:

Websites For Vulnerability Search

Here is a list of websites you can refer to for more details about each vulnerability:

- *Exploit Database.* https://www.exploit-db.com/.
- *Security Focus.* http://www.securityfocus.com/.
- *Packet Storm.* https://packetstormsecurity.com/.
- *CVE Details.* http://www.cvedetails.com/.

Chapter 16 Learning How to Carry Out an Effective Attack

Now that you have a good understanding of hacking concepts and what is involved in the penetration of a system as well as how you can turn hacking into a career, we want to get into the heart of the action and learning how to carry out an effective attack. This is for demonstration purposes to help strengthen your knowledge and ideally stem further education. If you are still unsure on the basics of hacking, have a read through and study this book thoroughly as we will be going through this step by step guide with the assumption that you have a solid grasp of the topics of hacking and computer security and we wouldn't want you to get lost along the way.

Before you do get started, you will need to utilize a tool to help with the pen-test. For this example, we will be using Metasploit, an open source tool which has a number of functions which pen-testers and black hat hackers alike will find incredibly useful. The tool has a database filled with a large number of known exploits which can be picked up during the vulnerability test by the variety of scanners. Metasploit is one of the more popular pen-testing software applications and as an open source program, there is a large community which you can interact with in case you have any questions or concerns.

For the purpose of this example, we will be hacking into a virtual machine as this is a great way to practice and scan for weaknesses without actually breaking into an established machine. We will be scanning our virtual machine for exploits upon which we will then penetrate the system and extract the information we require. The virtual machine will also have limited access meaning it won't actually be accessible as easy to other people who may be scanning your network, leaving you in complete control. In order to create a virtual machine, we will be using VirtualBox, a software that allows you to establish a hacking lab in order to test your skills on a simulated machine. VirtualBox is another open source software that allows you to have access to the source code free of charge, allowing you to customise your build to your specifications.

Before continuing with your experiment ensure that the techniques and tools you use throughout this test are confined only to your machine and never used on other computers as this is not only illegal, it is also potentially dangerous. Even if you are simply learning how to carry out an attack for the purpose of your own education, if you are caught you can be prosecuted, and as you should have a good understanding from reading this book, this can be quite a serious crime and yes, it is possible to be caught. Keeping this in mind, let us go through with our virtual pen-test.

Initial Preparation

The first step toward setting up your environment is creating virtual machine to run on VirtualBox. You will need two machines, a target and a victim. You are able to download these online, they will come with files that we can extract as well as vulnerabilities to exploit. Once you have the files in place, extract them and create a new machine on VirtualBox and choose the type of machine you will be using. From there you decide how much RAM your machine will be running with, this isn't too important so selecting a small amount won't affect your test, 512MB is a good starting point.

Your next task is then to select a hard disk by checking the Use an Existing Disk option. You are able to click on the folder option and select the appropriate file that you had extracted from your download files and once that is all done, click create and your virtual machine and you are ready to move onto the next step.

Creating a Network

In order to access your machine, you will need to establish a virtual network. This is to keep your machine safe from existing threats outside your control. You are able to do this through VirtualBox by going through File > Preferences > Network >

Host Only Network. Once you click the plus sign, you are able to add a new entry which will be your virtual network. Now is time to add your virtual machine to the virtual network. You are able to do this by selecting your virtual machine and clicking settings from the menu. From there you will see the network tab which will allow you to click 'Attacked to' from and Host-Only Adaptor from the drop-down menu.

Attacking Tools

Now that your network and machine have been set up it is time to acquire the tools to launch your attack. In this example, we will be using Kali as it is simple to set up and you can also run it live in a virtual machine. Once you have downloaded Kali as an ISO file, open VirtualBox and click Add to allow you to create another machine which will be your attacker. For your attacker, you want to allocate some more memory to the machine of around 2GB, if your machine has less than 4GB on the system, you may need to allocate less. You will not need to allocate any hard drive space, Kali is running live so check the box Do Not Add a Virtual Hard Drive. Once you are ready, hit create and your offending machine will be created. Ensure that you attach the machine to your network and change the adapter to host-holy. From here, you will start both machines and run Kali on your attack machine when prompted to add a bootable CD. You are then presented with the interface, and are ready to start scanning and gathering information from the Kali desktop interface.

Gathering Information

The next step in carrying out your attack is deciding upon your target. For the purpose of this experiment, we will be carrying out the attack on our victim server. In reality, this is a simple surface attack rather than focusing on the entire network that we had set up or the virtualization tools. From there it is time to gather information to discover the vulnerabilities that we will be exploiting. In order to do this, we will need to set this up in the software. This is where Metasploit will come into play as our framework for carrying out the pen-test, taking us through the process.

It is now time to begin collecting information. To do this, we must first we must initiate the services through Kali by entering:

"service postgresql start"

"service metasploit start"

Metasploit is best used through the console interface known as MSFConsole which is opened with

"Msfconsole"

Now you are ready to start your scan.

Scanning for Ports

In order to gather information on ports, you can use Nmap which is built into MSFconsole. In order to set this up, you will first need to enter the IP address of the target which you can find by typing in

"ifconfig"

This will then bring up information on the IP address, labelled inet addr within the eth0 block. The IP address should be similar to other machines found on your network. By running a scan of the IP address by using

Db_map -sS -A *TARGET IP ADDRESS*

You are able to have detailed list of all services running on the machine. From there you are able gather further information on each of the services to discover any vulnerabilities to exploit. Once you have found the weakest point, you are able to move into attack mode.

Exploitation

By enter services into MSFconsole, you are able to access the database of information on the services running on the machine. Once you have discovered a service that is particularly vulnerable, you are able to scan this service to assess points of weakness. This is done by typing

Search *service name*

Once you have done this, you will be provided a list of exploits which you can take advantage and can then tell MSFconsole to exploit the model. Once you have set the target, you simply need to type the command "run" for the program to work its magic and access the port. You will then be able to see what you are able to do once operating from the computer with a number of commands at your disposal with the permissions provided to you by the service. From here you are able to extract data as well as upload data depending on your objective.

Once you have accessed the machine, you will obviously want to ensure that you remained in control and fortunately Metasploit has a number of tools to assist.

Having a deeper understanding of the meaning behind the word hacker can open up new doors for you not just within your career if you decide to explore IT security but also within your business and personal life as you become better equipped in dealing with external threats to your networks and systems. Before reading this book, you like many other people, may have had some misconceptions about what hacking actually means, who is behind it, why they do it, what they have to gain from it and what can be done to prevent them.

Now that you have reached the end of our book on hacking, you should have a much greater insight into the world of hacking including what it means to be an ethical hacker and how they operate. Knowing that an ethical hacker is also known as a white hat hacker, you also learnt the difference between white and black hat hackers, who are motivated by personal reasons whether that could be financial or ideological. You also gained some insight into the hackers that lie on the boundaries of ethics such as those known as grey hats and red hats as well the hacktivists that so often capture our awareness in the media.

We also explored the techniques used by hackers to attack your computer and what each of these attacks can do to a system, the seriousness behind them and the types of hackers that employ these tactics to achieve their motivations. Upon learning these techniques, you also learnt how it was possible to avoid becoming a target through precautions which can protect your system and the information contained on it.

We then moved onto the topic on penetration testing and how organizations are able to simulate attacks on their own systems in order to expose weaknesses and vulnerabilities that could be exploited by external hackers. We learnt the basic process of how a pen-test works and why it is performed. This gave us some insight into the world of ethical hackers and what their job is comprised of. Once learning this, we took a deeper look into careers in IT security, how the indri is moving and the qualifications that are widely recognised in the industry.

We then took a look at the other side of the coin into the world of cyber terrorism. We explored the reasoning's behind why terrorists carry out these attacks as well as how organizations are able to better equip themselves for dealing with these threats. In looking at each type of attack, we gained an understand how businesses need to be extra vigilant to avoid suffering losses both financial and intangible.

Towards the end of the book we walked through the basic setup of a pen-test and how it can be performed using a lab type scenario on a virtual machine. While this was just a brief cover of a pen-test, it hopefully spurred some curiosity for you to continue your education further and develop new skills in hacking. With the now solid understanding of hacking in your possession, it is worth exploring further certifications and courses that will allow you to get closer to a career in security as a white hat hacker and expressing your skills in a healthy environment or just to expand your knowledge and become more aware.

Conclusion

I want to thank you once again for choosing this book.

Kali Linux is a very advanced flavor of Linux, which is used for Security Auditing and Penetration Testing. After all the tools that we have looked at, it is pretty clear that if you want to succeed in the domain of Security Research, Kali Linux will provide with unlimited power to achieve the same. It is also clear that if you are just beginning with Linux, Kali Linux is not the place that you would want to start with as it is a highly complex operating system created and aimed at achieving one goal and that is security.

PYTHON FOR BEGINNERS:

Introduction

Basics of Programming

Before we take a plunge into the world of computer programming, let us take a closer look at what computer programs are and what they are supposed to be. The standard defining of a computer program is as follows:

> A sequence of instructions for performing a particular task that has been written in a specific programming language is commonly referred to as a computer program.

As you can see in the given definition, two phrases have been written in bold namely, 'sequence of instructions' and 'programming language'. To understand the meaning and significance of these two terms, let us take an example. For instance, you have a household help and you have to tell her the procedure to prepare 2 cups of coffee. What will be the set of instructions that you will give to her? In all probability, you will tell her something like this –

1. Firstly, take two cups and keep them on the kitchen slab.

2. Take a boiling pan and using one of these cups for measurement, add two cups of water to it.

3. Switch on the stove.

4. Put the boiling pan on medium heat and wait until the water starts boiling.

5. In the two cups, add 1 teaspoon of coffee, 1 teaspoon of sugar and 1 teaspoon of milk powder.

6. Add boiling water to the cups.

7. Lastly, serve.

The seven steps mentioned above form what can be called 'human program'. It is a set of instructions that you have given to a human to perform a specific task. Since the language used for this human program is English, the programming language used for writing this human program is English. If your household help doesn't understand English, this human program will fail. Therefore, you will have to translate this program to the language she understands, which can be French, Arabic, Hindi, Spanish or any other language for that matter.

Analogously, when you have to tell the computer to do something for you, you have to give it a set of instructions in the language that it can understand. The language that it understands is the computer programming language and the set of instructions written in that language and given to the computer to perform a specific task is simply a computer program.

There are some other terms that you may also encounter in the world of computer programming. One such term is software. A computer program is usually also referred to as software. Besides this, you may also see phrases like source code and program coding. These are terms usually used for referring to the set of instructions written in a computer program.

Computer Programs

Computer programs are the heart and soul of a computer. The hardware is just a dead body unless you have active computer programs running on the system. All the capabilities of the computer can be used only after you tell the computer what it should do for you in the form of computer programs.

We unconsciously use many computer programs everyday. For instance, Google Chrome or Internet Explorer that you use to browse Internet is a computer program. The chat programs you use on your computer or mobile phone is a computer program. Moreover, the voice calls and SMS capabilities of mobile phones are also computer programs. You name it and there is a computer program associated with it. Whenever and whenever you use a computer to do a task, you are using a computer program.

Since computer programming is a skilled job, the individual who has an expertise in computer programming is referred to as a computer programmer. Depending on the programming language in which the computer programmer has expertise, he or she is called Python/C/HTML/Java/CSS/SQL/JavaScript programmer.

Algorithm

Now that you are thorough with the concept of computer program, you can simply relate computer programming to the process and art of writing computer programs. These programs should not only perform the specified task, but they should also do them well. This is where the concept of effective and efficient programming came into existence.

In order to make the process of program designing simpler, several approaches have been designed. The systematic procedure developed to solve a problem is called an algorithm. It is one of the most effective approaches for creation of a sequence of well-defined instructions aimed towards performing a task. You will hear this term just as much as you shall counter computer programs as they essentially go hand in hand.

In simple words, an algorithm is an English language equivalent of the computer program, written in the form of a list, by the programmer, before transforming it into a programming language – specific code. A sample algorithm has been given below to help you understand how an algorithm typically looks like. This algorithm given below computes the largest number from a list of numbers.

Algorithm for Computing Largest Number From Given List of Numbers

1. Get the given list of numbers.
2. Assume a variable L, which will hold the largest number.
3. Initialize L with the first number of the list.
4. Go to the next number of the list.
5. If L is less than this number, put this new number in L
6. Repeat step 4 and step 5 till the list is completely scanned.
7. Print L on the screen

This is a raw algorithm written in simple language to make it easy to understand for beginners. There is a standard procedure that needs to be followed for writing algorithms. However, this is part of advanced programming fundamentals and is beyond the scope of this book.

Programming Languages

Just like we have innumerable languages that are used for communication between humans, scientists have developed a plethora of computer programming languages to serve and meet the varied requirements of developers and applications.

We will introduce some of the key languages to you in the chapters to come. A list of the programming languages that we shall cover is as follows –

1. Java
2. **SQL**
3. C
4. C++
5. C#
6. Python
7. HTML
8. CSS
9. JavaScript

In order to understand the concept of programming languages, their structure and how they work, let us look at English, which is a standard human interface language. It is used by billions of people around the world to communicate with each other. As we know, English language makes words from a set of alphabets and these words are used to make sentences.

In order to make sure that the sentences are understandable to one and all, several grammar rules have to be applied. Besides this, language elements like conjunctions, verbs, nouns and adverbs, in addition to several others, have to be kept in mind while forming sentences. Likewise, other languages like French, Spanish, Russian, Arabic or Hindi also have their own set of rules that need to be followed for effective communication between two humans.

In the same manner, computer languages also have rules and elements that need to be understood before you can write programs to communicate with the computer. Some of these basic elements are as follows –

- Syntax
- Data types
- Keywords
- Variables
- Operators
- Loops
- Decision Making
- Program organization elements like Functions
- File I/O
- Programming environment

Most of the languages that we shall deal with in this book will have most of these elements. However, how they are included in the programming language varies. In this book, we shall introduce you to the different programming languages listed above and deal with the different elements and advanced programming concepts specific to the programming language in books specifically written for the language.

Chapter 1 Programming Environment

Although, programming environment does not form one of the core elements of a programming language, it would not be wrong to state that it is one of the prerequisites that you need to learn and get acquainted with even before you have written your first program. You will never know if your program is right or wrong unless you have a programming environment that can test the same for you. This is the reason why we are going to introduce you to programming environment before we jump to languages.

Simply, programming environment is software that will allow you to create, compile and execute computer programs on the system. It is an interface between the programmer and the computer, which will convert the programs that you will write into the computer's language and ask it to execute the same for you. Therefore, before you pick up any programming language, be sure to enquire about the required programming environment and how the same can be set up on the computer that you intend to use for your programming course.

Digging deeper into the programming environment and its setup, it is made up of three basic elements namely text editor, compiler and interpreter. In all probability, you will need all these three components for your course. So, before you go searching for them, let us help you understand what they exactly are and why you will need them.

Text Editor

A text editor is a simple text program that will allow you to create text files in which you will write you code. Depending on the programming language you are working on, the extension of the text file will change. For instance, if you programming in C language, your text files will have the extension .c.

If you are working on a Windows machine, you can simply search for Notepad in the search bar and use it as a text editor for your programs. You can also explore Notepad++ for some advanced options. It is freely available and you will just need to download and install it on your machine. On the other hand, if you are a Mac user, you can explore text editor options like BBEdit and TextEdit.

Compiler

Now that you have written the program and you are all ready to test if you have written it correctly or not, you have to give it to the computer and see if it understands what you are trying to communicate. However, the computer only understands binary language and what you have written is far from what it can directly digest. Therefore, this file needs to be converted into binary format.

If you have made syntactical errors and not followed the rules of the programming language, the compiler will not be able to make this conversion smoothly and will raise an error message for you. Therefore, the compiler is a program that checks if you have followed the syntactical rules of the chosen programming language and converts the text file into its binary form. Moreover, this process of conversion is referred to as compilation.

Most programming languages like C, Java, C++ and Pascal, besides many others require compilation and you will need to install their respective compilers before you can execute any programs written using them.

Interpreter

Unlike the programming languages mentioned above, there are some other programming languages like Python and Perl that do not require compiler. Therefore, instead of a compiler, they need an interpreter, which is also software. The interpreter simply reads the program from the text file and as it parses the file, it converts the contents of the file and executes them. If you are working on any such programming languages, remember to install the corresponding interpreter on your system before starting.

If you haven't worked with a computer before or have little to no experience in installing software on the computer, technical advice from an expert is recommended. However, be sure to do the installation yourself, as it will help you build an acquaintance with the device that you will work with in the near future.

Besides this, if your computer does not support installation of any of the programming environment elements, you can also make use of the online compilers and interpreters that are available for all the different programming languages nowadays. All you need is a good Internet connection and a web browser to open these online facilities and get started with your programming lessons and practice sessions right away.

Chapter 2 Data Analysis with Python

Another topic that we need to explore a bit here is how Python, and some of the libraries that come with it, can work with the process of data analysis. This is an important process for any businesses because it allows them to take all of the data and information they have been collecting for a long time, and then can put it to good use once they understand what has been said within the information. It can be hard for a person to go through all of this information and figure out what is there, but for a data analyst who is able to use Python to complete the process, it is easy to find the information and the trends that you need.

The first thing that we need to look at here though is what data analysis is all about. Data analysis is going to be the process that companies can use in order to extract out useful, relevant, and even meaningful information from the data they collect, in a manner that is systematic. This ensures that they are able to get the full information out of everything and see some great results in the process. There are a number of reasons that a company would choose to work on their own data analysis, and this can include:

- Parameter estimation, which helps them to infer some of the unknowns that they are dealing with.
- Model development and prediction. This is going to be a lot of forecasting in the mix.
- Feature extraction which means that we are going to identify some of the patterns that are there.
- Hypothesis testing. This is going to allow us to verify the information and trends that we have found.
- Fault detection. This is going to be the monitoring of the process that you are working on to make sure that there aren't any biases that happen in the information.

One thing that we need to make sure that we are watching out for is the idea of bias in the information that we have. If you go into the data analysis with the idea that something should turn out a certain way, or that you are going to manipulate the data so it fits the ideas that you have, there are going to be some problems. You can always change the data to say what you would like, but this doesn't mean that you are getting the true trends that come with this information, and you may be missing out on some of the things that you actually need to know about.

This is why a lot of data analysts will start this without any kind of hypothesis at all. This allows them to see the actual trends that come with this, and then see where the information is going to take you, without any kind of slant with the information that you have. This can make life easier and ensures that you are actually able to see what is truly in the information, rather than what you would like to see in that information.

Now, there are going to be a few different types of data that you can work with. First, there is going to be the deterministic. This is going to also be known as the data analysis that is non-random. And then there is going to be the stochastic, which is pretty much any kind that is not going to fit into the category of deterministic.

The Data Life Cycle

As we go through this information, it is important to understand some of the different phases that come with the data life cycle. Each of these comes together to ensure that we are able to understand the information that is presented to us and that we are able to use all of the data in the most efficient and best way possible.

There are a few stages that are going to come with this data life cycle, and we are going to start out with some of the basics to discuss each one to help us see what we are able to do with the data available to us. First, we work with data capture. The first experience that an individual or a company should have with a data item is to have it pass through the firewalls of the enterprise. This is going to be known as the Data Capture, which is basically going to be the act of creating values of data that do not exist yet and have never actually existed in that enterprise either. There are three ways that you can capture the data including:

- Data acquisition: This is going to be the ingestion of data that is already existing that was produced by the organization but outside of the chosen enterprise.
- Data entry: This is when we are dealing with the creation of new data values to help with the enterprise and it is done by devices or human operators that can help to generate the data needed.
- Signal reception: This is where we are going to capture the data that a device has created with us, typically in the control system, but can be found in the Internet of Things if we would like.

The next part is going to be known as Data Maintenance. This is going to be where you supply the data to points at which data synthesis and data usage can occur in the next few steps. And it is best if you are able to work out the points so that they are going to be ready to go in this kind of phase.

What we will see during the data maintenance is that we are working to process the data, without really working to derive any value out of it yet. This is going to include integration changed data, cleansing, and making sure that the data is in the right format and as complete as possible before we get started. This ensures that no matter what method or algorithm you choose to work with here, you are going to be able to have the data ready to go.

Once you have been able to maintain the data and get it all cleaned up, it is time to work on the part known as data synthesis. This is a newer phase in the cycle and there are some places where you may not see this happen. This is going to be where we create some of the values of data through inductive logic, and using some of the data that we have from somewhere else as the input. The data synthesis is going to be the arena of analytics that is going to use modeling of some kind to help you get the right results in the end.

Data usage comes next. This data usage is going to be the part of the process where we are going to apply the data as information to tasks that the enterprise needs to run and then handle the management on its own. This would be a task that normally falls outside of your life cycle for the data. However, data is becoming such a central part of the model for most businesses and having this part done can make a big difference.

For example, the data itself can be a service or a product, or at least part of this service or product. This would then make it a part of the data usage as well. The usage of the data is going to have some special challenges when it comes to data governance. One of these is whether it is legal to use the data in the ways that most people in business would like. There could be some issues like contractual or regulatory constraints on how we can use this data and it is important that these are maintained as much as possible.

Once we have figured out the data usage, it is time to move on to data publication. In being used, it may be possible that our single data value may be sent outside of the enterprise. This is going to be known as the data publication, which we can define as the sending of data to a location that is not within the enterprise.

A good example of this would be when you have a brokerage that sends out some monthly statements to their client. Once the data has been sent outside the enterprise, it is de facto impossible to get that information back. When the values of data are wrong and you publish it, it is impossible to correct them because they are now beyond the reach of your enterprise. The idea of Data Governance, like we talked about before, is going to have to handle how this information that is incorrect can be handled with.

Next on the list is the data archival. We will see that the single data value that we are working with can sometimes experience a lot of different rounds of usage and then publication, but eventually, it is going to reach the very end of its life. The first part of this means that we need to be able to take the value of the data and archive it. When we work on the process of Data Archival, it is going to mean that we are copying the data to an environment where it is stored in case we need it again, in an active production environment, and then we will remove the data from all of those active environments as well.

This kind of archive for the data is simply going to be a place where the data is stored, but where no publication, usage, or maintenance is going to happen. If necessary, it is possible to take any of the data that is in the archive and bring it back out to use again.

And finally, we reach the part of data purging. This is going to be the end that comes with our single data value and the life cycle that it has gone through. Data purging is going to be when we remove every copy of data from the enterprise. If possible, you will reach this information through the archive. If there is a challenge from Data Governance at this point, it is just there to prove that the information and the data have gone through the proper purging procedure at that time.

–

Working with data analysis and why it is important

With this in mind, we need to pay attention to why we would want to work on data analysis to start with? Do we really need to be able to look through all of this information to find the trends, or is there another method? Let's look at an example of what can happen when we do this data analysis and why you would want to use it.

Let's consider that we are looking at a set of data that includes information about the weather that occurred across the globe between the years 2015 to 2018. We are also going to have information that is base don the country between these years as well. So, there is going to be a percentage of ran within that country and we are going to have some data that concerns this in our set of data as well.

Now, what if you would like to go through all of that data, but you would like to only take a look at the data that comes with one specific country. Let's say that you would like to look at America and you want to see what percentage of rain it received between 2016 and 2017. Now, how are you going to get this information in a quick and efficient manner?

What we would need to do to make sure that we were able to get ahold of this particular set of data is to work with the data analysis. There are several algorithms, especially those that come from machine learning, that would help you to figure out the percentage of rain that America gets between 2016 to 2017. And this whole process is going to be known as what data analysis is really all about.

The Python Panda Library

When it comes to doing some data analysis in Python, the best extension that you can use is Pandas. This is an open-sourced library that works well with Python and it is going to provide you with a high level of performance, data structures that are easy for even a beginner to use, and tools to make data analysis easy with Python. There are a lot of things to enjoy about this language, and if you want to be able to sort through all of the great information that you have available with the help of Python, then this is the library that you need to work with.

There are a lot of things that you can enjoy when it comes to working on the Python library. First off, this is one of the most popular and easy to use libraries when it comes to data science and it is going to work on top of the NumPy library. The name of Pandas that was given to this library is derived from the word of Panel Data, which is going to be an Econometrics from Multidimensional data. And one thing that a lot of coders are going to like about working with Pandas is that it is able to take a lot of the data that you need, including a SQL database or a TSV and CSV file, and will use it to create an object in Python. This object is going to have columns as well as rows called the data frame, something that looks very similar to what we see with a table in statistical software including Excel.

There are many different features that are going to set Pandas apart from some of the other libraries that are out there. Some of the benefits that you are going to enjoy the most will include:

- There are some data frames or data structures that are going to be high level compared to some of the others that you can use.
- There is going to be a streamlined process in place to handle the tabular data, and then there is also a functionality that is rich for the time series that you want to work with.

- There is going to be the benefit of data alignment, missing data-friendly statistics, merge, join, and groupby methods to help you handle the data that you have.
- You are able to use the variety of structures for data in Pandas, and you will be able to freely draw on the functions that are present in SciPy and NumPy to help make sure manipulation and other work can be done the way that you want.

Before we move on from here, we also need to have a good look at what some of the types of data are when it comes to Pandas. Pandas is going to be well suited when it comes to a large amount of data and will be able to help you sort through almost any kind of data that you would like. Some of the data types that are going to be the most suitable for working with the Pandas library with Python will include:

- Any kind of tabular data that is going to have columns that are heterogeneously typed.
- Arbitrary matrix data that has labels for the columns and rows.
- Unordered and ordered time-series data

- Any other kinds of sets of data that are statistical and observational.

Working with the Pandas library is one of the best ways to handle some of the Python codings that you want to do with the help of data analysis. As a company, it is so important to be able to go through and not just collect data, but also to be able to read through that information and learn some of the trends and the information that is available there. being able to do this can provide your company with some of the insights that it needs to do better, and really grow while providing customer service.

There are a lot of different methods that you can use when it comes to performing data analysis. And some of them are going to work in a different way than we may see with Python or with the Pandas library. But when it comes to efficiently and quickly working through a lot of data, and having a multitude of algorithms and more that can sort through all of this information, working with the Python Pandas is the best option.

–

Chapter 3 Fundamentals of Statistics

Why Statistics is Important for Data Science?

Some of the algorithms in machine learning have been borrowed from statistics. So, we need some basic knowledge of statistics to understand how to extract useful information from data and how to build estimation models for data prediction based on hypothesis and assumptions. For example, linear regression is widely used in several machine learning problems. In statistics, it is used for fitting a line to data values while in machine learning, it is more like learning weights (constant values in line equation) through examples.

Some uses of statistics in machine learning are:

• Data Understanding: *Understanding distribution of data variables and their relationships. So, we can design a model predictor best suited for data. For this, we need to understand what data distribution is, what relationships our variables can have and how to understand those relationships.*

- Data Cleaning: *We cannot simply get raw data and feed it to machine learning models for our task. There are certain complexities within. For example, the data might be corrupted, erroneous or just missing. So, we need to fix those issues e.g. we can fill the missing data following the same data distribution, we can identify outliers and abnormal data distributions to eliminate corruption or errors.*

- *Data Preparation*: Sometimes, our data features are not all on the same scale which leads to some issues in model training (It is further explained in training models part). Sometimes, the data is textual and we need to encode it in numeric form to make it compatible for our model. So we need data scaling, sampling and encoding from statistics.

- Model Configuration and Selection: *Hyperparameters of a machine learning model control the learning method which can lead to different results from the model. Using statistical hypothesis testing technique from statistics, we can compare results of different hyperparameters. Similarly, we need such statistical techniques to select a model by comparing models' results and their properties.*

• Model Evaluation: *To evaluate a model, we need statistical methods for data sampling and resampling. We also need metrics to properly evaluate model and quantify the variability in predictions using estimation statistics.*

Data Types

Data in statistics is classified in following types and subtypes:

4) Qualitative Data
  a. Nominal/Categorical
  b. Ordinal
5) Quantitative Data
  a. Discrete
  b. Continuous
    i.   Interval
    ii. Ratio

Qualitative Data

Qualitative data is non-numerical and categorical data. Categorical data can be counted, grouped and ranked in order of importance. Such data is grouped to bring order or make sense of the data.

Nominal:

Nominal scales represent data that does not have quantitative values or any numerical significance. This scale is used for classification or categorization of the variables. These variables are simply labels of data without any specific order. Such scale is often used in surveys and questionnaires.

Of these three colors, which one do you like the most?

6) Red
7) Green
8) Blue

For example, in the above question, color is a categorical variable but there is no specific way to order these colors from low to high or high to low.

So, for a question in a survey:

Which pizza crust do you like?

5) Thin Crust
6) Stuffed Crust

7) Cheese Stuffed Crust

8) Hand Tossed Crust

Only the types of crust are significant of analysis and their order does not matter. The results of such questions are analyzed to provide the most common answer which describes the customers' preferences.

ORDINAL:

Ordinal scale represents data that has some specific order. That order relates elements of data to each other in a ranked fashion. Numbers can be assigned as labels and are not mathematically measured as scales.

How satisfied you are with your test scores:

Chapter 17 Extremely Unsatisfied

Chapter 18 Unsatisfied

Chapter 19 Neutral

Chapter 20 Satisfied

Chapter 21 Extremely Satisfied

Here, these options are assigned numbers, that is, a ranking of 5 is better than a ranking of 3 but we cannot quantify the difference between these two rankings (i.e. how good ranking 5 is compared to ranking 3).

Quantitative Data

Data that is numerical or can be measured is called quantitative data. For example, heights of 12 years old boys, GPA of a class, Distance of stars, Temperature of the day and so on. Numerical data have two sub data types:

5) Discrete
6) Continuous

DISCRETE:

Discrete data is numerical data that can not be subdivided into smaller parts. For example, number of people in a room, number of apples in a basket, number of planets in solar system, etc.

CONTINUOUS:

Continuous data can be broken down into smaller parts. For example, temperature, distance, weight of a person, etc. Continuous data can be further categorized into two types:

5) Interval
6) Ratio

Interval:

Interval scale represents data that has specific order and that order has mathematical significance, which means that unlike nominal and ordinal scales, the interval scale quantifies the difference between the order of variables. This scale is quite effective because we can apply statistical analysis on such data. The only drawback of this scale is that we cannot compute ratios because it does not have a true zero value (a starting point for values) and hence, a zero value does not mean "absence of value" and is therefore not meaningful.

For example, 70 degree Celcius is less than 90 degree Celcius and their difference is a measurable 20 C as is the difference between 90 C and 110 C. Also, 40 degree Celcius is not twice as hot as 20 degree Celcius. A value of 0 C is arbitrary as it does not mean "no temperature" and because negative values of temperature do exist.

Ratio:

Ratio scale has all the properties from Interval scale and also defines a true zero value. A meaningful zero in ratio scale means "absence of value". Because of the existence of a true zero value, variables of ratio scale does not have negative values and it allows to measure ratio between two variables. This scale allows to apply techniques of inferential and descriptive statistics to variables. Some examples of ratio variables are height, weight, money, age and time.

For example, what is your weight in pounds?

- *< 100 lbs*

- *100 lbs - 120 lbs*

- *121 lbs - 140 lbs*

- *141 lbs - 160 lbs*

- *> 160 lbs*

Similarly, there is no such thing as age 0, because that essentially means you don't exist. Because of this, we can compare that an age of 24 is twice the age of 12 and that we cannot have negative age value.

Statistics in Practice

Statistics is defined as the collection, analysis and interpretation of data. It transforms raw data to useful information and helps us understand our data required to train our machine learning models and interpret their results. The field of statistics has two major divisions: Descriptive statistics and Inferential statistics. Both of these divisions combined are powerful tools for data understanding, description and data prediction. Descriptive statistics describes and interprets data and helps us understand how two variables or processes are related while inferential statistics is used to reason from available data.

Descriptive Statistics

Descriptive statistics describes features of data by summarizing it. For example we have test scores of 100 students from a class. Descriptive statistics gives detailed information about those scores e.g. how spread the scores are, if there are outliers (scores way above or lower than average score), how scores are distributed (how many students with low score, high score or average score) and many other similar stats of those results.

Basic Definitions

POPULATION

Population is something under observation for study. It is a set of observations. It also describes the subject of a particular study. For example, if we are studying weights of men, the population would be the set of weights of all men of the world.

Population Parameters

Population parameters are characteristics and stats about population such as mean, standard deviation.

Sample

Sample is a randomly taken small part of the population or just a subset of the population. The observations and conclusions made on sample data represent properties or attributes of the entire population. For example, consider a study where we want to know how many hours, on average, do a teenager spends in physical exercise. Since, surveying all the teenagers of the world or even a country is impractical because of time and resource constraint. So, we take a sample from the population that represents the entire population.

Descriptive statistics is further divided into measures of center and measures of dispersion.

3) Measures of Center
   a. Mean
   b. Median
   c. Mode
4) Measures of Dispersion
   a. Range
   b. Percentiles/Quartiles
   c. Interquartile range
   d. Variance
   e. Standard Deviation
   f. Kurtosis
   g. Skewness

Measure of Center/Central Tendency

Central tendency describes a dataset with a single value which is the central position within that dataset. This central position provides summary of the whole data.

Three measures of central tendency are:

- Mean

- Median

- Mode

189

Mean

It refers to the mean or average of data and is the sum of all values of the data divided by the number of values. It is represented by letter μ or $\underline{x}$ and is given by:

$$\mu = \frac{1}{n}\sum_{i=1}^{n} x_i$$

Some properties of mean make it very useful for measuring

For example, consider following array of numbers and their mean calculated:

Given Array: $\{-5, 6, 3, 0, 6\}$

$$\mu = \frac{(-5 + 6 + 3 + 0 + 6)}{5} = \frac{10}{5}$$

$$\mu = 2.0$$

A disadvantage of using statistical mean is that it can be biased because it is affected by outliers in the data. Consider the above example again and see how the existence of an outlier will affect the mean value:

Given Array: { − 5, 6, 3, 0, 6, 110 }

$$\mu = \frac{(-5 + 6 + 3 + 0 + 6 + 110)}{6} = \frac{120}{6}$$

$\mu = 20.0$

Median

Median is another measure of central tendency and is the middle value of ascendingly sorted data. If the number of values in dataset is even, the median is the mean value of two middle values in sorted array.

Given Array { − 5, 6, 3, 0, 6 }

Sorted in Ascending Order { − 5, 0, 3, 6, 6 }

Median is our middle value in sorted array = 3

One important property of median is that it is not affected by outliers. Consider the example of statistical mean with outlier:

Given Array { − 5, 6, 3, 0, 6, 110 }

Sorted in Ascending Order { − 5, 0, 3, 6, 6, 110 }

$$Median = \frac{(3 + 6)}{2} = \frac{9}{2}$$

$$Median = 4.5$$

So, median should be used when data is skewed (not symmetric).

Mode

Mode is the most frequently occurring value in the data. Some datasets can be multimodal (having more than one modes) and some may not have any mode at all. For example,

Given Array $\{1, 6, 0, 9, 3, -2, 4, -1, -1, 5, 1, 5, 3, 1, 7, -3, -4, 7, 8, -1\}$

Modes: $-1, 1$

Given Array: $\{-1, 7, 3, 15, 2\}$

This data does not have any mode

Mode is rarely used as central measure of tendency. One problem with mode is that there can be multiple modes in data and they can be spread out.

Following three histograms with different symmetric and skewed distributions show three measures of center. In case of symmetric (normal) distribution, mean, median and mode are all same. Although we can use any of these three measures but mean is usually preferred because it considers all the values of data in calculation, which is not the case for median and mode.

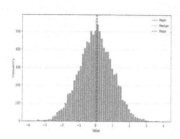

Now consider when the data is right skewed. Here, mean is not a good representation of the center of dataset and so, we can better choose median measure.

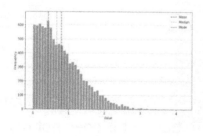

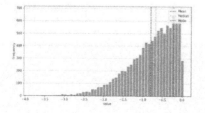

Measures of Dispersion

Measure of dispersion tells how much the data distribution is stretched out or how variable the data is. Sometimes, measure of central tendency is not enough to grasp the distribution of data. For example, two data distributions can have same mean but one distribution can be more spread out than the other.

Range

It is the simplest measure of dispersion. It is the difference between the maximum value and the minimum value of the data.

Given Array: $\{-4, 7, 1, 7, -5, 6, 3, 0\}$

Range: $7 - (-5) = 12$

Range provides us a quick way to get a rough idea of the spread of distribution but it does not give much detail about the data. Two datasets can have same range but their values can vary significantly. Also, range is sensitive to outliers or extreme values.

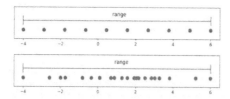

Percentile

A percentile represents a value below which a given percentage of data falls. In other words, percentile is the relative position of a value in sorted dataset. A student scored 89 out of 100 in a test. This figure alone does not have significant meaning unless we know what was his/her position in class. May be, a score of 89 falls in the 30th percentile which means that it is better than 30% of the class or may be 70th percentile (70% of students have scored less than 89 on test).

Index of a number at Pth percentile in an ordered list of values is given by:

$$Index = \frac{P}{100} * N$$

For example,

Given Sorted Values: { − 1,5,12,13,30,50}

For example, for list of numbers given above,

$15th\ percentile: P_{15}$
$$= \frac{15}{100} * 6 = 0.9 \approx 1\ (1st\ number\ in\ the\ list)$$

$30th\ percentile: P_{30}$
$$= \frac{30}{100} * 6 = 1.8 \approx 2\ (2nd\ number\ in\ the\ list)$$

$60th\ percentile: P_{60}$
$$= \frac{60}{100} * 6 = 3.6 \approx 4\ (4th\ number\ in\ the\ list)$$

$99th\ percentile: P_{99}$
$$= \frac{99}{100} * 6 = 5.9 \approx 6\ (6th\ number\ in\ the\ list)$$

Quartiles

Quartiles are three values that divide a dataset into 4 parts where each part contains 25% of the total data. First, second and third quartiles are actually 25th, 50th and 75th percentiles respectively. First quartile divides the data in 1:3 parts and has 25% of data on the left side(or below it). Second quartile divides the data in 1:1 while the third quartile divides the data in 3:1 parts (75% data on left side). So, second quartile is actually the middle value (or median) of the dataset and it divides the data into two equal parts. Then, first quartile is the middle value (or median) of the first part and third quartile is the middle value (or median) of the second part.

For example,

Given array:

$[\,10,\,-9,\,-7,10,3,\,-10,\,-2,\,-3,14,\,-2,\,-6,$
$-9,14,16,0\,]$

Sorted array:

$[\,-10,\,-9,\,-9,\,-7,\,-6,\,-3,\,-2,$
$-2,\ 0,\ 3,10,10,14,14,16\,]$

$Q_1 = -2$

InterQuartile Range

Interquartile range (IRQ) is the difference between third quartile and first quartile. An important property of IQR is that it is not affected by outlier values, which makes it preferable over range. It focuses on the middle 50% values of data.

Sorted array:

$[-10, -9, -9, -7, -6, -3, -2, -2, 0, 3, 10, 10, 14, 14, 16]$

IRQ: 16.5

Visual representation of some of these measures is shown in following boxplot.

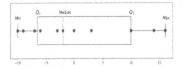

Variance

It is a measure of the spread of data. It quantifies how far, on average, the data is from the mean value.

$$Var(X) = \frac{1}{N}\sum_{i=1}^{N}(x_i - \mu)^2$$

Standard Deviation

Standard deviation is just the square root of variance. The difference between variance and standard deviation is that variance value is on a large scale while standard deviation has the same scale as other dataset values. It is represented by the greek letter σ and is given by:

$$\sigma = \sqrt{Var(X)}$$

For example, consider following values, their mean and standard deviation has been calculated:

$\{2, 8, 0, 2, -2, -4, 7, 1, 7, -5, 6, 3, 0, 6, 8, 6, 2, 6, -3, 9\}$

$\mu = 2.95$

$\sigma = 4.2$

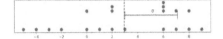

Skewness

Skewness is a measure of data asymmetry. A symmetric distribution means that the data values are equally distributed around the mean value, as in the case of a normal distribution. In case of asymmetry, data is distributed unevenly or the distribution is not symmetrical about the mean. In positively skewed data distribution, values are concentrated to the left and in negatively skewed data, values are concentrated to the right as shown in figure below. If data skewness is not close to zero, the data is not normally distributed.

$$Skewness = \frac{\frac{1}{N}\sum_{i=1}^{N}(x_i - \mu)^3}{\sigma^3}$$

Kurtosis

Kurtosis describes the tail of a distribution with reference to a normal distribution. A normal distribution has a kurtosis equal to 3 and is called mesokurtic. A distribution with shorter and thinner tails, broader and lower peaks than a normal distribution is called platykurtic and has kurtosis less than 3. A distribution with longer tails, higher and sharper peaks than a normal distribution is called leptykurtic and has kurtosis greater than 3.

$$Kurtosis = \frac{\frac{1}{N}\sum_{i=1}^{N}(x_i - \mu)^4}{\sigma^4}$$

Where N is the number of values, μ is mean of values and σ is standard deviation.

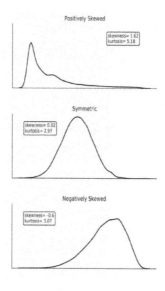

Chapter 4 Visualization and results

In the previous chapters we learnt how to handle data. In this chapter we are going to learn methods of visualizing data as well as creating figures to present analysis of data. In order to develop figures, many libraries are available in Python. This section presents only functionalities of the matplolib library which is an advanced library in Python to develop figures.

Matplotlib library in Python

Matplolib library is an open source advanced package available in Python for data visualization. Data visualization is crucial in data analysis as well as to communicate the results to stakeholders. This library is based on the NumPy library too. One module of matplotlib library that is very used is the Pyplot. This module has similar interface as Matlab a programming tool that is efficient for numerical programming. If you did not install matplotlib yet, you can do so by typing the following command in python prompt:

pip install matplotlib

If you have installed Anaconda and you are using Jupyter, this library should be already installed by default. All you have to do is import the package.

Before dining into examples and how to use the matplotlib library, let's see the component of a figure that we can set. A figure is entire figure that is formed by one or more axes which are called a plot. Axes is what is commonly named as a plot. A figure can be formed by different axes depending on the type of plotting we are making 1D, 2D or 3D. Axis are responsible of setting the limits of a plot. Artist is all the components that can be in a figure like a text object, collection objects.

Basic plot in matplotlib

We will start first in this chapter by the Pyplot module in matplotlib. This module offers the basic functions to supplement components to the current axes of a figure. To use this module, it should be imported as follows:

>>> import numpy as np

>>> import matplotlib.pyplot as plt

Note here we imported the Numpy library as well because we will be working with numpy arrays.

Now we can create a single plot of a data using the function plot(). Let's create a series of data and plot these data.

```
>>> X = np.array([1,2,3,4])
>>> Y = X ** 2
>>> plt.plot(X,Y)
>>> plt.show()
```

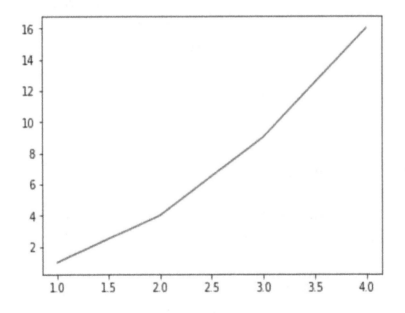

In this example, we created an array of values and computed the square of each value. The plot function is supplied with 2 inputs where the 1st argument is values of X-axis and the 2nd argument is corresponding values of Y-axis. Now it would be helpful to understand the plotting if we had a legend of the axis and a title for the plot. To add these elements into our plotting, we can use the *xlabel()* function that adds a label to the x-axis and *ylabel()* function that adds a label to the y-axis. The *title()* function adds a title to the plot.

```
>>> A = np.array([1,2,3,4])

>>> B = A ** 2

>>> plt.plot(A,B)

>>> plt.xlabel('A labels')

>>> plt.ylabel('B= A**2')

>>> plt.title('My first in Python')

>>> plt.show()
```

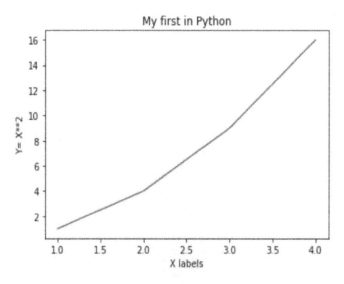

Now we can change the size of the figure using the figure function and passing argument that specifies the size of the figure. For example, let's change the size of the previous figure we created.

```
>>> A = np.array([1,2,3,4])

>>> B = A ** 2

>>> plt.figure(figsize=(5,5))

>>> plt.plot(A,B)

>>> plt.xlabel('A labels')

>>> plt.ylabel('B= A**2')

>>> plt.title('My first in Python with different size')

>>> plt.show()
```

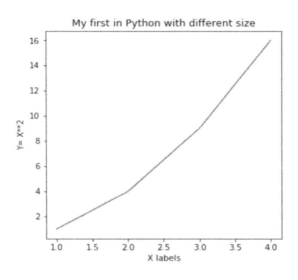

The plot function can take other input argument. In fact, we can plot two different datasets in the same plot. Let's define compute the values of X ** 3 and plot it in the same figure as an example.

```
>>> A = np.array([1,2,3,4])
>>> B = A ** 2
>>> B2 = A ** 3
>>> plt.figure(figsize=(10,5))
>>> plt.plot(A,B, A,B2)
>>> plt.xlabel('A labels')
>>> plt.ylabel('B= A**2')
>>> plt.title('My first in Python with two dataset')
>>> plt.show()
```

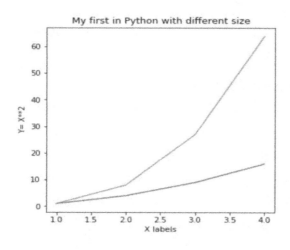

Note that by default the plot function used a different color to plot the second dataset. Also, by default plot function draws the data as a line. In fact, we can pass another argument to the plot function that will specify how the data is plot. In other words, we specify if data is plotted as a line or using another marker such '+', '*', '0'. We can also specify the color. For instance, 'go' will make the plot function to use o to plot the data and the data will be plotted in green. We can also specify the line width if the data is plotted as a line. For example:

```
>>> A = np.array([1,2,3,4])
>>> B=A ** 2
>>> B2 = A ** 3
>>> plt.figure(figsize=(10,5))
>>> plt.plot(A,B,A,B2,linewidth=5)
>>> plt.xlabel('A labels')
>>> plt.ylabel('B= A**2')
>>> plt.title('My first in Python with two datasets and Line width=5')
>>> plt.show()
```

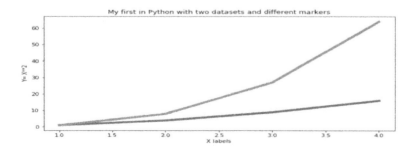

The following example uses different markers to plot two datasets:

```
>>> X = np.array([1,2,3,4])

>>> Y = X ** 2

>>> Y2 = X ** 3

>>> plt.figure(figsize=(5,5))

>>> plt.plot(X,Y,'r*', X,Y2, 'ko')

>>> plt.xlabel('X labels')

>>> plt.ylabel('Y= X**2')

>>> plt.title('My first in Python with two datasets and different markers')

>>> plt.show()
```

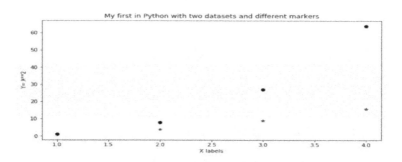

Multiple plots in same figure

You plot several plots in the same figure using the *subplot()* function. Note the datasets that we plotted in the previous section in the same plot can be plotted in different plots in the same figure. The *subplot()* function takes as inputs the following arguments ncols, nrows and finally index. The ncols indicate the number of columns in the figure, nrows the numbers of rows in the figure and the index point toward which plot. For example, we can plot our two datasets in a figure with two rows as follows:

```
>>> X = np.array([1,2,3,4])
>>> Y = X ** 2
>>> Y2 = X ** 3
>>> plt.figure(figsize=(10,10))
>>> plt.subplot(2,1,1)
>>> plt.plot(X,Y,linewidth=5)
>>> plt.xlabel('X labels')
>>> plt.ylabel('Y= X**2')
>>> plt.title('My first subplot in Python')
>>> plt.subplot(2,1,2)
>>> plt.plot(X,Y2,linewidth=5)
>>> plt.xlabel('X labels')
>>> plt.ylabel('Y= X**3')
>>> plt.title('My second subplot in Python')
```

```
>>> plt.show()
```

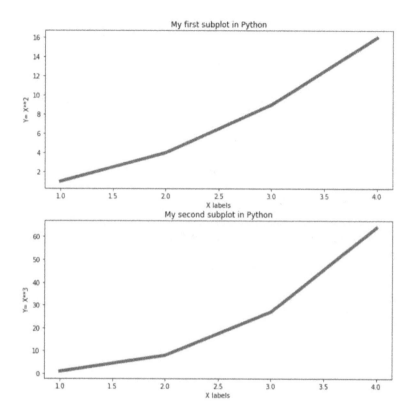

We can plot the two data set in a figure with two columns and two rows by passing as argument to the subplot (1,2,1) and (1,2,2) as follows:

```
>>> X = np.array([1,2,3,4])

>>> Y = X ** 2

>>> Y2 = X ** 3

>>> plt.figure(figsize=(10,10))
```

```
>>> plt.subplot(1,2,1)

>>> plt.plot(X,Y,linewidth=5)

>>> plt.xlabel('X labels')

>>> plt.ylabel('Y= X**2')

>>> plt.title('My first subplot in Python')

>>> plt.subplot(1,2,2)

>>> plt.plot(X,Y2,linewidth=5)

>>> plt.xlabel('X labels')

>>> plt.ylabel('Y= X**3')

>>> plt.title('My second subplot in Python')

>>> plt.show()
```

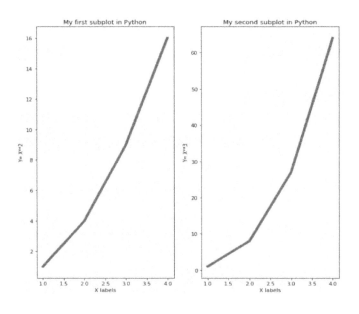

Type of plots

The matplotlib offers several functions to create different graphs that are useful in data science and statistical analysis. The bar graphs are a handy graph to assess and compare different groups among data and explore their distribution. The *bar()* function take as input argument a set of categorial data and their associated values. It takes also optionally a color if you want to make a bar graph where each category is represented with a specific color. For example, let's take the Iris data from the example in the previous chapter about Data frame data structure. Remember the Iris data is formed by a by a sample of 3 species of the Iris flower. Each species is described by sepals and petals length and sepals and petals width. This dataset is available in the sklearn library from which we are going to import the dataset. Because we will be using DataFrame structure we will import the Pandas library as well and we are going to create a Dataframe for the Iris dataset.

>>> import pandas as pd

>>> import numpy as np

>>> from sklearn import datasets

>>> Iris = datasets.load_iris()

I>>> Iris_d = Iris.data

>>> Iris_DF = pd.DataFrame(Iris_d, columns=Iris.feature_names)

213

The Iris data set has also a variable associated with each value of the sepal length and width as well as lengths and width of the petal. This variable indicates the Iris follower's species and is stored in the variable target. In the following command we are going to create a variable for this variable target:

>>> Y = Iris.target

Now that we have our data ready, we are going to plot a bar graph of the sepal length as follows:

>>> plt.bar(Y, Iris_DF['sepal length (cm)'])

>>> plt.title(' Bar Graph of the Sepal length')

>>> plt.xlabel(' Iris Species')

>>> plt.ylabel(' Count')

>>> plt.show()

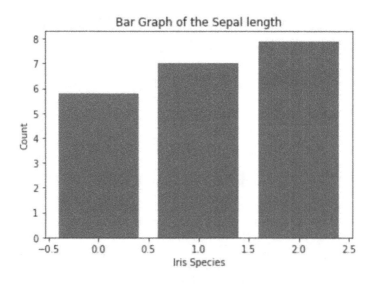

By default, Python plot figures in blue. We can change the color of the bars in the graph by passing the argument color as follows:

>>> plt.bar(Y, Iris_DF['sepal length (cm)'], color='black')

>>> plt.title(' Bar Graph of the Sepal length')

>>> plt.xlabel(' Iris Species')

>>> plt.ylabel(' Count')

>>> plt.show()

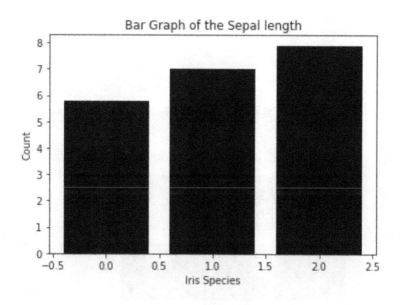

We can also change the orientation of the bars from vertical bars to horizontal bars using the function *barh()*. The barh() function takes the same input argument as the *bar()* function. Let's plot horizontal bar graph for the sepal width length for each Iris species.

>>> plt.barh(Y,Iris_DF['sepal length (cm)'], color='black')

>>> plt.title(' Bar Graph of the Sepal length')

>>> plt.xlabel(' Iris Species')

>>> plt.ylabel(' Count')

>>> plt.show()

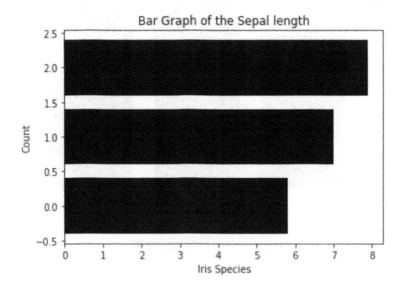

We can also supply the *bar()* or the *barh()* function with an extra argument xerr or yerr(if using the *bar()* function) and its values. For example, if we want o plot also the variance of the variable for which the bar graph is plotted. For example, in the case of the sepal length we can do if we are using *barh()* function:

>>> # Computing the variance with Numpy library

>>> V = np.var(Iris_DF['sepal length (cm)'])

>>> plt.barh(Y, Iris_DF['sepal length (cm)'], xerr = V, color = 'grey')

>>> plt.title(' Bar Graph of the Sepal length with Variance')

>>> plt.xlabel(' Iris Species')

>>> plt.ylabel(' Count')

>>> plt.show()

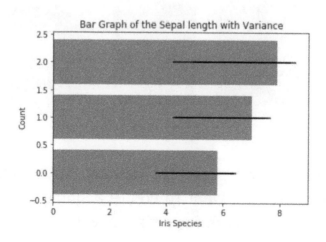

If the function *bar()* is used for vertical bars, to plot the variance with bars we pass as argument yerr as follows:

>>> plt.bar(Y, Iris_DF['sepal length (cm)'], yerr = V, color = 'grey')

>>> plt.title(' Bar Graph of the Sepal length with Variance')

>>> plt.xlabel(' Iris Species')

>>> plt.ylabel(' Count')

>>> plt.show()

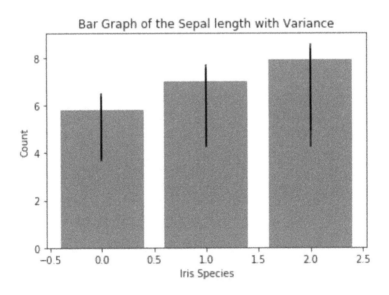

Sometimes, we have a dataset with multiple variables and we want to create a single bar graph that shows the bars for different variables for each category like in the case of the Iris data set we are using in this chapter. To plot or stack multiple bars in the same graph, we need to use the *bar()* function as many times as the number of the variables for which the graph are plotted. In this case, we need to specify the index and width for the bars to stack them together. Let's see how we can use this in order to plot in the same graph sepal length and sepal width bars. First, we need to group the Iris flowers according to the species and compute the mean sepal length and mean sepal width for each species. Remember we can do that using the *groupby()* function like we did in the previous chapter. We also need to add the Y variable which indicates the Iris species into our DataFrame.

>>> data = Iris_DF

>>> data['Y'] = Y # Adding the Y variable to the Dataframe

>>> grouped_data = data.groupby(' Y ') # Grouping the Iris flowers according to the species

>>> # Computing the mean sepal length and width for each species

>>> M = grouped_data['sepal length (cm)'].agg(np.mean)

```
>>> M2 = grouped_data['sepal width
(cm)'].agg(np.mean)
```

```
>>> print(' The mean sepal length (cm) for
each species is:', M)
```

The mean sepal length (cm) for each
species is: Y
0   5.006
1   5.936
2   6.588
Name: sepal length (cm), dtype: float64

```
>>> print(' The mean width (cm) of the sepal
for each species is:', M)
```

The mean sepal width (cm) for each species is: Y

0   5.006

1 5.936

2 6.588

Name: sepal length (cm), dtype: float64

Now that the data is ready, we plot the stacked bar
graph as follows:

```
>>> ind = np.arange(3)
```

```
>>> width = 0.3

>>> plt.bar (ind, M, width, color = 'grey')

>>> plt.bar (ind + width, M2, width, color = 'blue')

>>> plt.title(' Bar Graph of the Sepal length
and width (cm)')

>>> plt.xlabel(' Iris Species')

>>> plt.ylabel(' Count')

>>> plt.show()
```

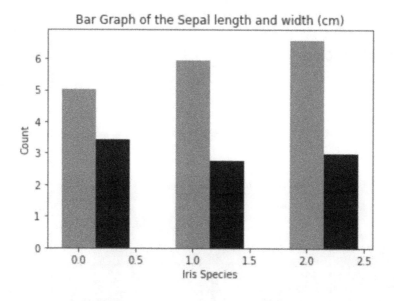

We can add a legend to our graph using the *legend()* function in oder to distinguish between the graphs. We can also define specify in the graph the position of ticks in axis. The following statements how we can do that:

```
>>> ind = np.arange(3)

>>> width = 0.3

>>> plt.bar (ind, M, width, color = 'grey',
label = 'Sepal length(cm)')

>>> plt.bar (ind + width, M2, width, color =
'blue', label = 'Sepal width(cm)')

>>> plt.title(' Bar Graph of the Sepal length
and width (cm)')

>>> plt.xlabel(' Iris Species')

>>> plt.ylabel(' Count')

>>> plt.xticks(ind + width/2, ind) # Position
of the xticks

>>> plt.legend(loc = 'best') # Position of the
legend

>>> plt.show()
```

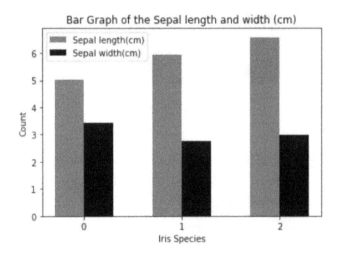

We can also stack the bars vertically. In this case we pass an argument to the *bar()* function fro the second variable and specify the bar graph of the values below. For example, to stack vertically the sepal lenght and width we follow the code presented in below:

```
>>> ind = np.arange(3)

>>> width = 0.3

>>> plt.bar (ind, M, width, color = 'grey', label = 'Sepal length(cm)')

>>> plt.bar (ind, M2, width, color = 'blue', label = 'Sepal width(cm)', bottom = M)

>>> plt.title(' Bar Graph of the Sepal length and width (cm)')

>>> plt.xlabel(' Iris Species')

>>> plt.ylabel(' Count')

>>> plt.xticks(ind + width/2, ind) # Position of the xticks

>>> plt.legend(loc = 'best') # Position of the legend

>>> plt.show()
```

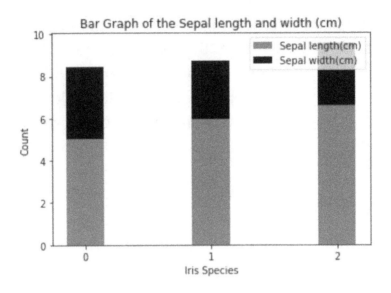

Histograms are another common graph in data analysis and statistical analysis that show the distribution of a variable. The histogram is a plot that shows the frequency of the values that a variable can take. In other words, we plot the range values of a variable against its frequency which describe the distribution of the variable. The *hist()* function allows to plot histograms with matplotlib library. For example, let's plot the histogram of the sepal length of the Iris data:

>>> plt.title(' Histogram of the Iris sepal length')

>>> plt.xlabel ('Sepal length (cm)')

>>> plt.ylabel (' Frequency')

>>> plt.hist(Iris_DF['sepal length (cm)'])

```
>>> plt.show()
```

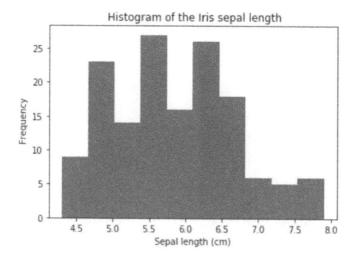

Like the other plot functions, color of the histogram can be changed by passing a color input argument like in the following example:

```
>>> plt.title(' Histogram of the Iris sepal
length')

>>> plt.xlabel ('Sepal length (cm)')

>>> plt.ylabel (' Frequency')

>>> plt.hist(Iris_DF['sepal length (cm)'],
color = 'grey')

>>> plt.show()
```

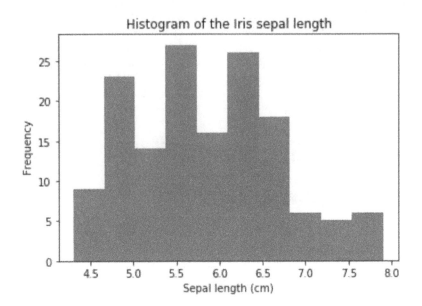

In order to detect visually correlation between the variables we can use scatter plots that plots variables against each other in 2-dimensional space. To plot a scatter plot, we use the function *scatter()*. For example, we plot the sepal length against the sepal width:

>>> plt.scatter(Iris_DF['sepal length (cm)'], Iris_DF['sepal width (cm)'])

>>> plt.title(' Scatter plot of sepal length and sepal width')

>>> plt.xlabel(' Sepal length (cm)')

>>> plt.ylabel (' Sepal width (cm)')

>>> plt.show()

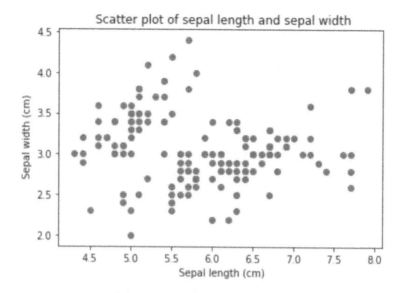

The scatter plot in the figure above is in a 2-dimensional space. We can also visualize the same scatter in a 3-dimensional space using *scatter3D()* function. This function is part of the mplot3d for 3 dimensional plots. So, we import first the module than plot the scatter plot in a 3-dimensional plot as follows:

>>> from mpl_toolkits import mplot3d

>>> ax = plt.axes(projection='3d')

>>> ax.scatter3D (Iris_DF['sepal length (cm)'], Iris_DF['sepal width (cm)'])

>>> ax.set_xlabel(' Sepal length (cm)')

```
>>> ax.set_ylabel (' Sepal width (cm)')
```

```
>>> ax.set_title(' 3-D scatter plot of sepal
length and sepal width')
```

```
>>> plt.show()
```

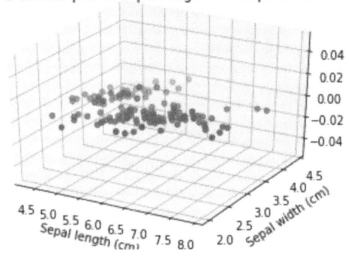

3-D scatter plot of sepal length and sepal width

Chapter 5 Writing Loops in Python

The next thing that we need to take a look at when it is time to write some of your own codes in Python will be looped. Creating loops can help you to make a code that is more efficient, and will ensure that you are able to get codes written quickly and without a ton of work in the process. These loops work well with some of the conditional statements that we are going to talk about, later on, helping you to clear up your code while getting a lot done in a short amount of time.

Loops are helpful because they are going to speed up how long it is going to take you to write out some codes, can help to clean it all up, and can take hundreds of lines of code (potentially), and put it in just a few lines if needed. Think about how much time that is going to save when you can get all of that code into a few lines with the help of the loops.

If you are working on your code and you find that there are parts of the program that can repeat them over and over again, at least a few times, then the loops are going to help make this happen. You will be able to get the code to repeat as many times as you would like, without having to rewrite the same codes over and over again.

Let's say that you would like to work on some kind of program that has a multiplication table that is going to go from 1 to 10 and all of the answers that are needed for it. Maybe you would choose to do some of the beginner codes and write it all line by line while wasting a ton of time and making it so that the code looks kind of messy in the process. But you are able to use the idea of a lop and write it out with the help of a few lines. We will explore some of the different options that are available for the loops and using them, while also seeing how you would be able to do the example above in just a few lines.

While this may seem like a complex thing to work within the coding, it is actually pretty easy to work with, and even a beginner is going to be able to write out some of these codes. The way that these codes will work is that it tells the compiler to keep reading the same part of the code until there is some condition that is met. Once that condition is met, the compiler will get out of the loop and start working on the next part of the code.

So, let's say that you are working on a program, and a part of it needs to be able to count from one to ten. You would be able to use the idea of the loop in order to tell the compiler to keep going through the code until it reaches higher than ten. We can take a look at a few of the different examples that you are able to do with the ideas of the loop.

One thing to remember here is that when you write out some of these loops, it is important to set up the conditions in the right manner. It is easy to forget to set up these conditions when you first get started, but if you forget them right from the beginning of the code, then you will end up in a loop that is not going to stop. You will get stuck in a continuous loop because the code doesn't know when it needs to stop going through the loop.

When you decide to work with some of the methods that are considered more traditional with coding, or using some of the other methods that are found throughout this guidebook, your whole goal here will be to write out all of the lines of code to get things done. Even if you see some parts of the code repeating, then you would still need to rewrite it out. This could take a long time and may not be as easy to work with as well. But when you work with loops, this is not going to be something that is going to be that big of a deal.

When working with these loops, you are able to get rid of some of the traditional ways of coding and change it up and make things easier. You will be able to combine together a ton of lines of code, or as many as you would need in order to get things done. The compiler will still be able to read through it when the loop is done in the proper way, just as long as you make sure that all of your conditions are put in place.

Now that we have spent some time looking at what the loops mean and why they are going to be so important to your code writing, it is time to divide up some of the different types of loops that are available to help you get this done inside the codes you write.

The first loop: the while loop

      So, the first type of loop that we are going to explore is the idea of the while loop in Python. This loop is a good one to bring out and use when you want to make sure that your code is able to go through the loop or the cycle for a predetermined number of times. You can pick out how many times you would like the code to go through this kind of loop to get the best results out of it. This makes it easy to get the number of times you would like the loop to go through.

When you work with the while loop, the goal is not to make the code that you write go through the cycle an indefinite amount of times. But you do have in mind a number of times that you would like the code to do its work. So, if you want to count from one to ten in the code, your goal is to use the while loop in order to go through the loop that many times.

With the while loop, you will see that the code is going to go through the loop, and then it will double check to see if the conditions are met or not. Then, if the conditions are not met, they will go through the loop again and then check again. It will continue doing this over and over again until it has met the conditions, and then it will go on to the other part of the code when the loop is all gone.

To see how the while loop is going to work, and to gain a better understanding of the loop works in general, let's look at some examples of a code that has a while loop inside of it:

```
counter = 1

while(counter <= 3):

principal = int(input("Enter the principal amount:"))

numberofyeras = int(input("Enter the number of years:"))

rateofinterest = float(input("Enter the rate of interest:"))

simpleinterest = principal * numberofyears * rateofinterest/100

print("Simple interest = %.2f" %simpleinterest)

#increase the counter by 1

counter = counter + 1

print("You have calculated simple interest for 3 times!")
```

Before we take a look at some of the other types of loops that we are able to work with, let's open up the compiler on Python and type in the code to see what is going to happen when we execute it. You will then be able to see how the while loop is able to work. The program is able to go through and figure out the interest rates, along with the final amounts that are associated with it, based on the numbers that the user, or you, will put into the system.

With the example from the code that was above, we have the loop set up so that it is going to go through three times. This means that the user gets a chance to put in different numbers and see the results three times, and then the system will be able to move on. You do get the chance to add in more or take out some loops based on what is the best for your needs.

The second loop: the for loop

At this point, we have been able to take a look at the while loop and what it is all going to entail, it is time to take a look at the for loop so that we are able to see how this in order to do more with loops, and how this is going to be different than the while loop overall. When you work with the while loops, you will notice that the code is going to go through a loop a certain number of times. But it is not always going to work for all of the situations where you want to bring in a loop. And the for loop is going to help us to fill in the blanks that the while loop is not able to do.

When you are ready to work with the for loop, you will be able to set up the code in a manner that the user isn't going to be the one who will go into the code and provide the program with the information that it needs. They do not have the control that is needed to stop the loop from running.

Instead of the user being able to hold the control, the for loop is going to be set up so that it will go over the iteration of your choice in the order that you place the items into your code. This information, when the for loop is going to list them out in the exact way that they are listed in the code. The user will not need to input anything for the for loop to work.

A good example of how this is going to work inside your code so that you are able to make it work for your needs will include the following syntax:

```
# Measure some strings:
words = ['apple,' 'mango,' 'banana,' 'orange']
for w in words:
print(w, len(w))
```

When you work with the for loop example that is above, you are able to add it to your compiler and see what happens when it gets executed. When you do this, the four fruits that come out on your screen will show up in the exact order that you have them written out. If you would like to have them show up in a different order, you can do that, but then you need to go back to your code and rewrite them in the right order, or your chosen order. Once you have then written out in the syntax and they are ready to be executed in the code, you can't make any changes to them.

The third loop: the nested loop

The third and final loop that we are going to work within Python is going to be known as the nested loop. You will find that when we look at the nested loop, there are going to be some parts that are similar to what we looked at with the while loop and with the for loop, but it is going to use these topics in a different way. when you decide to work with a nested loop, you will just take one loop, and then make sure that it is placed inside of another loop. Then, both of these loops will work together and continue on with their work until both have had a chance to finish.

This may seem really hard to work with when it comes to the loops, and you may wonder if there is actually any time that you, as a beginner, would need to work with this loop. But there are often a lot more chances to work with the nested loop than you may think in the beginning. For example, if you are working some kind of code that needs to have a multiplication table inside of it, and you want the answers listed all the way up, then you are going to work with the nested loop.

Imagine how long this kind of process is going to take if you have to go out and list each and every part of the code without using a loop to make it happen. You would have to write out the lines of codes to do one time one, one's times two, and so on until you reach the point where you are at ten times ten. This would end up being a ton of lines of code just to make this kind of table work in your code. But you are able to work with the idea of the nested loop in order to see the results that you want.

A good example that you will be able to work with to show how a nested loop works and to make sure that you are able to make a full multiplication table of your own, includes the following:

#write a multiplication table from 1 to 10

For x in xrange(1, 11):

For y in xrange(1, 11):

Print '%d = %d' % (x, y, x*x)

When you got the output of this program, it is going to look similar to this:

1*1 = 1

1*2 = 2

1*3 = 3

1*4 = 4

All the way up to 1*10 = 2

Then it would move on to do the table by twos such as this:

2*1 =2

2*2 = 4

And so on until you end up with 10*10 = 100 as your final spot in the sequence.

Go ahead and put this into the compiler and see what happens. You will simply have four lines of code, and end up with a whole multiplication table that shows up on your program. Think of how many lines of code you would have to write out to get this table the traditional way that you did before? This table only took a few lines to accomplish, which shows how powerful and great the nested loop can be.

As you can see, there are a lot of different things that you are able to do when you start to implement some loops into the codes that you are writing. There are a ton of reasons why you should add a loop into the code you are writing. You will be able to use it in most cases to take a large amount of code and write it in just a few lines instead. This saves you time, cleans up the code that you are trying to light, and the compiler is going to be able to still help you do some things that are super powerful!

Chapter 6 K-Means Clustering

Clustering falls under the category of unsupervised machine learning algorithms. It is often applied when the data is not labeled. The goal of the algorithm is to identify clusters or groups within the data.

The idea behind the clusters is that the objects contained one cluster is more related to one another than the objects in the other clusters. The similarity is a metric reflecting the strength of the relationship between two data objects. Clustering is highly applied in exploratory data mining. In have many uses in diverse fields such as pattern recognition, machine learning, information retrieval, image analysis, data compression, bio-informatics, and computer graphics.

The algorithm forms clusters of data based on the similarity between data values. You are required to specify the value of K, which are the number of clusters that you expect the algorithm to make from the data. The algorithm first selects a centroid value for every cluster. After that, it performs three steps in an iterative manner:

- Calculate the Euclidian distance between every data instance and the centroids for all clusters.
- Assign the instances of data to the cluster of centroid with the nearest distance.
- Calculate the new centroid values depending on the mean values of the coordinates of the data instances from the corresponding cluster.

Let us manually demonstrate how this algorithm works before implementing it on Scikit-Learn:

Suppose we have two dimensional data instances given below and by the name D:
D = { (5,3), (10,15), (15,12), (24,10), (30,45), (85,70), (71,80), (60,78), (55,52), (80,91) }

Our goal is to divide the data into two clusters, namely C1 and C2 depending on the similarity between the data points.

We should first initialize the values for the centroids of both clusters, and this should be done randomly. The centroids will be named C1 and C2 for clusters C1 and C2 respectively, and we will initialize them with the values for the first two data points, that is, (5,3) and (10,15). It is after this that you should begin the iterations.

Anytime that you calculate the Euclidean distance, the data point should be assigned to the cluster with the shortest Euclidean distance. Let us take the example of the data point (5,3):

Euclidean Distance from the Cluster Centroid $C1 = (5,3) = 0$

Euclidean Distance from the Cluster Centroid $C2 = (10,15) = 13$

The Euclidean distance for the data point from point centroid c1 is shorter compared to the distance of the same data point from centroid C2. This means that this data point will be assigned to the cluster C1.

Let us take another data point, (15,12):

Euclidean Distance from the Cluster Centroid $C1 = (5,3)$ IS 13.45

Euclidean Distance from the Cluster Centroid $C2 = (10,15)$ IS 5.83

The distance from the data point to the centroid C2 is shorter, hence it will be assigned to the cluster C2.

Now that the data points have been assigned to the right clusters, the next step should involve calculation of the new centroid values. The values should be calculated by determining the means of the coordinates for the data points belonging to a certain cluster.

If for example for C1 we had allocated the following two data points to the cluster:

(5, 3) and (24, 10). The new value for x coordinate will be the mean of the two:

x = (5 + 24) / 2

x = 14.5

The new value for y will be:

y = (3 + 10) / 2

y = 13/2

y = 6.5

The new centroid value for the c1 will be (14.5, 6.5).

This should be done for c2 and the entire process be repeated. The iterations should be repeated until when the centroid values do not update any more. This means if for example, you do three iterations, you may find that the updated values for centroids c1 and c2 in the fourth iterations are equal to what we had in iteration 3. This means that your data cannot be clustered any further.

You are now familiar with how the K-Means algorithm works. Let us discuss how you can implement it in the Scikit-Learn library.

Let us first import all the libraries that we need to use:

import matplotlib.pyplot as plt

import numpy as np

from sklearn.cluster import KMeans

Data Preparation

We should now prepare the data that is to be used. We will be creating a **numpy array** with a total of 10 rows and 2 columns. So, why have we chosen to work with a numpy array? It is because Scikit-Learn library can work with the numpy array data inputs without the need for preprocessing. Let us create it:

X = np.array([[5,3], [10,15], [15,12], [24,10], [30,45], [85,70], [71,80], [60,78], [55,52], [80,91],])

Visualizing the Data

Now that we have the data, we can create a plot and see how the data points are distributed. We will then be able to tell whether there are any clusters at the moment:

plt.scatter(X[:,0],X[:,1], label='True Position')

```
plt.show()
```

The code gives the following plot:

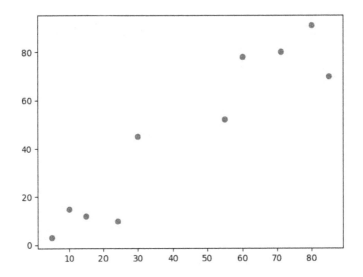

If we use our eyes, we will probably make two clusters from the above data, one at the bottom with five points and another one at the top with five points. We now need to investigate whether this is what the K-Means clustering algorithm will do.

Creating Clusters

We have seen that we can form two clusters from the data points, hence the value of K is now 2. These two clusters can be created by running the following code:

```
kmeans_clusters = KMeans(n_clusters=2)

kmeans_clusters.fit(X)
```

We have created an object named *kmeans_clusters* and 2 have been used as the value for the parameter *n_clusters*. We have then called the *fit()* method on this object and passed the data we have in our numpy array as the parameter to the method.

We can now have a look at the centroid values that the algorithm has created for the final clusters:

print (kmeans_clusters.cluster_centers_)

This returns the following:

```
[[ 16.8    17. ]
 [ 70.2    74.2]]
```

The first row above gives us the coordinates for the first centroid, which is, (16.8, 17). The second row gives us the coordinates of the second centroid, which is, (70.2, 74.2). If you followed the manual process of calculating the values of these, they should be the same. This will be an indication that the K-Means algorithm worked well.

The following script will help us see the data point labels:

print(kmeans_clusters.labels_)

This returns the following:

```
[0 0 0 0 0 1 1 1 1 1]
```

The above output shows a one-dimensional array of 10 elements which correspond to the clusters that are assigned to the 10 data points. You clearly see that we first have a sequence of zeroes which shows that the first 5 points have been clusterd together while the last five points have been clustered together. Note that the 0 and 1 have no mathematical significance but they have simply been used to represent the cluster IDs. If we had three clusters, then the last one would have been represented using 2's.

We can now plot the data points and see how they have been clustered. We need to plot the data points alongside their assigned labels to be able to distinguish the clusters. Just execute the script given below:

```
plt.scatter(X[:,0],X[:,1],
c=kmeans_clusters.labels_, cmap='rainbow')
        plt.show()
```

The script returns the following plot:

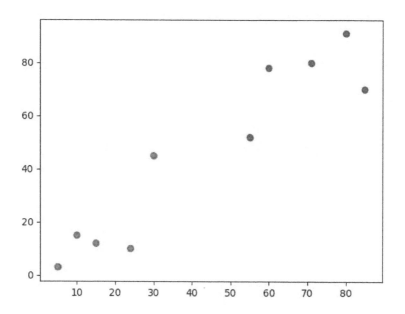

We have simply plotted the first column of the array named X against the second column. At the same time, we have passed *kmeans_labels_* as the value for parameter c which corresponds to the labels.

Note the use of the parameter *cmap='rainbow'*. This parameter helps us to choose the color type for the different data points.

As you expected, the first five points have been clustered together at the bottom left and assigned a similar color. The remaining five points have been clustered together at the top right and assigned one unique color.

We can choose to plot the points together with the centroid coordinates for every cluster to see how the positioning of the centroid affects clustering. Let us use three clusters to see how they affect the centroids. The following script will help you to create the plot:

plt.scatter(X[:,0],   X[:,1], c=kmeans_clusters.labels_, cmap='rainbow')

plt.scatter(kmeans_clusters.cluster_centers_[:,0] ,kmeans_clusters.cluster_centers_[:,1], color='black')

    plt.show()

The script returns the following plot:

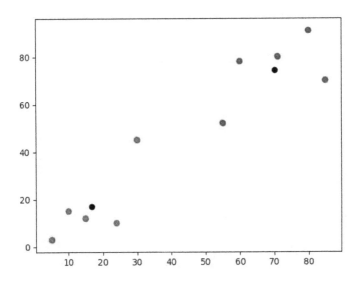

We have chosen to plot the centroid points in black color.

Chapter 7 Support Vector Machines

SVMs fall under the category of supervised machine learning algorithms and are highly applied classification and regression problems. It is known for its ability to handle nonlinear input spaces. It is highly applied in applications like intrusion detection, face detection, classification of news articles, emails and web pages, handwriting recognition and classification of genes.

The algorithm works by segregating the data points in the best way possible. The distance between the nearest points is referred to as the *margin*. The goal is to choose a hyperplane with the maximum possible margin between the support vectors in a given dataset.

To best understand how this algorithm works, let us first implement it in Scikit-Learn library. Our goal is to predict whether a bank currency note is fake or authentic. We will use the attributes of the note including variance of the image, the skewness of the wavelet transformed image, curtosis of the image and entropy of the image. Since this is a binary classification algorithm, let us use the SVM classification algorithm.

If we have a linearly separable data with two dimensions, the goal of a typical machine learning algorithm is to identify a boundary that will divide the data so as to minimize the misclassification error. In most cases, one gets several lines with all these lines correctly classifying the data.

SVM is different from the other classification algorithms in the way it selects the decision boundary maximizing the distance from the nearest data points for all classes. The goal of SVM is not to find the decision boundary only, but to find the most optimal decision boundary.

The most optimal decision boundary refers to the decision boundary with the maximum margin from nearest points of all classes. The nearest points from the decision boundary maximizing the distance between the decision boundary and the points are known as *support vectors*. For the case of support vector machines, the decision boundary is known as *maximum margin classifier* **or** *maximum margin hyper plane.*

A complex mathematics is involved in the calculation of the support vectors; determine the margin between the decision boundary and support vectors and maximizing the margin.

Let us begin by importing the necessary libraries:

```
import numpy as np

import pandas as pd

import matplotlib.pyplot as plt
```

This dataset can be downloaded from the following URL:

https://drive.google.com/file/d/13nw-uRXPY8XIZQxKRNZ3yYlho-CYm_Qt/view

Download and store it on your local machine. I have saved the file in the same directory as my Python scripts and given it the name *bank_note.csv*.

Importing the Dataset

We will use the *read_csv* method provided by the Pandas library to read the data and import it into our workspace. This can be done as follows:

```
dataset = pd.read_csv("bank_note.csv")
```

Let us call the **shape** method to print the shape of the data for us:

```
print(dataset.shape)
```

This returns the following:

```
(1372, 5)
```

This shows that there are 1372 columns and 5 columns in the dataset. Let us print the first 5 rows of the dataset:

```
print(dataset.head())
```

Again, this may return an error because of lack of the output information. Let us solve this using the Python's sys library. You should now have the following code:

import numpy as np

import pandas as pd

import matplotlib.pyplot as plt

import sys

```
sys.__stdout__=sys.stdout
```
dataset = pd.read_csv("bank_note.csv")

```
print(dataset.head())
```

The code returns the following output:

	Variance	Skewness	Curtosis	Entropy	Class
0	3.62160	8.6661	-2.8073	-0.44699	0
1	4.54590	8.1674	-2.4586	-1.46210	0
2	3.86600	-2.6383	1.9242	0.10645	0
3	3.45660	9.5228	-4.0112	-3.59440	0
4	0.32924	-4.4552	4.5718	-0.98880	0

All attributes of the data are numeric as shown above. Even the last attribute is numeric as its values are either 0 or 1.

Preprocessing the Data

It is now time to subdivide the above data into attributes and labels as well as training and test sets. The following code will help us subdivide the data into attributes and labels:

X = dataset.drop('Class', axis=1)

y = dataset['Class']

The first line above helps us store all the columns of the dataset into variable **X**, except the *class* column. The *drop()* function has helped us exclude the *Class* column from this. The second line has then helped us store the *Class* column into variable *y*. The variable **X** now has attributes while the variable *y* now has the corresponding labels.

We have achieved the goal of diving the dataset into attributes and labels. The next step is to divide the dataset into training and test sets. Scikit-learn has a library known as *model_selection* which provides us with a method named *train_test_split* that we can use to divide the data into training and test sets.

First, let us import the *train_test_split* method:

from   sklearn.model_selection   import train_test_split

The following script will then help us to perform the split:

```
X_train, X_test, y_train, y_test = train_test_split(X,
y, test_size = 0.20)
```

Training the Algorithm

Now that the data has been split into training and test sets, we should now train the SVM on the training set. Scikit-Learn comes with a library known as *svm* which has built-in classes for various SVM algorithms.

In this case, we will be doing a classification task, hence we will use the support vector classifier class (SVC). The takes a single parameter, that is, the kernel type. For a simple SVM, the parameter should be set to **"linear"** since the simple SVMs can only classify data that is linearly separable.

We will call the *fit* method of SVC to train the algorithm on our training set. The training set should be passed as a parameter to the *fit* method. Let us first import the SVC class from Scikit-Learn:

```
from sklearn.svm import SVC
```

Now run the following code:

```
svc_classifier = SVC(kernel='linear')

svc_classifier.fit(X_train, y_train)
```

Making Predicting

We should use the SVC class for making predictions. Note that the predictions will be made on the test data. Here is the code for making predictions:

```
pred_y = svc_classifier.predict(X_test)
```

Evaluating the Accuracy of the Algorithm

In classification tasks, we use confusion matrix, recall, precision and F1 as the metrics. Scikit-Learn has the *metrics* library which provides us with the *confusion_matrix* and *classification_report* methods which can help us find the values of these metrics. The following code can help us find the value for these metrics:

First, let us import the above methods from the Scikit-Learn library:

```
from sklearn.metrics import confusion_matrix, classification_report
```

Here is the code that can help in doing the evaluation:

```
print(confusion_matrix(y_test,pred_y))
        print(classification_report(y_test,pred_y))
```

The code returns the following:

```
[[160    1]
 [   1 113]]
            precision    recall  f1-score   support

        0       0.99      0.99      0.99       161
        1       0.99      0.99      0.99       114

avg / total     0.99      0.99      0.99       275
```

The output given above shows that the algorithm did a good task. An average of 99% for the above metrics is not bad.

Let us give another example of how to implement SVM in Scikit-Learn using the Iris dataset. We had already loaded the Iris dataset, a dataset that shows details of flowers in terms of sepal and petal measurements, that is, width and length. We can now learn from the data, and then make a prediction for unknown data. These calls for us to create an estimator then call its fit method.

This is demonstrated in the script given below:

from sklearn import svm

from sklearn import datasets

Loading the dataset

iris = datasets.load_iris()

clf = svm.LinearSVC()

learn from the dataset

clf.fit(iris.data, iris.target)

```
# predict unseen data
```

```
clf.predict([[ 6.2,  4.2,  3.5,  0.35]])
```

```
# Changing model parameters using the attributes
ending with an underscore
```

```
print(clf.coef_ )
```

The code will return the following output:

```
[[ 0.18423824  0.45123312 -0.80793878 -0.45071592]
 [ 0.05187834 -0.88969839  0.40345845 -0.93664852]
 [-0.85062306 -0.98667154  1.38105171  1.86536558]]
```

We now have the predicted values for our data. Note that we imported both *datasets* and *svm* from the scikit-learn library. After loading the dataset, a model was fitted/created by learning patterns from the data. This was done by calling the *fit()* method. Note that the *LinearSVC()*method helps us to create an estimator for the support vector classifier, on which we are to create the model. We have then passed in new data for which we need to make a prediction.

Chapter 8 Variables and Data Types

A software application consists of two fundamental parts: Logic and Data. Logic consists of the functionalities that are applied on data to accomplish a particular task. Application data can be stored in memory or hard disk. Files and databases are used to store data on hard disk. In memory, data is stored in the form of variables.

Definition of Variable

Variable in programming is a memory location used to store some value. Whenever you store a value in a variable, that value is actually being stored at physical location in memory. Variables can be thought of as reference to physical memory location. The size of the memory reserved for a variable depends upon the type of value stored in the variable.

Creating a Variable

It is very easy to create a variable in Python. The assignment operator "=" is used for this purpose. The value to the left of the assignment operator is the variable identifier or name of the variable. The value to the right of the operator is the value assigned to the variable. Take a look at the following code snippet.

```python
Name  = 'Mike'        # A string variable

Age   = 15            # An integer variable

Score = 102.5         # A floating type variable

Pass  = True          # A boolean Variable
```

In the script above we created four different types of variables. You can see that we did not specify the type of variable with the variable name. For instance we did not write "string Name" or "int Age". We only wrote the variable name. This is because Python is a loosely typed language. Depending upon the value being stored in a variable, Python assigns type to the variable at runtime. For instance when Python interpreter interprets the line "Age = 15", it checks the type of the value which is integer in this case. Hence, Python understands that Age is an integer type variable.

To check type of a variable, pass the variable name to "type" function as shown below:

```python
type(Age)
```

You will see that the above script, when run, prints "int" in the output which is basically the type of Age variable.

Python allows multiple assignment which means that you can assign one value to multiple variables at the same time. Take a look at the following script:

Age = Number = Point = 20 #Multiple Assignment

print (Age)

print (Number)

print (Point)

In the script above, integer 20 is assigned to three variables: Age, Number and Point. If you print the value of these three variables, you will see 20 thrice in the output.

Python Data Types

A programming application needs to store variety of data. Consider scenario of a banking application that needs to store customer information. For instance, a person's name and mobile number; whether he is a defaulter or not; collection of items that he/she has loaned and so on. To store such variety of information, different data types are required. While you can create custom data types in the form of classes, Python provides six standard data types out of the box. They are:

- Strings
- Numbers
- Booleans

- Lists
- Tuples
- Dictionaries

Strings

Python treats string as sequence of characters. To create strings in Python, you can use single as well as double quotes. Take a look at the following script:

first_name = 'mike' # String with single quotation

last_name = " johns" # String with double quotation

full_name = first_name + last_name # string concatenation using +

print(full_name)

In the above script we created three string variables: first_name, last_name and full_name. String with single quotes is used to initialize the variable "first_name" while string with double quotes initializes the variable "last_name". The variable full_name contains the concatenation of the first_name and last_name variables. Running the above script returns following output:

mike johns

Numbers

There are four types of numeric data in python:

- int (Stores integer e.g 10)
- float (Stores floating point numbers e.g 2.5)
- long (Stores long integer such as 48646684333)
- complex (Complex number such as 7j+4847k)

To create a numeric Python variable, simply assign a number to variable. In the following script we create four different types of numeric objects and print them on the console.

```
int_num = 10      # integer

float_num = 156.2  #float

long_num = -0.5977485613454646  #long

complex_num = -.785+7J #Complex


print(int_num)

print(float_num)

print(long_num)

print(complex_num)
```

The output of the above script will be as follows:

```
10
156.2
-0.5977485613454646
(-0.785+7j)
```

Boolean

Boolean variables are used to store Boolean values. True and False are the two Boolean values in Python. Take a look at the following example:

defaulter = True

has_car = False

print(defaulter and has_car)

In the script above we created two Boolean variables "defaulter" and "has_car" with values True and False respectively. We then print the result of the AND operation on both of these variables. Since the AND operation between True and False returns false, you will see false in the output. We will study more about the logical operators in the next chapter.

Lists

In Python, List data type is used to store collection of values. Lists are similar to arrays in any other programming language. However Python lists can store values of different types. To create a list opening and closing square brackets are used. Each item in the list is separated from the other with a comma. Take a look at the following example.

```
cars = ['Honda', 'Toyota', 'Audi', 'Ford', 'Suzuki', 'Mercedez']
print(len(cars))    #finds total items in string
print(cars)
```

In the script above we created a list named cars. The list contains six string values i.e. car names. Next we printed the size of the list using len function. Finally we print the list on console.

The output looks like this:

```
6
['Honda', 'Toyota', 'Audi', 'Ford', 'Suzuki', 'Mercedez']
```

Tuples

Tuples are similar to lists with two major differences. Firstly, opening and closing braces are used to create tuples instead of lists that use square brackets. Secondly, tuple once created is immutable which means that you cannot change tuple values once it is created. The following example clarifies this concept.

```
cars = ['Honda', 'Toyota', 'Audi', 'Ford', 'Suzuki',
'Mercedez']


cars2 = ('Honda', 'Toyota', 'Audi', 'Ford', 'Suzuki',
'Mercedez')


cars [3] = 'WV'


cars2 [3] = 'WV'
```

In the above script we created a list named cars and a tuple named cars2. Both the list and tuple contains list of car names. We then try to update the third index of the list as well as tuple with a new value. The list will be updated but an error will be thrown while trying to update the tuple's third index. This is due to the fact that tuple, once created cannot be modified with new values. The error looks like this:

Dictionaries

Dictionaries store collection of data in the form of key-value pairs. Each key-value pair is separated from the other via comma. Keys and values are separated from each other via colon. Dictionary items can be accessed via index as well as keys. To create dictionaries you need to add key-value pairs inside opening and closing parenthesis. Take a look at the following example.

cars = {'Name':'Audi', 'Model': 2008, 'Color':'Black'}

print(cars['Color'])

print(cars.keys())

print(cars.values())

In the above script we created a dictionary named cars. The dictionary contains three key-value pairs i.e. 3 items. To access value, we can pass key to the brackets that follow dictionary name. Similarly we can use keys() and values() methods to retrieve all the keys and values from a dictionary, respectively. The output of the script above looks like this:

```
Black
dict_keys(['Name', 'Model', 'Color'])
dict_values(['Audi', 2008, 'Black'])
```

Chapter 9 How to install the Python Interpreter, how to use the Python Shell, IDLE and write your first program ✄

Python installation is dependent upon the OS on your computer as well as the source of the Python installation you are using. Python can be obtained from a number of different sources, some of which are modified versions of the official releases.

The following discussion will look at the installation procedure for the 3 major supported operating systems from the official source at python.org. Installation for other operating systems should be similar to one of these three. Please see python.org for installers and instructions for those systems.

The installers on pythons.org contain the python interpreter, the IDLE integrated development environment and the python shell.

Following is an OS specific description to installing and accessing each.

Mac OS X:

Mac OS X comes with Python 2 preinstalled. The exact version of python will depend on the version of OS X currently running on your system and can be determined by opening the terminal app and entering the following at the prompt:

python -V

which should return a result similar to:

Python 2.6.1

Python 3 can also be installed on OS X with no need to uninstall 2.x. To check for a 3.x installation open the terminal app and enter the following at the prompt:

Python3 -V

which should return a result similar to:

Python 3.6.4

By default, OS X will not have python 3.x installed. If you wish to use python 3.x, it can be installed with binary installers for OS X available at python.org.

Those installers will install the interpreter, the IDLE development tools and the python shell for python 3.x. Unlike python 2.x, those tools are installed as standard applications in the applications folder.

Running IDLE and the python shell in OS X is dependent on the version of Python you are using and your personal preference. The IDLE/shell applications in Python 2.x and 3.x can be started from the terminal window by entering the following commands:

For python 2.x:

Idle

For Python 3.x:

idle3

As mentioned above, Python 3 also installs IDLE as a standard application in the Python folder within the Applications older. To start the IDLE/Shell program from the desktop simply open that folder and double click the IDLE application.

Python can also be accessed as a command line terminal application within OS X. With a terminal window open, simply enter the following:

Python 2.x:

Python

and you will get a response like:

Python 2.6.1 (r261:67515, Jun 24 2010, 21:47:49) [GCC 4.2.1 (Apple Inc. build 5646)] on darwin Type "help", "copyright", "credits" or "license" for more information.

>>>

Python 3.x:

python3

and you will get a response like:

Python 3.6.4 (v3.6.4:d48ecebad5, Dec 18 2017, 21:07:28)
 [GCC 4.2.1 (Apple Inc. build 5666) (dot 3)] on darwin
 Type "help", "copyright", "credits" or "license" for more information.

>>>

The >>> prompt allows direct entry of python commands which will be detailed in greater depth later.

Windows:

Once setup correctly, python can used from the command line with either command.exe or the windows power shell.

Alternatively, the standard installation adds Python IDLE to the start menu. Selecting that will bring up the IDLE application to allow you to start creating your first script.

Linux

If you are using one of the many flavors of Linux you can check for the presence of python by typing

python -V

at a shell command prompt. If python is installed, the installed version should be returned like

Python 3.6.4

If not, an error should be returned.

Installing and/or updating can vary depending on the Linux distribution you are using. Please consult the documentation for your linux distribution for more information.

Python Interpreter, IDLE, and the Shell

A standard installation of Python from python.org, contains documentation, licensing information and 3 main executable files which are used to develop and run python scripts.

Let's take a brief look at each of these three programs and the role each plays in python programming.

Python Interpreter

The python interpreter is the program responsible for executing the scripts you write. The interpreter converts the .py script files into bytecode instructions and then processes them according to the code written in the file.

Python IDLE

IDLE is the Python integrated development and learning environment. It contains all of the tools you will need to develop programs in Python including the shell, a text editor and debugging tools.

Depending on your python version and operating system, IDLE can be very basic or have an extensive array of options that can be setup.

For example, on Mac OS X, the text editor can be setup with several code indentation and highlighting options which can make your programs much easier to read and work with.

If the text editor in IDLE does not offer the sophistication you need, there are several aftermarket text editors which support Python script highlighting, autocomplete and other features that make script writing easier.

Python Shell

The shell is an interactive, command line driven interface to the python interpreter.

In the python shell, commands are entered at the >>> prompt. Anything that is entered at the prompt must be in proper python syntax, incorrect entries will return a syntax error like

SyntaxError: invalid syntax

When a command is entered, it is specific to that shell and has the lifetime of the shell.

For example, if you assign a variable a value such as:

```
>>>X=10
```

Then the variable is assigned an integer value of 10.

That value will be maintained until the shell is closed, restarted or the value is changed.

If another shell window is opened, the value of X will not be accessible in the new window.

When a command is entered and accepted, the code is executed. If the entered code generates a response, the response will be output to the specified device. If it does not, such as simply assigning a variable as above, then another prompt (>>>) is shown and additional commands can be entered.

This can be useful for a number of simple tasks, testing simple functions and getting a feel for how commands work.

As an example, enter the following:

```
>>>X=10
 >>>Y=5
 >>>print(X)
10
 >>>print(Y)
5
 >>>print(X+Y)
15
```

This demonstrates a couple of things.
First, we assign the two variables X and Y values.

Both variables retain their values within the shell. It also shows that the way we defined the variables was acceptable. If it is acceptable in the shell, it will be acceptable in a script.

If a command is not acceptable, it will return an error or exception.

For example if we ask for the length of X with the following command

>>>print(len(X))

Then the following is returned:

Traceback (most recent call last):
  File "<pyshell#12>", line 1, in <module>
    print(len(X))
 TypeError: object of type 'int' has no len()

The error returned usually will provide some valuable information as to why the error occurred.

In this case, it is telling us that we assigned an integer value to X.

The len() command gives the length of a string so we are getting this error because the type of data held by the variable does not match the requirements of the function called.

If instead we had used

```
>>>print(len(str(X)))
2
```

In this case, we are using the str() command to convert the value of X into a string.

We are then using len() to get the length of that string, which is 2 characters.

This can be loosely translated into

$$X=12 \Rightarrow str(X)='12' \Rightarrow len('12')=2$$

We can continue to use the shell to explore other things like different ways to assign variable values.

For example, rather than explicitly assigning values on a per line basis, variables can be assigned as comma separated groups.

```
>>>X,Y = 20,12
>>>print(X,Y)
20 12
```

Script Editor

To create our first program, open the text editor.

To open it in a GUI OS like OS X or Windows, select File->New from the IDLE menus.

In non-GUI implementations .py files can be created in a terminal text editor like VI or VIM. Please see documentation on those programs for information on working in them.

Once a text window is open we can simply enter our program code.

In this case, we will write a quick program for calculating the volume of a cylinder. The formula is $V=(\pi r^2)*h$ where r is the radius and h is the height.

While this program will be extremely simple, and could easily be done just using the shell, it will show several fundamentally important things in Python programming.

The first step will be to import the math library.

Many functions available in python are stored in libraries. These libraries typically house functions which are grouped by task such as math.

If the proper library is not loaded when prior to making a call to that library, an error such as

```
Traceback      (most      recent      call      last):
    File  "<pyshell#22>",  line  1,  in  <module>
                                    print(math.exp(2))
    NameError: name 'math' is not defined
```

will be displayed. This error is telling you that math is not defined.

Since math is part of a Python standard library this tells you that the library was not imported prior to execution of the request for the math keyword.

In the text editor, enter the lines as follows

```
# import math library
 import math
```

The #is the python comment symbol. Anything between that and the end of the line is ignored by the interpreter.

One of the key advantages of Python scripting is readability so it is very important (as it is in all programing) to be diligent about commenting.

Comments will make it easier to debug your code later and will make it easier for someone else to look at your work and see how the program works.

In many cases, it also forces you to slow down and think out the programming process as you go which will lead to cleaner and better organized code.

Next, we need to set up our variables.

This can be done anywhere within a script as long as they are defined prior to calling for their value.

If a variable is called before it is defined, a 'name not defined' exception will be displayed and program execution will halt.

```
# assign variables

r=5 # radius
 h=10 # height
 V=0 # volume
```

While V does not need to be explicitly defined, here it is considered good practice to do so because it makes the code is easier to understand.

Next, we do the actual volume calculation.

```
# calculate volume of a cylinder
V=(math.pi*math.pow(r,2))*h #
volume=(π*r^2)*h
```

Next, to see the result we use the print function, which will output the result to the console.

```
# output the result
print(V)
```

The complete program looks like this

```
# import math

import math

# assign variables
r=5 # radius
h=10 # height
V=0 # volume

# calculate volume of a cylinder
V=(math.pi*math.pow(r,2))*h #
volume=(π*r^2)*h

# output the result
print(V)
```

You can save the program to your hard drive, let's call it cylinder.py.

Python views files ending in .py as script files so it is important to always save your scripts with the .py extension. Once we have a saved script file, we can go ahead and run it.

Chapter 10 Strings

Earlier in the variables section we learned a little about strings. Strings and string functions are one of the strengths of the Python language.

It has many built in string handling and manipulation features and many more are available through external libraries. Previously, we discussed accessing substrings using the [:] nomenclature, as well as concatenating strings using the '+' operator.

Python offers inline string formatting similar to that in C/C++ through the use of the % special character. % followed by any one of a number of formatting characters allows variable information to be inserted into formatted strings for display or storage.

Those special characters include:

%c – character
%d – signed decimal
%e – lower case e exponent
%E – upper case E exponent
%f – floating point number
%g – the smaller of %e/%f
%G – the smaller of %E/%F
%i – signed integer
%s – string
%u – unsigned integer

%o – octal

%x – lower case hexadecimal

%X – upper case hexadecimal

These can be used as follows to format text on the fly:

>>> print('%s scored %i in game one of the playoffs' % ('John', 32))

John scored 32 in game one of the playoffs

As shown the values for %s and %i are dynamically inserted into the output text based on the input values provided in parenthesis.

While in this example, the values are given explicitly, they can also be provided as variables. Care must be taken to insure the variable types and the formatting characters match. In other words, do not specify %i and provide a string variable as the source.

These formatting characters also have a number of modifiers that alter or specify their output.

These include:
*   specifies width or precision
-    justify left
+   show sign
<sp>   left padding with spaces
show leading 0's in octal output or leading 0x in hexidecimal
0   left padding with 0's

%%   literal % (allows printing a % symbol in the string)

(var)   key value for dictionary elements

m.n.   for floating point numbers this is the minimum width and number of decimal places

>>> print('%s spent $%3.2f at the store last night' % ('John', 12.8975))

John spent $12.90 at the store last night

%3.2f formats the floating point number to 2 decimal places.

The % nomenclature is considered the 'old way' of handling string formatting. The new format is to enclose the formatted text in braces while calling the format function like this:

>>> print('{} spent ${:2.2f} at the store last night'.format('John', 12.8975))

John spent $12.90 at the store last night

In this case, the first insert is a set of empty braces. This is what is classified as an autofill, or more specifically that it is filled by the items in the format command in the order it's called.

The second set of braces then autofills with the second item in the format statement. In that second statement we used a ':' to specify that a formatting modifier is included.

Alternatively, we can manually select which items within the format command get inserted into the string as follows:

>>> print('Item 3={2}, Item 2={1}, Item 4={3}, Item 1={0}'.format('1','2','3','4'))

Item 3=3, Item 2=2, Item 4=4, Item 1=1

A dictionaries key value pair can also be used to fill in strings dynamically as well. For example:

>>> 'My Name is {firstname} and I am {age} years old'.format(firstname='John', age=29)

'My Name is John and I am 29 years old'

     Or..

>>> testd={'firstname': 'John', 'age': 29}
>>> 'My Name is {firstname} and I am {age} years old'.format(**testd)

'My Name is John and I am 29 years old'

The ** operator is the exponent operator when applied to numerical variables. When applied as shown to a dictionary, it force splits the dictionary into its component entities.

If testd={'firstname': 'John', 'age': 29} then **testd=(firstname='John', age=29) so the use of the operator functionally converts the contents of the dictionary variable in the second example into the format of the first example.

Python has a large number of built in string methods. These do a wide range of everyday string manipulation functions in a single command that would require more elaborate programming in other languages.

As of this writing there are 44 different methods available and as the language evolves more are added. Due that evolution, the not all of the 44 will be available on all versions of Python.

Because of that fact, and the sheer volume of methods, covering all of them and their use is beyond the scope of this book.

Here are a few of the more commonly used examples and how to use them. Reference to all of them is available from the docs on python.org.

> *str.lower()* - converts a string to all lower case

```
>>> str.lower('Hello')
 'hello'
```

str.upper() - converts a string to all upper case

```
>>> str.upper('Hello')
 'HELLO'
```

These functions convert text to all lower or upper case respectively. This is a common operation when checking for non-case sensitive equality in string values.

```
>>> print('Hello'=='hello')
False
```

```
>>> print(str.lower('Hello')=='hello')
True
```

str.strip([char]) – strips characters from the beginning and end of a string. It removes only the characters specified by char. If char is not specified, it strips whitespace. This is a commonly used command to remove leading and trailing spaces from user input.

```
>>> print(str.strip('    Hello    '))
Hello
```

```
>>> print(str.strip('    #--Comments--#    ', ' #-'))
Comments
```

str.split([,delimiter]) – splits a string into individual list entries using delimiter as the split point.

```
>>> str.split('A,b,CC,ASD,The end', ',')
['A', 'b', 'CC', 'ASD', 'The end']
```

```
>>> str.split('www.mywebsite.com', '.')
['www', 'mywebsite', 'com']
```

```
>>> myweb='WWW.WEBSITE.COM'
>>> myweb.split('.')
['www', 'website', 'com']
```

Chapter 11 Control Flow
Introduction

Went to sleep you starts execution of the program code, it starts from the main function and terminates at the end of the code, which is usually the end of main function. The statements that are executed in sequence are nothing but the part of the program. Most of the programs, which we have learned until now are simple straight line programs. These programs have a steady and sequential flow.

To break the flow of control, we have control flow statements in C++. Please control flow statements help the programmer to change the path of the CPU. Some of the control flow statements discussed below.

Halt: this is the most widely used and the basic control statement in C++. You can perform a halt with the exit function. The exit functional is defined in the header cstdlib. Here is a small example showing the use of exit function.

```cpp
#include <cstdlib> // needed for exit()
#include <iostream>
int main()
{
    std::cout << 1;
    exit(0); // terminate and return 0 to operating system
    // The following statements never execute
    std::cout << 2;
    return 0;
}
```

In the above sample code the flow of control is broken and it will never reach the statements that are written below the exit statement. These types of statements give the programmer the authority to stop the program when required.

Jumps: Jump is also a basic controls statement in C++. Using this statement will make the CPU to jump to a different statement. Continue, break and goto are used to perform different types of jumping operations.

Conditional branches: these are flow control statements which change the part of the flow of control depending on the value of a given expression. The 'if' statement is the most basic type of the conditional branch statements. Example:

```
1  int main()
2  {
3      // do A
4      if (expression)
5          // do B
6      else
7          // do C
8      // do D
9  }
```

In the sample code given above, there are two possible paths the flow of control can take. If it is it true the CPU will go and execute A, B and D. But if the condition turns out to be false the flow of control will go and execute A, C and D statements.

Conditionals

Conditionals allow you to form a junction in the code and send it off on various paths, rather than keeping it as a linear code. C++ conditionals are if statements - if something is false, the program should execute one piece of code, another if it is true:

```
1  int a = 1;
2
3  if(a < 2)
4  {
5      cout << "a is less than 2!\n";
6  }
```

You know what lines 1 and 5 mean but line 3 is a little different – this is an if statement. What it is doing is checking to see if the integer variable is less than 2. If it is, it will run one piece of code, if not, it will carry on as normal. If you compile and run what is written here, you will see printed on your screen "a is less than 2!".

Loops

Loops are used in the programs where the code is to be used repeatedly. They will put the code into a loop till the condition is satisfied. Imagine if you have to write a code, which prints numbers from 1 to 100 in a new line each. Writing the code for such programs will be very difficult and time taking. For such situations we use loops. Loops keep the flow of control in the loop till the condition is satisfied.

So our code now reads user inputs, it can do a variety of different things based on those inputs but now we are going to look at making that code do the same things over and over again but with slightly different parameters. To do this, we need to use a loop, which is a piece of code that is repeated a number of different times until it's achieved what it needed to do and a specific C++ condition has been met. C++ has three different types of loop:

- while
- for
- do

The WHILE loop is the easiest and looks very similar to an if statement:

```
1  int userInput = 0;
2  {
3  while(userInput != 10)
4  {
5      cin >> userInput;
6  }
```

What the WHILE loop is doing here is saying that while whatever the user input variable is not equal to 10, the ode needs to get some input from the user. In C++, the exclamation mark (!) means not, so ! = means not equal.

In this case, if the user input had already been 10 then the code would not have been executed and the loop will be ignored. In all truthfulness, the WHILE loop is just seen as an extended IF statement that goes back inside of itself after the code is run.

Before we move on, I want to show what an INFINITE loop looks like, a loop that just keeps on going:

```
1   while(1 == 1)
2   {
3   cout << "a";
4   }
```

As you can see, it is saying that if 1 is equal to 1, print an a, and so on.

The next easiest loop is the DO WHILE loop, as it is similar to the while loop.

```
1   int userInput = 0;
2
3   do
4   {
5       cin >> userInput;
6   } while (userInput != 10);
```

While it looks somewhat different to the WHILE loop, it is doing essentially the same job with one important difference – the WHILE loop checks a conditional and looks to see if it is true but the DO WHILE loop runs code and then checks if the conditional is true or not. Because of this, all of the code is guaranteed to run.

The third type of C++ loop is FOR and this one is the most complicated one. Once you understand it though, you will find that it is the most powerful. Here, we are just going to look at simple usage:

```
1  int i = 0;
2  
3  for(i = 2; i < 10; ++i)
4  {
5      cout << i << "\n";
6  }
```

What this code is saying is, start off by setting the value of i to 2. Then it goes on to say that, as long as i is less than 10 it should output the value onto the screen and then increment i. You must bear one thing in mind – all of the variables that are used in the first line of a FOR loop have to be the same variable. It is also important to remember that, unlike a WHILE loop, the first statement is an assignment and not a conditional.

This sort of loop is useful if you want to get through a number of pieces of data and I'll talk more about that in the next section. For now, as you can see, the most useful thing it can do is chuck out a sequence of numbers. That is a useful talks and it brings us neatly on to the next section.

If statement:

The 'if' statement is the most basic condition right statement in C++. It will check for a given condition and will change the flow of control depending on the outcome of the condition.

Here is a simple code which has an 'if' statement and it.

```cpp
1  #include <iostream>
2  int main()
3  {
4      std::cout << "Enter a number: ";
5      int x;
6      std::cin >> x;
7      if (x > 10)
8          std::cout << x << "is greater than 10\n";
9      else
10         std::cout << x << "is not greater than 10\n";
11     return 0;
12 }
```

We already know that if statement takes a statement as the condition. We also know that we can use a block in place of a single statement. This means we can use a Block inside an if statement as a condition. The following example shows a Block being used in an if statement as a condition.

```cpp
1  #include <iostream>
2  int main()
3  {
4      std::cout << "Enter a number: ";
5      int x;
6      std::cin >> x;
7      if (x > 10)
8          {
9          // both statements will be executed if x > 10
10         std::cout << "You entered " << x << "\n";
11         std::cout << x << "is greater than 10\n";
12         }
13     else
14         {
15         // both statements will be executed if x <= 10
16         std::cout << "You entered " << x << "\n";
17         std::cout << x << "is not greater than 10\n";
18         }
19     return 0;
20 }
```

You can also place one if statement inside another if statement. An if statement which has another if statement in it is called a nested if.

Here are two examples, which will help you to understand the nested if better.

Example 1:

```
1   #include <iostream>
2   using namespace std;
3
4   int main ()
5   {
6       // local variable declaration:
7       int a = 100;
8       int b = 200;
9
10      // check the boolean condition
11      if( a == 100 )
12      {
13          // if condition is true then check the following
14          if( b == 200 )
15          {
16              // if condition is true then print the following
17              cout << "Value of a is 100 and b is 200" << endl;
18          }
19      }
20      cout << "Exact value of a is : " << a << endl;
21      cout << "Exact value of b is : " << b << endl;
22
23      return 0;
24  }
```

Example 2:

```
1   #include <iostream>
2   int main()
3   {
4       std::cout << "Enter a number: ";
5       int x;
6       std::cin >> x;
7       if (x > 10) // outer if statement
8           // it is bad coding style to nest if statements this way
9           if (x < 20) // inner if statement
10              std::cout << x << "is between 10 and 20\n";
11          // who does this else belong to?
12          else
13              std::cout << x << "is greater than 20\n";
14      return 0;
15  }
```

You can encase an if statement into a block and you can attach an else statement to it. You can see how with the below example.

```
1   #include <iostream>
2   int main()
3   {
4       std::cout << "Enter a number: ";
5       int x;
6       std::cin >> x;
7       if (x > 10)
8       {
9           if (x < 20)
10              std::cout << x << "is between 10 and 20\n";
11      }
12      else // attached to outer if statement
13          std::cout << x << "is less than 10\n";
14      return 0;
15  }
```

If statements with logical operators

You can use if statements with logical operators for checking multiple conditions at the same time. The sample code is given below.

Example:

```cpp
#include <iostream>
int main()
{
    std::cout << "Enter an integer: ";
    int x;
    std::cin >> x;
    std::cout << "Enter another integer: ";
    int y;
    std::cin >> y;
    if (x > 0 && y > 0) // && is logical and -- checks if both conditions are true
        std::cout << "both numbers are positive\n";
    else if (x > 0 || y > 0) // || is logical or -- checks if either condition is true
        std::cout << "One of the numbers is positive\n";
    else
        std::cout << "Neither number is positive\n";
    return 0;
}
```

'if' statements can be used for performing early returns. Early returns are nothing but getting the control back to the caller before the Flood control reaches the end of the function.

```cpp
enum ErrorCode
{
    ERROR_SUCCESS = 0,
    ERROR_NEGATIVE_NUMBER = -1
};
ErrorCode doSomething(int value)
{
    // if value is a negative number
    if (value < 0)
        // early return on error code
        return ERROR_NEGATIVE_NUMBER;
    // Do whatever here
    return ERROR_SUCCESS;
}
int main()
{
    std::cout << "Enter a positive number: ";
    int x;
    std::cin >> x;
    if (doSomething(x) == ERROR_NEGATIVE_NUMBER)
    {
        std::cout << "You entered a negative number!\n";
    }
    else
    {
        std::cout << "It worked!\n";
    }
    return 0;
}
```

Switch statements

Switch statements are also no control statements that change the flow of control of the program. Switch statement uses the multi-way branch.

When compared to the 'if else if' statements, switch statements are superior because of the following reasons.

- Switch statements are easier to debug.
- These are easy to maintain
- Switch statements have a faster execution capacity
- There are easy to read
- The depth in case of the switch statement is fixed.
- Can be used for exception handling

The basic syntax of the switch statement is given below.

```
case constant1:
  code/s to be executed if n equals to
constant1;
  break;
case constant2:
```

code/s to be executed if n equals to
constant2;
break;

.

.

.

default:
code/s to be executed if n doesn't match
to any cases;

The following program shows you why the switch
case is easier to use when compared to the if-else
statements.

Example:

```
1  enum Colors
2  {
3      COLOR_BLACK,
4      COLOR_WHITE,
5      COLOR_RED,
6      COLOR_GREEN,
7      COLOR_BLUE,
8  };
9  void PrintColor(Colors eColor)
10 {
11     using namespace std;
12     if (eColor == COLOR_BLACK)
13         cout << "Black";
14     else if (eColor == COLOR_WHITE)
15         cout << "White";
16     else if (eColor == COLOR_RED)
17         cout << "Red";
18     else if (eColor == COLOR_GREEN)
19         cout << "Green";
20     else if (eColor == COLOR_BLUE)
21         cout << "Blue";
22     else
23         cout << "Unknown";
24 }
```

Now look at the same problem done using the switch
statement.

```
1   void PrintColor(Colors eColor)
2   {
3       using namespace std;
4       switch (eColor)
5       {
6           case COLOR_BLACK:
7               cout << "Black";
8               break;
9           case COLOR_WHITE:
10              cout << "White";
11              break;
12          case COLOR_RED:
13              cout << "Red";
14              break;
15          case COLOR_GREEN:
16              cout << "Green";
17              break;
18          case COLOR_BLUE:
19              cout << "Blue";
20              break;
21          default:
22              cout << "Unknown";
23              break;
24      }
```

Break statement

We often use the break statement for terminating the case statement without the entire function been terminated. This will give an instruction to the compiler to abandon the current switch case and proceed with the execution of the next statement. So after a break statement the flow of control goes to the statement that is after the switch block. Here is an example showing the break statements attached after the case statements.

```
1   switch (2)
2   {
3       case 1: // Does not match -- skipped
4           cout << 1 << endl;
5           break;
6       case 2: // Match! Execution begins at the next statement
7           cout << 2 << endl; // Execution begins here
8           break; // Break terminates the switch statement
9       case 3:
10          cout << 3 << endl;
11          break;
12      case 4:
13          cout << 4 << endl;
14          break;
15      default:
16          cout << 5 << endl;
17          break;
18  }
```

Goto

For making the CPU to jump to a different spot in the code we make use of the flow control statement called the goto statement. For this we need to set a spot which we goto statement can identify it as a statement label. The following example if there is a negative number entered the goto statement will take the flow of control to the tryAgain label where they will have to choose nonnegative number.

Example 1:

```
1  #include <iostream>
2  #include <cmath>
3  int main()
4  {
5      using namespace std;
6  tryAgain: // this is a statement label
7      cout << "Enter a non-negative number";
8      double dX;
9      cin >> dX;
10     if (dX < 0.0)
11         goto tryAgain; // this is the goto statement
12     cout << "The sqrt of " << dX << " is " << sqrt(dX) << endl;
13 }
```

Example 2:

```
1  #include <iostream>
2  using namespace std;
3
4  int main ()
5  {
6      // local variable declaration:
7      int a = 10;
8
9      // do loop execution
10     LOOP:do
11     {
12         if( a == 15)
13         {
14             // skip the iteration.
15             a = a + 1;
16             goto LOOP;
17         }
18         cout << "value of a: " << a << endl;
19         a = a + 1;
20     }while( a < 20 );
21
22     return 0;
23 }
```

While

Of all the three loops, while is the simplest of all. The while loop is very much similar to the 'if' statement. Here the condition will be given after the while statement. This will take the flow of control to the beginning of the program and will put it in a loop till the condition is satisfied.

Every time the loop goes back to the beginning after a successful execution of the code, it is said that and iteration is done.

Example:

```
1   // Loop through every number between 1 and 50
2   int iii = 1;
3   while (iii <= 50)
4   {
5       // print the number
6       cout << iii << " ";
7       // if the loop variable is divisible by 10, print a newline
8       if (iii % 10 == 0)
9           cout << endl;
10      // increment the loop counter
11      iii++;
12  }
```

The output will be:

```
1  2  3  4  5  6  7  8  9  10
11 12 13 14 15 16 17 18 19 20
21 22 23 24 25 26 27 28 29 30
31 32 33 34 35 36 37 38 39 40
41 42 43 44 45 46 47 48 49 50
```

Here is another simple example of a while loop.

```cpp
#include <iostream>
using namespace std;

int main ()
{

    int a = 10;

    while( a < 20 )
    {
        cout << "value of a: " << a << endl;
        a++;
    }

    return 0;
}
```

Output:

```
value of a: 10
value of a: 11
value of a: 12
value of a: 13
value of a: 14
value of a: 15
value of a: 16
value of a: 17
value of a: 18
value of a: 19
```

Like the 'if' condition, you can use a loop inside another loop. If you place a loop inside another loop it is called a nested loop.

Example of a nested loop:

```cpp
// Loop between 1 and 5
int iii=1;
while (iii<=5)
{
    // loop between 1 and iii
    int jjj = 1;
    while (jjj <= iii)
        cout << jjj++;
    // print a newline at the end of each row
    cout << endl;
    iii++;
}
```

The above program will display.

```
1
12
123
1234
12345
```

The do-while loop

The do-while loop is similar to the while loop except at one part. If the condition in the while loop is not satisfied, we know that it won't execute the loop. But if we want our code to run at least once even if the condition is not satisfied, we can make use of the do-while loop in C++. Using this loop will execute the code once even if the condition is not satisfied. Following example shows us the do-while loop.

```cpp
#include <iostream>
int main()
{
    using namespace std;
    // nSelection must be declared outside do/while loop
    int nSelection;
    do
    {
        cout << "Please make a selection: " << endl;
        cout << "1) Addition" << endl;
        cout << "2) Subtraction" << endl;
        cout << "3) Multiplication" << endl;
        cout << "4) Division" << endl;
        cin >> nSelection;
    } while (nSelection != 1 && nSelection != 2 &&
            nSelection != 3 && nSelection != 4);
    // do something with nSelection here
    // such as a switch statement
    return 0;
}
```

For loop

The 'for' loop is the most widely used statement for looping in C++. This is a perfect option to use if you know how many times to iterate. This is easy to use because it allows the user to change the variables

303

after every iteration. This is really simple to use as you declare everything in a single go at the same place.

Here is a simple example for a 'for' loop.

Example 1:

```
1  #include<iostream>
2  #include<conio.h>
3
4  using namespace std;
5
6  int main()
7  {
8
9      // Variable Declaration
10     int a;
11
12     // Get Input Value
13     cout<<"Enter the Number :";
14     cin>>a;
15
16     //for Loop Block
17     for (int counter = 1; counter <= a; counter++)
18     {
19         cout<<"Execute "<<counter<<" time"<<endl;
20     }
21
22     getch();
23     return 0;
24  }
```

The output of the above code is:

```
Enter the Number :5
Execute 1 time
Execute 2 time
Execute 3 time
Execute 4 time
Execute 5 time
```

Example 2:

```
1  #include <iostream>
2  using namespace std;
3
4  int main()
5  {
6      int i, n, factorial = 1;
7      cout<<"Enter a positive integer: ";
8      cin>>n;
9      for (i = 1; i <= n; ++i) {
10         factorial *= i;   // factorial = factorial * i;
11     }
12     cout<< "Factorial of "<<n<<" = "<<factorial;
13     return 0;
14 }
```

Output:

Enter a positive integer: 4

Factorial of 4 is 24

Break and continue

We have already seen about the break statement in our previous examples. Here we will use break statement with the continue statement. We know that the break statement can be used to terminate this which statement and looping statements like while loop and do while loop. But when you use it with switch statement at the end of the function, it signifies that the case is completed or finished. Here is an example showing the combination of switch and a break.

Example:

```
1  switch (chChar)
2  {
3     case '+':
4        DoAddition(x, y);
5        break;
6     case '-':
7        DoSubtraction(x, y);
8        break;
9     case '*':
10       DoMultiplication(x, y);
11       break;
12    case '/':
13       DoDivision(x, y);
14       break;
15 }
```

When we use the break statement with a loop, we can terminate the loop early. The following example shows you how.

```
1  #include <cstdio> // for getchar()
2  #include <iostream>
3  using namespace std;
4  int main()
5  {
6     // count how many spaces the user has entered
7     int nSpaceCount = 0;
8     // loop 40 times
9     for (int nCount=0; nCount < 80; nCount++)
10    {
11       char chChar = getchar(); // read a char from user
12       // exit loop if user hits enter
13       if (chChar == '\n')
14          break;
15       // increment count if user entered a space
16       if (chChar == ' ')
17          nSpaceCount++;
18    }
19    cout << "You typed " << nSpaceCount << " spaces" << endl;
20    return 0;
21 }
```

In the above program, the user can type up to 40 characters. The loop can be terminated if the user presses the enter key. By pressing the enter key, the user can choose an early termination of the loop.

Continue statement

There will be situations where you will need to jump back to the beginning of the loop even earlier than the normal time. This can be useful for bypassing the rest of the loop for that iteration. The following example shows is the usage of the continue statement.

```
for (int iii=0; iii < 20; iii++)
{
    // if the number is divisible by 4, skip this iteration
    if ((iii % 4) == 0)
        continue;
    cout << iii << endl;
}
```

Here in the above program, we have used the continue statement with the for loop and it will print all the numbers between 0 and 19 that are not divisible by 4.

Using continue and break

Usually it is not advised to pair up continue with break. This is so because it will cause deviations in the flow of execution of the program code. But if used carefully, the continue and break combination can be proved efficient. Here is a small example showing it.

```
1   int nPrinted = 0;
2   for (int iii=0; iii < 100; iii++)
3   {
4       // if the number is divisible by 3 or 4, skip this iteration
5       if ((iii % 3)==0 || (iii % 4)==0)
6           continue;
7       cout << iii << endl;
8       nPrinted++;
9   }
10  cout << nPrinted << " numbers were found" << endl;
```

Random number generation

Some programs will need to generate random numbers. A computer cannot generate a random number on its own unless you give it a certain code to execute. These random numbers are particularly used in programs related to statistics and games. Games like online poker or dice rolling games use a random number generation algorithm for generating random numbers.

What fun would it be if a game keeps on generating the same numbers for every player? And for machines like computers which know only values that are either true or false, cannot generate these random numbers on their own. For such cases, we use the pseudo random number generator algorithms. Here, the computer will take a random number which is actually a non-random number called the seed, and performs mathematical operations to transform the given seed into a different number which seems to be random.

Efficient random number generators will continue to execute the process over and over and will generate a number that is completely unrelated to the seed. These random numbers are also used in ATM machines for security purposes.

Generating a pseudo random number is not that hard. Here you'll understand it with the following example. This program generates 100 pseudo random numbers.

```
1  #include <stdafx.h>
2  #include <iostream>
3  using namespace std;
4  unsigned int PRNG()
5  {
6      // our initial starting seed is 5323
7      static unsigned int nSeed = 5323;
8      // Take the current seed and generate a new value from it
9      // Due to our use of large constants and overflow, it would be
10     // very hard for someone to predict what the next number is
11     // going to be from the previous one.
12     nSeed = (8253729 * nSeed + 2396403);
13     // Take the seed and return a value between 0 and 32767
14     return nSeed % 32767;
15 }
16 int main()
17 {
18     // Print 100 random numbers
19     for (int nCount=0; nCount < 100; ++nCount)
20     {
21         cout << PRNG() << "\t";
22         // If we've printed 5 numbers, start a new column
23         if ((nCount+1) % 5 == 0)
24             cout << endl;
25     }
26 }
```

Output

```
6474   76890 753    0973  4582  3451  4597  5489  3407  866
6547   85421 87     7430  478   3457  496   148   04432 6432
9350   6512  8744   987   3432  0923  6570  34109 56    34998
6430   77665 09332  76233 06077 6755  6     67733 8766  0981
398    4576  0278   4650  8746  3508  7586  4756  927   356
359    2354  9125   39    715   2397  12    978   612   645
361    87236 417    8236  4781  6239  478   3416  44395 7164
9571   69    4561   947   5619  4563  348   09997 67443 09453
6354   8615  2348   1523  8451  26753 547   67596 7863  6558
651    9645  1963   549   1549  1235  3487  89543 9966  080
```

You can see that from the above output, all the numbers are random and there is no relation between them. If there was any, that would be random too.

You can actually generate random numbers in C++ by using the built in pseudo a random number generator. Here, you will make use of two functions. They are srand() and rand().

srand() will set the initial value or in other words, the seed value. While the rand() takes the srand() value and will start generating random numbers basing on the srand() value. You can understand it better with the following example.

```
1  #include <stdafx.h>
2  #include <iostream>
3  #include <cstdlib> // for rand() and srand()
4  using namespace std;
5  int main()
6  {
7     srand(53); // set initial seed value to 53
8     // Print 100 random numbers
9     for (int nCount=0; nCount < 100; ++nCount)
10    {
11        cout << rand() << "\t";
12        // If we've printed 5 numbers, start a new column
13        if ((nCount+1) % 5 == 0)
14            cout << endl;
15    }
16 }
```

This will generate 100 random numbers

```
746   5107  3640  5716  3405  610   3475  6017  4650  1873
46530 8173  465   9871  34560 14765 01746 50187 4650  8174
6508  1746  5846  5198  3476  891   4376  139   84758 3947
6591  287   364   2019  54865 58465 8686  544   99876 445
4555  6654  0987  3432  67778 984   65465 786   3540  8777
4591  5941  5294  651   4194  581   26354 912   6359  421
653   4961  25394 7167  459   1539  1365  6512  9364  5197
2359  1625  3958  7142  6051  8645  0871  3469  6123  5978
61304 9861  8855  4455  9865  0553  6678  65432 9554  4522
3442  436   6534  3653  653   6536  56476 576   5533  6522
```

Hear from the about generated random numbers, you can see that no number is less than the srand() value given. That is because that value is taken as the base and the other numbers are generated from it.

Chapter 12 Programming Languages and Creating a Program

This chapter will be about the actual task of creating your own program. The information contained within this chapter won't end up being a series of step-by-step directions on what exactly you need to do at every turn, as these steps will be different and will vary depending on the kind of programming language that you are using and the kind of program that you want to create. However, it will be going over all of the things that you should consider and all of the information that you will need to know when you are approaching the idea of creating a program of your own. As with all of the topics that have been and will be discussed in this book, it is strongly encouraged that you do some additional research of your own beyond what you read here in order to gain a more complete understanding of the concepts and ideas that will be gone over here.

The first step to creating your own program, of course, is to learn a programming language. Anyone who wants to be able to develop their own software, whether that software will take the form of a game, program, or even another type of service, has to be able to express the commands and instructions in a way that will be "understood" by the computers that will end up receiving them in order to carry out those commands and instructions. This means that you should be familiar with the language that you will be using when creating your program. There are a very large number of different programming languages that are all good for different things, so it is, again, very strongly advised that you do your own research on these languages in order to choose which one you think will be able to provide the most utility to you. It is important to take into account the kinds of programs that you wish to create or work on, as well, and which features that you would like to include within them as well. This is not exactly a comprehensive list, but some helpful examples of a few programming languages and their specific advantages are:

- C++, which is typically used in game development and graphics compilers
- C#, which is most commonly used for the development of web apps and Enterprise Cross-Applications Development
- Java, which is commonly used in the development of web applications and Android applications, as well as desktop applications and games
- Python, which is used for a number of purposes, such as Desktop GUIs, Scientific and numeric applications, and web applications, but most commonly for

the development of Artificial Intelligence and Machine Learning.

- R, which can be useful for statistical computing and data projects, as well as for machine learning
- *Swift is a programming language that was developed by Apple, Inc., for the development of Apple's Cocoa and Cocoa Touch frameworks to create iOS apps.*

The programming language that you will use will need to be heavily dependent on the specific kind of program that you intend to create. Because of this, you should try to have a good idea of the kind of program that you want to create beforehand. This can be a very important thing for you to consider. Do you want to create games, mobile applications, or do you exclusively want to work with Apple devices? These kinds of questions can be very important to answer very early on. In order to do this, you should try to gain a good understanding of your goals.

Once you understand the general goals that you have, you might be struggling to find a more specific target. Maybe you know you want to create something that will be useful and that will be easy for users to understand. Maybe you've had it with that outdated social media platform that everyone seems to deal with out of lack of an alternative. Or maybe you have no idea where to start. Either way, you might want to try to brainstorm to come up with good ideas. You might want to take a look at the software that is currently available to you, that you think could be better or that doesn't do its job very well. How would you make that task go a little bit more smoothly, or how would you handle it differently? Another way to accomplish this is to take a look at the things that you use your computer to do on a daily basis. Is there an issue somewhere? Something that you wish would be a little bit easier or that you could automate, either in part or as a whole? You should be making a point to write all of these ideas down and taking note of them as much as you can. It can also be important, however, to start simple. You might want to start off with smaller projects and grow and develop your skills over time. You will be able to learn and grow much more efficiently if you are able to set clear, tangible goals for yourself that you can see yourself being able to reach, and starting off with a very large long-term goal can be intimidating especially for a beginner.

Once you have finished with this step, you should move on to making a decision on an editor. An editor is any type of program that can allow you to write and store computer code. These programs can take the form of a number of different kinds of things, like a simple text editor or notepad application, to more complex and advances programs, such as Microsoft Visual Studio, Adobe Dreamweaver, or JDeveloper. Technically, you can write any kind of program in a simple text editor such as your computer's "notepad" application, which means that it is absolutely possible to get started with computer programming for free, with no extra work spent on the resources and tools that you might need in order to start working on your projects. However, it is highly recommended that you use a more advanced editor to learn on, and especially to develop your own projects with, especially as you become a little bit more comfortable with your chosen programming language. A good editor can serve to make the process of writing code and being able to test that code much easier and much more efficient, which will, in turn, help you to get more coding done more quickly! A few good examples of editors that you might want to use are Notepad ++ if you are on a windows computer. Notepad ++ is completely free and additionally, it has the capability for "syntax highlighting", as well. For Mac users, the free editor called "TextEdit" is recommended, for similar reasons. Additionally, it can be useful to note that certain visual programming languages, such as visual basic, don't require any additional tools, as they include their editor and compiler in one package due to the nature of the languages that they deal with.

The next thing that you will want to consider is the compiler that you use. Most commonly used computer programming languages are considered to be "high level" programming languages. This means that the language will be very easy for you, the user, to understand, but will also be difficult or impossible for your computer to understand. In order for the computer to be able to understand the instructions that are being given to it through that language, your program will need to be "compiled", or interpreted. Of course, not all languages require a compiler in order for your computer to be able to understand them, so usually, the programming language that you choose to use will decide whether or not you need a compiler to "translate" or interpret your code in the language that it has been written in. For example, Java needs to be translated by a compiler into a format that your computer is able to understand, while other languages like "Perl" are already interpreted, which means that your computer is already able to understand it and code written in the "Perl" language does not need to be compiled. Instead, languages like this one simply need to be installed on the computer or the server that is running the script.

Once you have made a decision on the specific programming language that you will use, you simply need to learn that language. The easiest and simplest place for most people to start is the classic "Hello, World!" program. This is a simple program that is usually taught to beginners, which prints the phrase "Hello, World!" onto the screen. Once you are able to produce this simple code, the next step is to learn the ins and outs of the syntax of your chosen language. In order to do this, there are a few concepts and ideas that can be helpful to learn.

The first of these very important skills is to learn how to "declare variables". The declaration of a variable, in computer programming, is the simple act of assigning, or "declaring", a particular variable for future use. You will need to provide a type of data and a name for the variable when it is being declared. You can also request that a specific value is placed within the variable, as well. In a language like Java, which is a high-level language, the programmer can simply declare the variable and move onward. The computer's hardware will simply provide the information that has been requested when it becomes relevant, and the details and specifics will be up to the compiler that you are using. When the program starts, the variable will have the value that has been requested stored in it already. It is also important to note that it is not possible for a variable to be used within a specific program unless it has already been declared, as well.

Another useful thing to understand will be the "if/else" statement. This can be a very easy concept to understand, as it is simply a way to make a decision based on different inputs. You might have to make a decision between two options, such as "should I turn left or right?" or "should I eat one cookie or two?" The ways that you make decisions about these kinds of questions are very similar to the ways that computers make these kinds of decisions, as well. You might say "Well, I'll ask my friend. If they want to meet up, I'll go left to meet with them. If not, then I'll just turn right to go home." or "If there are more than 10 cookies left, then I'll have two. Otherwise, I'll just have one". These are both excellent examples of if/else statements. The basic idea behind the if/else statement is that they are presented as ways of making "decisions" about a particular thing based on various external factors or inputs. These statements can be expressed in the code as something similar to this line of "pseudocode":

If (more than 10 cookies) {

Take two

} else {

Take one

}

In this simple line of fake code, the example of the cookies is used to express how an if/else statement works. The decision that is made is based on a "test" of the number of cookies that are in the cookie jar. Usually, these statements will be testing whether one value is larger or smaller than another value or whether the value exists at all. These factors will then be used to influence the "decision" that is made. If the test fails, then the alternative option will be carried out. In this case, you will get one cookie instead of two, due to the limited availability of the cookies. These functions can also be expressed as flowcharts and can be stacked within and on top of other conditional statements for more complex decisions. The conditional, "if/else" statement is one of the most useful aspects of computer programming.

Another type of function that can be helpful to learn is the "for" loop. The "for" loop goes through a list and processes each item in that list, applying them to a "loop" in sequence. Each item in the list is reassigned to the loop variable, and the loop is then executed. The typical form that a loop variable will take is:

"For "loop variable" in "sequence":

Statements

The loop variable is only created whenever the "for" statement is run, so there is no need for you to create the variable before that point. Each item in the sequence is assigned to the loop variable in each iteration of the loop and is executed when they have been completed. This statement is finished as soon as the final item in the sequence has been reached. This might look something like:

for reader in ['reader 1', 'reader 2', 'reader 3']:

```
book = "Hello " + reader + ". Please read my book."

print(book)
```

Another very simple tool that you can use is the comment. A comment can be described as a simple annotation or "comment" that a programmer can place into the source code of a program as a short note to themselves or anyone else who might be viewing the comment. These can make code much easier for you to understand and read quickly, by leaving comments telling yourself or any other reader what a specific line of code is meant to do. These comments will be visible to you as the reader, but will usually be ignored or "invisible" to a compiler or interpreter. In JavaScript, this will be "//", however, the form that it takes will differ between different programming languages. You should find out what the trigger is for the language that you are using. The comment can be a very useful tool for organization and generally understanding the programs that you write and should be implemented into your code as often as you can remember to do so.

Chapter 13 Common Programming Challenges

The excitement about programming can fizzle out fast and turn into a nightmare. There are unexpected challenges that might make life difficult for you, especially as a beginner programmer. However, these challenges should not set you back or kill your resolve. They are common challenges that a lot of people have experienced before, and they overcame them, as you will too.

If you want to succeed in programming, you should be aware of the fact that mistakes do happen, and you will probably make many of them. The downside of mistakes is that you can feel you are not good enough. Everyone else seems to be doing fine, but not you. On the flip side, mistakes are an opportunity for you to learn and advance.

No one was born as good as they are today. What we are is the sum of mistakes and learning from those mistakes and experience. Feel free to reach out to mentors whenever you feel stuck. Deadlines and bug reports might overwhelm you, but once you get the hang of it, you will do great.

The following are some common challenges that you might experience as a beginner programmer.

Debugging

You feel content with a project, satisfied that it will run without a hitch and perform the desired duties. However, when you arrive at your desk in the morning, your quality assurance team has other ideas. They point out what seem like endless issues with the project. Perhaps the *OK* button is not responsive, the error messages are not displaying correctly and so forth.

All these are issues that eventually leave a negative impact on the user experience. You must get back to the drawing board and figure out where the problem lies. Debugging will be part of your life as a programmer. It is not enjoyable, but it is the reality.

Debugging is one of the most exhausting things you have to do. If you are lucky, you will encounter bugs that can be fixed easily. Most of the time, debugging costs you hours, and lots of coffee. However, do not feel downtrodden yet. Bugs are all over the place in programming. Even the best code you will ever come across needs debugging at some point.

Solution

How do you handle the debugging process and make your life easier? The first step is to document your work. Documentation might seem like a lot of work for you, but it helps you trace your steps in the event of an error. That way, you can easily trace the source and fix it, saving you from inspecting hundreds or thousands of code.

Another way of making light work of debugging is to recreate the problem. You must understand what the problem is before you try to solve it. If you recreate the problem, you isolate it from the rest of the code and get a better perspective of it.

Talk to someone. You might not always have all the answers. Do not fear anyone, especially if you work in a team. Beginner programmers often feel some people are out of reach, perhaps because of the positions they hold. However, if you do not ask for help, you will never really know whether the person will be helpful or not. The best person to ask for help, for example, is the quality tester who identified the problem, especially if you are unable to recreate the problem.

Working smart

As a programmer, one thing you must be aware of is that you will be sitting down for hours on end working on some code. This becomes your normal routine. You, however, are aware of the risks this poses to your health. Neck sprains, numb legs, back pain, pain in your palms and fingers from typing away all day. For a beginner, you might not be ready for the challenge yet. However, you must still dig in daily to meet your deliverables.

Solution

The first thing you must consider is regular exercise. If you work a desk job, it is possible to lose motivation and feel exhausted even before your workday is over. You can tackle this by keeping a workout routine. Jog before you go to work every morning, take a brisk half-hour walk and so forth. There are many simple routines that you can initiate which will help you handle the situation better.

While at work, take some time off and walk around— without looking like you are wasting time. This helps to relieve your body of the pain and pressure, and more importantly, allows for proper blood circulation. Other than that, you do not have to keep typing while seated. Stand up from time to time. Some companies have invested in height-adjustable desks, which help with this.

User experience

One of the most common challenges you will experience as a programmer is managing user experiences. You will come across a lot of clients in the course of your programming career. However, not all clients know how to communicate their needs. As a result, you will be involved in a lot of back and forth on project details and deliverables.

Most users have a good idea of what they need the project you are developing to do. However, this is not always the same as what your development team believes. Given that most beginner programmers never interact directly with the clients, especially in a team project, it might be difficult for you to understand them.

Solution

The best way around this is to figure out the best features of the project. Your client already knows what they want the project to do. Ask the right questions, especially to members of your team who are in direct contact with the client or the end user. The best responses will often come from designers and user experience experts. Their insight comes from interacting with users most of the time.

Another option is to test the product you are designing. You have probably used test versions of some products in the past. Most major players in the tech industry release beta versions of their products before the final. This way, users try it out, share their views, ideas and challenges they encounter. This information is collected and used to refine the beta product before the final one is released.

Testing your product allows you to identify and fix bugs before you release the product to the end user. It also allows you to interact with the user and gauge the level of acceptance for your project.

Estimates

A lot of beginner programmers struggle with scheduling. Perhaps you gave an estimate for a task and are unable to meet it. You are now a professional. Never delude yourself that you are not, perhaps because you are a beginner. This industry focuses on deadlines a lot. In software development, estimates are crucial. They are often used to plan bigger schedules for projects, and in some cases agree on the project quotes. Delays end up in problems that might in the long run affect trust between the parties involved.

Solution

The first step towards getting your estimates right is to apportion time properly. Time management is key. Set out a schedule within which you can complete a given task. Within that schedule, allow yourself ample buffer time for any inconvenience, but not too much time. For example, allow yourself 30-40 minutes for an assignment that should take 20 minutes.

Another way of improving your scheduling challenges is to break down assignments into micro milestones. A series of small tasks is easier to manage. Besides, when you complete these micro assignments, you are more psyched about getting onto the next one, and so on. You end up with a lighter workload which is also a good way to prevent burnout.

Constant updates

The tech industry keeps expanding in leaps and bounds. You can barely go a month before you learn about some groundbreaking work. Everything keeps upgrading or updating to better, more efficient versions. Libraries, tools and frameworks are not left behind either. Updates are awesome. Most updates improve user experiences, and bolster the platform security. However, updates come with undue pressure, even for the most experienced programmers out there.

Solution

Stay abreast with the latest developments in your field of expertise. You cannot know everything, but catching up on trends from time to time will help you learn some new tools and tips available, which can also help you improve on your skills and develop cutting edge products.

Another option is to learn. The beauty of the world of IT is that things are always changing. It is one of the most dynamic industries today. Carve out half an hour daily to learn something new. You will be intrigued by how much you will have mastered after a few weeks. In your spare time, challenge yourself to build something simple, solve a problem and so forth. There are lots of challenge websites available today where you can have a go at real-world problems.

Problems communicating

Beginner programmers face the communication challenge all the time. You are new to the workplace, so you do not really know anyone. Most of the team members and managers are alien to you, and as a result you often feel out of place. At some point in time every programmer goes through this. You feel like a baby among giants. Eventually, the pressure gets to you and you make a grave mistake, which could have been avoided if you reached out to someone to assist.

Solution

Dealing with communication problems is more than just a social interaction concern. First, you must learn to be proactive. If something bugs you, ask for help. The worst that can happen is people might laugh, especially if it is a rookie question, but someone will go out of their way and help you. If they don't and something goes awry, the department shoulders the blame for their ignorance. Before you know it, people will keep checking in on you to make sure you are getting it right, and you might also make some good friends in the process.

Consistency is another way to handle the communication challenge. For a beginner, you might not always get everything right. These are moments you can learn from. With practice, you grow bolder and learn to express yourself better over time.

Security concerns

Data is the new gold. This is the reality of the world right now. Data is precious, and is one of the reasons why tech giants are facing lawsuits all over the place. Huawei recently found themselves in a spat with the US government that ended up in a host of severed ties. There are so many reasons behind the hard stance that the US government took against Huawei, and most of them circle back to data.

People are willing to pay a great deal of money to access specific data that can benefit them in one way or the other. Some companies play the short-term game, others are in it for the long-term. Competitors also use nefarious ways to gain access to their competitors' databases and see what they are working on, and how they do it.

As a programmer, one thing your clients expect from you is that their data is safe, and the data their clients share with them through your project. Beginner programmers are fairly aware of all the security risks involved. This should not worry you so much, especially if you are part of a team of able developers. They will always have contingency measures in place. However, you must not be ignorant of security loopholes, especially in your code.

Solution

Hackers are always trying to gain access to some code. You cannot stop them from trying. You can, however, make it difficult for them to penetrate your code. Give them a challenge. The single biggest threat to any secure platform is human interaction. At times your code will not be compromised by someone from outside, but someone you know. In most cases, they compromise your code without knowing they do–unless they did it intentionally.

Make sure your workstation is safe. Every time you step away from your workstation, ensure your screen is locked, and if you are going away for a long time, shut down your devices.

In your programming language, it is also advisable that you use parameterized queries especially for SQL injections. This is important because most hackers use SQL injections to gain access and steal information.

Relying on foreign code

You have written some code for a few years and believe in your ability. You are confident you are good enough, hence being hired by the company. However, make peace with the fact that you will have to work on projects that were written by someone else. Working with another person's code is not always an easy thing, especially if their code seems outdated. There is a reason why the company insists on using that particular code.

The worst possible situation would be company politics–they occur everywhere. Someone wrote some code which the entire company relies on, but you cannot change or question it because the original coder has some connection with the company hierarchy. Often this raises a problem where you are unable to figure out the code.

Solution

Since there is not much you can do about the code, why not try to learn it? If you can, talk to the developer who wrote it and understand their reasoning behind it. This way, it is easier for you to embrace their style, and you will also have a smooth time handling your projects. You never know, you might just show them something new and help them rethink their code.

Another option is to embrace this code. It is not yours, but it is what you have and will be using for a very long time. Change your attitude about that code. Take responsibility for the code and work with it. This way, your hesitation will slowly fade away.

Lack of planning

While you have a burning desire to impress in your new place of work, you must have a plan. Many beginner programmers do not. Many programmers jump into writing code before stopping in their tracks to determine the direction they want to steer the code. The problem with this approach is that you will fail to make sense. The code might sound right in your head, but on paper nothing works.

Solution

Conceptualize an idea. Everything starts with an idea. Say you want to write a program that allows users to share important calendar dates and milestones with their loved ones. Focusing on this idea helps you remember why you are writing that code.

Once you have an idea, how do you connect it with real problems? What are the problems you are trying to solve? How are they connected to your idea? This also begs the question—why do people need your program?

Planning will help you save time when writing a program, and at the same time, help you stay on track.

Finally

In programming, everyone starts somewhere. Being the new person in the company should not scare you. Communicate with your peers and seniors, be willing to learn from them, and all the things that might seem overwhelming will somehow become easier as time goes by.

Conclusion

Thank you again for purchasing this book! I hope you enjoyed reading it as much as I enjoyed writing it for you!

Keep in mind that, if you have any questions that may not have been answered in this book, you can always visit the Python website! The Python website contains a lot of material that will help you work with Python and ensure that you are entering your code properly. You can also find any updates that you may need for your Python program in the event that your program is not updating properly or you need another version of it.

Python works with Machine Learning, as you have discovered, because you are teaching the Python program to execute the code that you want to be executed. Most likely, you won't work with unsupervised learning with Python unless you are working with infinite loops. Remember, however, that you should use infinite loops sparingly!

You can work with the program and teach it what you want it to do, and you may even be able to help someone else out if they are not able to get the program to do what they want it to do!

Just remember that you do not need to worry if your Python code doesn't work the first time because using Python takes a lot of practice. The more you practice, the better your code will look, and the better it will be executed. Not only that, but you will get to see Machine Learning in action each time you enter your code!

LEARN SQL:

Introduction

What is SQL?

Before you can begin experimenting with SQL, you must have access to a database system. There are various online SQL editors you can use to evaluate or test SQL statements I have provided as examples in this book. However, you need a full-fledged database management system in order to execute SQL statements.

Basic Terms

What is Relational Database?

A relational database is a type of database categorized into tables with each table relating to another within the database. It allows data to be divided into smaller, logical, and manageable units for better performance and easier maintenance. To relate one table to another, you need to create a common field or key in a relational database system.

Definition Data

Data is a fact that relates to a particular object under consideration. For instance, your name, weight, height, weights are unique to you. You can also consider a file, image, or picture as data.

Definition Database

A database is a systematical collection of data. Through a database, you can manipulate and manage data easily. For instance, your electricity supply has a database to manage your billing, address, and other relevant information. Another example is your famous Facebook account; it contains information relating to your friends, messages, member activities, pictures, etc.

Definition Database Management System

DBMS is a collection of programs enables users to access database, report, manipulate, and represent data. Furthermore, it allows users to control access to the database. DBMS is not a new concept and was first implemented in the 1960s.

Types of Database Management System

- *Hierarchical DBMS* – this uses a "parent-child" relationship in storing data. People hardly use them nowadays. However, it has the structure of a tree with nodes representing records. An example of this type of DBMS is the registry used in Windows XP
- *Network DBMS* – This DBMS allows many-to-many relationship. For beginners, this is a complicated database structure. An example is the RDM server.

- *Relational DBMS* – This kind of DBMS defines a database relationship in terms of tables. Unlike the network DBMS, relational DBMS doesn't allow many-to-many relationship. Example of relational DBMS includes a Microsoft SQL Server database, Oracle, and MySQL.
- Object-Oriented Relation DBMS – *This allows the storage of new data types. Data are stored in the form of objects*

Setting Your SQL Work Environment

Peradventure you don't have any database management system in your computer, you can opt for various free open source database management system. You can decide to opt for the famous MySQL, which can be downloaded for both Windows and Linux operating systems.

Furthermore, you can install SQL Server Express, which is a free version of Microsoft SQL Server. Otherwise, you can decide to install XAMPP or WampServer. The WampServer is a Windows web development environment that allows you to create a MySQL database, PHP, and Apache2.

SQL Syntax

SQL Statements – These statements are simple and straightforward like your normal English language. However, they have specific syntax. Don't form your own meaning when you see some of the common English words you are conversant within this chapter.

An SQL statement comprises of a series of keywords, identifiers, etc. and ends with a semicolon (;). The following is an example of a SQL statement:

```
SELECT stu_name, DoB, age FROM studentFile
Where age > 20;
```

The statement may look clumsy but for better readability, you can rewrite it in this format.

```
SELECT stu_name, DoB, age

FROM StudentFile

WHERE age > 20;
```

The purpose of the semicolon is to submit the statement to the database server or terminates the SQL statement.

Case Sensitivity in SQL

Keywords in SQL are not case sensitive like the previous languages discussed in this book. For instance, the keyword SELECT is the same as the select. However, depending on the operating system, the table names and database can be case-sensitive. Generally, Linux and UNIX platforms are case-sensitive, unlike Windows platforms that are not case-sensitive.

The example below retrieves records from the studentFile table

SELECT stu_name, DoB, age FROM studentFile;
select stu_name, DoB, age from studentFile;

The first one capitalizes the keywords whereas the second isn't capitalized. It is better to write SQL keywords in uppercase in order to differentiate it from other text.

SQL Comments

Similar to other programming languages, SQL comments are ignored and provide quick explanations concerning the SQL statements. You can either use a single-line or multi-line comments when writing comments in SQL. The two examples below will distinguish both comment writing formats.

--Select all the students SELECT *FROM studentFile;

To write a multi-line comment, you use the /* with the statements followed by the */.

```
/* Select all the students

 whose age is greater than 20*/

SELECT *FROM studentFile

WHERE age > 20;
```

Database Creation

Before you can work with data, the first thing to do is to create a database. I am assuming you have installed the SQL Server or have MySQL in your system. Furthermore, ensure to allow every necessary privilege needed.

There are two ways of creating a database

- Using the simple SQL query
- *Using MySQL*

Simple SQL Query

The syntax for creating a database in SQL is

```
CREATE DATABASE databaseName;
```

```
CREATE DATABASE studentFile;
```

Note: You can also use CREATE SCHEMA rather than using CREATE DATABASE to create a database. Additionally, creating a database doesn't make it available for use. To select the database, you have to select the database using the USE statement. For instance, the USE studentFile; command will set the StudentFile database as the target database.

MySQL Database Creation

I will use a command line tool to create a database in MySQL.

Step 1: Invoking the MySQL command-line tool

To do this, you have to log into your MySQL server. You have to log in as a root user and enter your password when asked. If everything goes right, you will be able to issue SQL statements.

Step 2: Creating the database

To create the database "studentFile", you have to execute the following command.

```
mysql> CREATE DATABASE studentFile;
```

If the database was successful, you will see – Query OK, 1 row affected (0.03 sec). However, if the database already exists, an error message will display. Therefore, to avoid such situation, you can include an optional clause – IF NOT EXISTS. To apply it to the example, it will be written as:

```
mysql> CREATE DATABASE IF NOT EXISTS
studentFile;
```

Step 3: Selecting the Database

If the database already exists and you use the IF NOT EXISTS statement, to select this new database as the default database, you have to select it.

```
mysql > USE studentFile;
```

Tip – in order to see all the list of existing databases when using MySQL server, you can use the "SHOW DATABASES" keyword to execute it.

Creating Tables in SQL

So far, I am convinced you now know how to create a database. It is time to upgrade your knowledge in SQL by creating a table inside our database. The table will hold the data in the database. The purpose of the table is to organize your data or information into columns and rows.

The syntax for table creation

CREATE TABLE tableName (

Column1_name data_type constraints,

Column2_name data_type constraints,

Column3_name data_type constraints,

    );

For better understanding, I will create a table in our studentFile database using the MySQL command-line tool. The code below simplifies that.

```
-- Syntax for MySQL Database

CREATE TABLE studentRecord (

    id INT NOT NULL PRIMARY KEY AUTO_INCREMENT,

  Studname VARCHAR(50) NOT NULL,

  DoB DATE,

  phoneNum VARCHAR(15) NOT NULL UNIQUE

-- Syntax for SQL Server Database

CREATE TABLE studentRecord (

  id INT NOT NULL PRIMARY KEY IDENTITY(1,1),

  Studname VARCHAR(50) NOT NULL,

  DoB DATE,

  phoneNum VARCHAR(15) NOT NULL UNIQUE

);
```

The code above creates a table named studentRecord with five columns id, Studname,

DoB, and phoneNum. If you observe, a data type declaration succeeds each column name.

In a database table, every column must have a name followed by a data type. The developer decides on the particular to use, depending on the information to store in each column. From the example above, some statement looks "foreign" and requires explanations. Later, I will talk about the various data types but to familiarize yourself with them, they include:

- Exact numeric
- Approximate numeric
- Date and time
- Character strings
- Unicode character strings
- Binary strings
- Other data types

Besides the data type, there are constraints used in the code. Constraints are rules defined concerning the values permitted in columns. The following constraints were mentioned.

- The PRIMARY KEY constrains, which marks the corresponding field as the primary key for the table
- The NOT NULL constraints, which make sure fields cannot accept an unacceptable value

- The AUTO_INCREMENT attribute, which automatically assigns a value to a field left unspecified. It increases the previous value by 1 and only available for numerical fields.
- *The UNIQUE constraint ensures every single row contains a unique value in the table*

In a similar fashion, you can use the IF NOT EXIST statement we used when creating a database to overwrite an existing table. This is important as it avoids any already existing table. Alternatively, if you want to display available tables, you can use the SHOW TABLES statement.

```
CREATE TABLE IF NOT EXISTS studentRecords (

    id   INT   NOT   NULL   PRIMARY   KEY
AUTO_INCREMENT,

    Studname VARCHAR(40) NOT NULL, DoB,

    phoneNum VARCHAR(25) NOT NULL UNIQUE

);
```

Constraints In SQL

As the name implies, it is a restriction or limitation imposed on a column (s) of a table in order to place a limitation on the type of values the table can store. They provide a better mechanism to retain the reliability and accuracy of the data contained in the table. We have several categories of constraints, which includes:

NOT NULL Constraint – This statement states that NULL values will not be accepted at the column. What it means is that a new row cannot be added in a table without the inclusion of a non-NULL value for such a column.

For instance, the statement below creates a table "studentRecords" with four columns and three of these columns (id, Studname, and phoneNum) do not accept NULL Values.

```
CREATE TABLE studentRecords (

    id INT NOT NULL,

    Studname VARCHAR(30) NOT NULL,

    DoB DATE,

    phoneNum VARCHAR(15) NOT NULL
);
```

Tip: A null value is not the same as blank, zero (0), or a zero-length character string. The meaning of a NULL is that there hasn't been any entry made in that field.

- PRIMARY KEY Constraint – *This classifies a column (s) with values that distinctively recognize a row in the table.*

You cannot have two rows simultaneously in a particular table having the same value for its primary key. The example below shows a SQL statement creating a table named "studentRecords" and identify the id column as the primary key.

```
CREATE TABLE studentRecords (

    id INT NOT NULL PRIMARY KEY,

    Studname VARCHAR(30) NOT NULL,

    DoB DATE,

    phoneNum VARCHAR(15) NOT NULL
);
```

- UNIQUE Constraint – *if you want to restrict a column (s) to contain unique values in a table, the UNIQUE statement is used. While the PRIMARY KEY and UNIQUE constraint enforce uniqueness in a table; however, the UNIQUE constraint is used when your goal is to enforce the exclusivity on a particular column (s). I will use our previous example to specify the phone column as unique. With this, the phone column won't allow duplicated values.*

```
CREATE TABLE studentRecords (

    id INT NOT NULL PRIMARY KEY,

    Studname VARCHAR(30) NOT NULL,
```

```
    DoB DATE,

    phoneNum VARCHAR(15) NOT NULL UNIQUE,

    country VARCHAR(30) NOT NULL DEFAULT
'England'

);
```

- *FOREIGN KEY Constraint* – This particular kind of constraint is a column (s) used to set up and implement a relationship among data in two different tables.
- CHECK constraint – *The purpose of this statement is to restrict values in a column. For instance, the range of student age column can be restricted by creating CHECK constraint, which allows values only 16 to 45. This hinders ages entered from exceeding the age range. Here is an example to illustrate it.*

```
CREATE TABLE studentRecords (

    stu_id INT NOT NULL PRIMARY KEY,

    stu_name VARCHAR(55) NOT NULL,

    stu_date DATE NOT NULL,

    age INT NOT NULL CHECK (age >= 16 AND age
<= 45),

    dept_id INT,
```

```
        FOREIGN   KEY   (dept_id)   REFERENCES
departments(dept_id)

);
```

Inserting Data in Tables

In previous examples, I created a table with the name "studentRecords" in our "studentFile" database. Now, we need to add information into the table. To do this, SQL has a unique keyword, which is the "INSERT INTO" statement.

Format:

INSERT INTO NameOfTable (columnA, columnB, columnC,...) VALUES (value1, value2, value3,...);

The syntax is self-explanatory but if you are unclear, the tableName is the name of your table. In our examples so far, we have used "studentRecords." However, the column1, column2, column3,... represents the name of the table columns with value1, value2, value3 the parallel values for the columns.

To insert records to our "studentRecords" table, we will use the following statement.

```
INSERT INTO studentRecords (FullName, Age,
Sex, PhoneNum) ;
```

```
VALUES ('Donald Williamson', '30', 'Male', '0722-
022569') ;
```

If you observe, there is no value inserted for the id field. Do you remember when we created the table (studentRecords), we mark the id field with an AUTO_INCREMENT flag. Let's add another record to our table.

```
INSERT INTO studentRecords (FullName, Age,
Sex, PhoneNum) ;

VALUES ('Jefferson Peterson', '45', 'Male', '0252-
027948') ;
```

Why don't you add another one?

```
INSERT INTO studentRecords (FullName, Age,
Sex, PhoneNum) ;

VALUES ('Mariah Lawson', '50', 'Female', '0722-
457906') ;
```

If you were to display the output of this table, it will look like this

id	FullName	Age	Sex	PhoneNum
1	Donald Williamson	30	Male	0722-022569
2	Jefferson Peterson	45	Male	0252-027948
3	Mariah Lawson	50	Female	0722-457906

Chapter 1 Creating a Database in SQL Server

Like I mentioned above, SQL databases are among the most used databases across the world. This is because of a number of reasons, for instance it is very easy to create. What you need is a graphical user interface program that comes freely like a SQL Server Management. With that in place, creating a database is easy and you can start entering your data in no time at all. Here is how:

- **Start by installing the software(SQL Server Management Studio) to your computer**

This is software that is freely available for Microsoft. It will allow you to gain access to and also to work with your SQL server from a graphical interface other than using a command line for the same. The software will also allow you to gain access to a remote request of an SQL server. If not this one, you will require a similar software.

There are other interfaces that are available for other platforms like Mac for instance SQuirreL SQL. Such interfaces may differ but they all work the same.

You can also create a database using the tools available in command line.

4. Once the software has been installed, start it up.

After the installation, you can now start your program. You will be required to choose if you want to connect to a certain server. If there is a server already that is already set and working and you have all the permissions connect access it, just enter its address and the authentication information. But if you want to build your own local database, you will create the Database name and the type of authentication under the **Windows Authentication**.

Chapter 22 Now locate your database folder

After a connection has been made to the server, whether it is a local connection or a remote one, the Object Explorer will now open on the left hand side of your screen. Right at the top part of your Object Explorer diagram, you will see the server that you are using to. If it has not been expanded, click on the "+" icon that is following it and it will expand.

2. You can now create a fresh database

Spot the database folder and right click on it. Click on New database option from the list that will come up. This will give you a new window which will allow you to organize your database before you start creating it. First of all, you need to give your database a new and unique name, which will make it easy for you to identify it. The other settings can be left just the way they are at default settings unless there is an important change that you want to make. When you give your database a name, there are two other additional files that will be formed automatically, which are log and data files. The data file will be the one that will host all your information in your database and the log file will be the one that will track all the changes that you will make on the database. When satisfied, you can hit OK in order to create your database. Your newly created database will now appear in the extended database Folder, with a cylindrical icon, it will be easy to spot it.

6. Start creating your table

You have to come up with a structure where you will start storing your data and this will be your table. With a table, you can hold all manner of information and data that you want stored in the database. This is an important part before you can go on. To do this, you enlarge the new database that is in your database folder and then right click on the table's icon to select a New Table option. Windows thereafter opens everything else on your screen to let you to work on your new table as much as you want.

• It's time for the primary key

Primary keys are very important, therefore it is important to let them be the first entry on the first column of your SQL table. They act as the ID number or the highest number that helps you quickly remember what you have put in record in that table. In order to create your primary keys, enter ID on the field that has the Column Name and enter INT into the field marked Data Type. As of the Allow Nulls, ensure that they are all unchecked. Now hit the key icon in your toolbar in order to make this column your primary key. With this, you will not have null values but if you want to have a null value as your principal entry, you will check to Allow Nulls.

Scroll down the column properties to find the option Identity Specification. Expanding this option and setting it to a YES will ensure that the values on the ID column increases automatically on every entry that you will make. With this, all your new entries will be effectively numbered in the right order.

5. It's time to understand how tables are designed

This is an important part so as to find it easy to enter information in your database. With tables, you will get different columns or fields and every column denotes an aspect of every database entry that you will make. If you have a database for people in an organization for instance, your will have a FirsName column entry, LastName column entry, Address, Phone Number and such like entries.

- **The other columns**

When all the fields of the Primary Key have been filled in, other fields will automatically form beneath it. These will be the fields where all your other data will be entered. You are now free to enter data in those fields the way you want to. The right data type has to be chosen though so that it will match the data that you have filled in that column.

nchar(#) represents the type of data that should be used for the text for instance addresses, names among others. In the parenthesis will be a number which is the highest number that will be allowed in that field. You can set the limit in order to allow the size of your database to remain manageable. You can for instance use this format for the phone numbers in order to make it hard for you to perform mathematical function on the numbers.

int on the other hand represents data in whole numbers. This is the one that is used in the field marked ID.

decimal(x,y) will save your numbers in a decimal format. The number within the parenthesis will signify the total number of numerals and the other number of digits that will follow the decimals respectively.

- **When all that is done, save the table**

First save the table then you can start entering information on your columns. To do this, click on the Save button on your toolbar, then enter the name for your table. It is important to have a unique and easy to understand name for your table so that you will be able to tell what the table is all about without going through the data in it. This will be very useful especially once you start using large databases that have so many tables.

Chapter 2 The SQL Structure

In this chapter you will learn the fundamental features of the SQL language and an overview of its programming aspect. In addition, you will be presented with a step-by-step instruction on where and how to download SQLite, a version of the SQL software that will be used all throughout the discussion of this e-Book.

SQL Fundamental Features

SQL is a flexible computer language that you can deploy in different ways to communicate with relational databases. This software has some distinct features that differentiates it from other programming applications. First and foremost, SQL is a nonprocedural language. Most computer programs (e.g., C, C++ and Java) solve problems by following a sequence of commands that is called a *procedure*. In this case, one specific operation is performed after another until the required task has been accomplished. The flow of operation can either be a linear sequence or a looping one, depending on what the programmer had specified. This is not the same for SQL. In using this application, you will just have to specify the output that you want, not how you want to generate the output. From the CUSTOMER TABLE, if you want to create a separate list of contacts whose company are located in Texas then you have to retrieve the rows where the STATE column contains "TX" as its value. In writing the SQL command, you don't have to indicate how the information should be retrieved. It is the primary role of the database management system to examine the database and decide how to generate the results you wanted.

Learning the SQL syntax is like understanding the English language structure. Its command language, comprised of a limited number of statements, performs three primary data functions - definition, manipulation and control. The SQL programming language also includes reserved words that are only to be used for specific purposes. Thus, you cannot use these words as names for variables, tables and columns; or in any other way apart from their intended use. Below are some of the most common reserved words in SQL:2011.

ABS	ALL	ALLOCATE	ALTER	AND	ANY
ARE	ARRAY	AS	AT	AVG	BEGIN
BETWEEN	BINARY	BOOLEAN	BOTH	BY	CALL
CASCADED	CASE	CEILING	CHAR	CHARACTER	CHECK

CLOSE	COLLATE	COLLECT	COLUMN	COMMIT	CONDITION
CONNECT	CONSTRAINT	CONVERT	COUNT	CREATE	CURSOR
CYCLE	DATE	DAY	DEALLOCATE	DEC	DECIMAL
DECLARE	DEFAULT	DELETE	DESCRIBE	DISCONNECT	DISTINCT
DOUBLE	DROP	DYNAMIC	EACH	ELEMENT	ELSE
END	ESCAPE	EVERY	EXCEPT	EXECUTE	EXISTS
EXTERNAL	EXTRACT	FALSE	FETCH	FILTER	FLOAT
FLOOR	FOR	FOREVER	FREE	FROM	FULL
FUNCTION	FUSION	GET	GLOBAL	GRANT	GROUP
GROUPING	HAVING	HOLD	HOUR	HOURS	IDENTITY
IN	INNER	INOUT	INSERT	INT	INTEGER
INTERSECT	INTERVAL	INTO	IS	JOIN	KEEP
LANGUAGE	LARGE	LEAD	LEFT	LIKE	LOCAL
LOWER	MATCH	MAX	MEMBER	MERGE	METHOD

MINUTE	MOD	MODULE	MONTH	MULTISET	NATIONAL
NATURAL	NEW	NIL	NO	NONE	NORMALIZE
NOT	NULL	NUMERIC	OF	OFFSET	OLD
ON	ONLY	OPEN	OR	ORDER	OUT
OVER	OVERLAY	PARAMETER	PARTITION	POSITION	POWER
PRECISION	PREPARE	PRIMARY	PROCEDURE	RANGE	RANK
REAL	RECURSIVE	REF	REFERENCES	REFERENCING	RELEASE
RESULT	RETURN	REVOKE	RIGHT	ROLLBACK	ROLLUP
ROW	ROWS	SCOPE	SCROLL	SEARCH	SECOND
SELECT	SET	SIMILAR	SOME	SPECIFIC	SQL
START	STATIC	SUM	SYMMETRIC	SYSTEM	TABLE
THEN	TIME	TIMESTAMP	TO	TRANSLATE	TREAT
TRIGGER	TRUNCATE	TRIM	TRUE	UNION	UNIQUE
UNKNOWN	UPDATE	UPPER	USER	USING	VALUE

VALUES	VARCHAR	VARYING	VERSION	WHEN	WHENEVER
WHERE	WINDOW	WITH	WITHIN	WITHOUT	YEAR

If you think that an SQL database is just a collection of tables, then you are wrong. There are additional structures that need to be specified to maintain the integrity of your data, such as schemas, domains and constraints.

- *Schema* – This is also called the *conceptual view* or the *complete logical view* that defines the entire database structure and provides overall table organization. Such schema is considered a metadata – stored in tables and part of the database (just like tables that consist of regular data).

- *Domain* – This specifies the set of all finite data values you can store in a particular table column or attribute. For example, in our previous CUSTOMER TABLE the STATE column can only contain the values "TX", "NY", "CA" and "NV" if you only provide products and services in the states of Texas, New York, California and Nevada respectively. So these four state abbreviations are the domain of the STATE attribute.

• *Constraint* – Often ignored but one of the important database components, this sets down the rules that identify what data values a specific table attribute can contain. Incorporating tight constraints assures that database users only enter valid data into a particular column. Together with defined table characteristics, column constraints determine its domain. Using the same STATE column as an example with the given constraint of only the four values, if a database user enters "NJ" for New Jersey, then the entry will not be accepted. The system will not proceed until a valid value is entered for the STATE attribute, unless the database structure needs to be updated due to sudden business changes.

ROLLBACK [WORK];

In the previous command line, the keyword *WORK* is optional.

• *SAVEPOINT* – This statement works with the ROLLBACK command, wherein it creates sections or points within groups of transactions in which you will be performing the ROLLBACK command. Its syntax is:

SAVEPOINT *SAVEPOINT_NAME*;

SQLite Installation Instructions and Database Features

Before you start overwhelming yourself with various database solutions and SQL command lines, you need to determine first your purpose why you are creating a database. This will further determine other database design considerations such as size, complexity, type of machine where the application will run, storage medium and more. When you start thinking of your database requirements, you need to know up to what level of detail should be considered in your design. Too much detail will result to a very complex design that further wastes time and effort, and even your computer's storage space. Too little will lead to a poor performing, corrupt and worthless database. Once you are done with the design phase, then you can decide which database software you can download to start your SQL experience.

For the sake of this e-Book's discussion, SQLite, a simple software library, will be used as a starter database engine to design, build and deploy applications. A free and stand-alone database software that is quick to download and easy to administer, SQLite was developed by Richard Hipp and his team of programmers. It is was designed so that it can be easily configured and implemented, which does not require any client-server setup at all.

Thus, SQLite is considered as one of the most widely used database software applications in the world.

Stated below are some of the major features of SQLite:

- Transactions are atomic, consistent, isolated and durable
- Compilation is simple and easy
- System crashes and power failures are supported
- Full SQL implementation with a stand-alone command-line interface client
- Code footprint is significantly small
- Adaptable and adjustable to larger projects
- Self-contained with no external dependencies
- *Portable and supports other platforms like Windows, Android, iOS, Mac, Solaris and more*

In using SQLite, you need to download *SQLiteStudio* as your database manager and editor. With its intuitive interface, this software is very light yet fast and powerful. You don't even need to install it, just download, unpack and run the application. Follow these simple steps in downloading SQLiteStudio on a Windows 10 computer:

- Go to http://sqlitestudio.pl/?act=about. You should get the following page:

2.   Check the version of your computer's operating system then click the appropriate link to start downloading the software.

After downloading the software, go to the folder where the application was saved (usually the Downloads Folder in Windows). Click on the *Extract* tab on top then choose the *Extract all* option.

You will get the *Extract Compressed (Zipped) Folders* dialog box. Change the destination folder to C:\SQL then click the *Extract* button. This will be the folder where all your SQLite files will be saved.

Chapter 14 Once all the files have been extracted, you will have the SQLiteStudio subfolder.

• Find the application program named SQLiteStudio inside the subfolder. To create a shortcut on your desktop (so you can quickly launch the application), right-click the filename, select *Send to* option then choose *Desktop (create shortcut)*.

7.   When you double-click the SQLiteStudio icon on your desktop,

• you should get the following screen:

Chapter 2 Database Administration

Once you have your database up and running with tables and queries it is up you to keep the production database running smoothly. The database will have to be regularly looked at in order to ensure that it continues to perform as originally intended. If a database is poorly maintained it can easily result in a website connected to it performing poorly or worse still result in down time or even data loss. There is usually a person designated to look after the database and their job is titled Database Administrator or DBA. However, it's usually a non-DBA person who needs help with the database.

There are a number of different tasks which you can perform when carrying out maintenance which include the following:

Database Integrity: When you check the integrity of the database you are running checks on the data to make sure that both the physical and logical structure of the database is consistent and accurate.

Index Reorganization: Once you start to insert and delete data on your database there is going to be fragmentation (or a scattering) of indexes. Reorganizing the index will bring everything back together again and increase speed.

Rebuild Index: You don't have to perform an index reorganization, you can drop an index and then recreate them.

Database Backup: One of the most important tasks to perform. There are a number of different ways in which you can back up the database, these include: Full which backs up the database entirely, Differential which backs up the database since the last full backup and Transaction log which only backs up the transactional log.

Check Database Statistics: You can check the statistics of the database which are kept on queries. If you update the statistics, which can get out of date, you can help aid the queries being run.

Data and Log File: In general, make sure the data and log files are kept separate from each other. These files will grow when your database is being used and its best to allocate them an appropriate size going forward (and not just enable them to grow).

Depending on your database some tasks may be more useful than others. Apart from database backup which probably mandatory if it's in production you can pick through the other tasks depending on the state of the database.

For example, should the fragmentation of the database be below 30% then you can choose to perform an index reorganization. However, if the database fragmentation is greater than 30% then you should rebuild the index. You can rebuild the index on a weekly basis or more often if possible.

You can run a maintenance plan on SQL Server via its Server Agent depending on database requirements. It's important to set the times right not when your application is expected to be busy. You can choose a time or you can run it when the server CPU is not busy. Choosing to run when the server is not busy is a more preferred option for larger databases than selecting a particular time as there is no guaranteed time which the CPU will be idle. However, it is usually only a concern if your application is quite big and has a lot of requests.

When you do rebuild the indexes, it is important that you have the results sorted in tempdb. When using tempdb the old indexes are kept until new ones are added. Normally rebuilding the indexes uses the fixed space which the database was allocated. So, if you run out of disk space then you would not be able to complete the rebuilding of indexes. It's possible to use the tempdb and not have to increase the database disk size. The database maintenance can be run both synchronous (wait for task completion) or asynchronous (together) to speed things up however you must make sure that the tasks run in the right order.

Setting up a maintenance plan in SQL Server

To set up a maintenance plan in SQL Server you first must get the server to show advanced options. This is done by running the following code in a new query in SQL Server:

sp_configure 'show advanced options', 1

GO

RECONFIGURE

GO

sp_configure 'Agent XPs', 1

GO

RECONFIGURE

GO

SQL Server will now display the advanced options. Left click the + icon to the left of Management which is on the left-hand side of SQL Server Management Studio. Now left click Maintenance Plans and then right click Maintenance Plans. Select New Maintenance Plan Wizard.

Enter an appropriate maintenance plan name and description. From here you can either run one or all tasks in one plan and have as many plans as you want. After you have given a name, choose single schedule and click next.

You will see a number of options which you can pick for your maintenance including: *Check Database Integrity, Shrink Database, Reorganize Index, Rebuild Index, Update Statistics, Clean up History, Execute SQL Server Agent Job, Back Up – full, differential or transaction log and Maintenance Cleanup Task.* Select which you want to perform (in this example select all) This wizard will bring you through each of the items you have selected to fine tune them.

Once you select the items you want in your plan click next, you can now rearrange them in the order you wish them to complete. It's best to have Database Backup first in case of power failure, so select it and move it to the top of the list. Click next.

Define Back Up Database (Full) Task

This screen allows you to pick which full database backup you wish to perform it on. Best practice is to keep one plan per database, select one database and select next.

Define Database Check Integrity Task

This screen – the integrity task is a SQL Server command which checks the integrity of the database to see if everything is not corrupt and stable. Select a database and click next.

Define Shrink Database Task

You can now configure to shrink the database in order to free up space in the next screen. It will only shrink space if available but should you need space in the future you will have to re allocate it. However, this step will help backup speeds. Most developers don't use this feature that much. Click next after selecting a database to shrink.

Define Reorganize Index Task

The next screen is the Define Reorganize Index Tag screen. When you add, modify and delete indexes you will, like tables, need to reorganize them. The process is the same as a hard disk where you have there are fragmented files and space scattered across the disk. Best practice is to perform this task once per week for a busy database. You can choose to compact large object which compacts any index which has large binary object data. Click next to proceed to the next screen.

Define Rebuild Index Task

This screen covers individual index rows. As mentioned either reorganize or reindexing. Doing both together in one plan is pointless. Depending on your fragmentation level pick one or the other. In this example select your database and sort results in tempdb. Click next to proceed.

Define Update Statistics Task

The update statistics task helps developer keep track of data retrieval as its created, modified and deleted. You can keep the statistics up to date by performing this plan. Both statistics for index and statistics for individual columns are kept. Select your database and click next to proceed.

Define History Cleanup Task

You should now see the Define maintenance cleanup task screen which specifies the historical data to delete. You can specify a shorter time frame to keep the backup and recovery, agent job history and maintenance place for on the drop down. Click next to proceed.

Define Back up Database (Differential) Task

This screen allows you to back up every page in the database which has been changed since the last full backup. Select a database you wish to use and click next.

Define Back Up Database (Transaction Log) Task

The transaction log backup backs up all the log records since the last backup. You can choose a folder to store it. Performing this type of backup is the least resource intensive backup. Select a database and storage location and click next.

Define Execute SQL Server Agent Job Task

The SQL Server Agent Job Task deals with jobs that are outside the wizard, for example it could be to check for nulls, check whether the database meets specified standards etc. Any jobs that are specified in SQL Server Agent Job Task are listed here. Click next to proceed.

Define Maintenance Cleanup Task

This screen defines the clean-up action of the maintenance task i.e. to ensure that the they are not taking up unnecessary space, so you can specify where to store them. You can delete specific backup files. Click next to proceed.

Report Options

The next screen covers where you want to store the report of the maintenance plan. Make a note of where you are going to store it. You need to have email set up on SQL Server in order to email it. Click next to proceed.

Complete the Wizard

The final screen is a complete review of the wizard. You can review the summary of the plan and which options were selected. Clicking finishes ends the wizard and creates the plan. You should now see a success screen with the tasks completed.

Running the maintenance plan

Once you successfully complete the maintenance wizard the next step is to run the plan you created. In order to get the plan to run you need to have the SQL Server Agent running. It is visible two down from where Management is on SQL Server Management Studio. You can left click SQL Server Agent and then right click and select Start.

Also, you can press the windows key + and press the letter r, then type in services.msc and hit return. Once Services appear scroll down and look for SQL Server Agent (MSSQLEXPRESS). SQL Server Express was installed in this EBook but you can select the other versions like (MSSQLSERVER) if you installed that. Left click it, then right click it and select Start.

You can go back to SSMS and right click on the maintenance plan you created under maintenance plans and then select Execute. This will now run your plan. One successful completion of the plan click ok and close the dialogue box. You can view the reports by right clicking the maintenance plan you created and selecting View history. On the left-hand side are all the different plans in SQL Server while on the right is the results of the specific plan.

Emailing the reports.

A lot of DBA's like to get their database reports via email. What you need to do is to set up a database mail before you can fire off emails and then set up a Server agent to send the email.

Setting up Database Mail.

The first step is to right click Database mail in SSMS and select configure database mail. A wizard screen will appear, click next. Now select the first choice – set up Database Mail and click next. Enter a profile name optional description of the profile. Now click on the Add button to the right.

This will bring you to an add New Database Mail Account – SMTP. You need to enter the STMP details for an email account. Maybe you can set up a new email account for this service. You can search online for SMTP details, Gmail works quite well (server name: smtp.gmail.com, port number 587, SSL required, tick basic authentication & confirm password). Click on ok. Click next, click on public (important: so it can be used by the rest of the database). Set it as default profile, click next, click next again. You should now get a success screen. Click close.

> Possible Error: It is important to ensure you select yes to public profile when you are at the Manage Profile Security part of the wizard above. If there is no public profile – no emails can be sent. You can check by running the following in a new query and check to ensure

SQL Server Agent

To send off the database email you need to set up a Server Agent. Start by right clicking on SQL Server

Agent – New – Operator. Give the operator a name like Maintenance Plan Operator and enter in the email address you wish to send the report to and click ok.

Now right the maintenance plan that you have successfully executed and select modify. The maintenance plan design screen will appear on the right-hand side where you can see some graphics of the tasks completed in it. Now click on Reporting and Logging – it is an icon situated on the menu bar of the design plan -   to the left of Manage Connections...

The Reporting and Logging window will appear. Select the tick box – Send report to an email recipient and select the Maintenance plan operator you just created. The next time you run the plan an email will be sent to the email address.

Summary

The running and maintenance of a database is an important job. Having the right plan for your database means it will continue to work as originally designed and you can quickly identify database errors or slowdowns early on and fix them quickly.

Chapter 3 Structure of the SELECT Statement

The SELECT Clause

The SELECT clause is the only required clause in a SELECT statement, all the other clauses are optional. The SELECT columns can be literals (constants), expressions, table columns and even subqueries. Lines can be commented with "--".

```
SELECT                    15                    *
15;                                      -- 225

SELECT       Today       =       convert(DATE,
getdate());           -- 2016-07-27

SELECT                    Color,

              ProdCnt                    =
COUNT(*),

              AvgPrice                   =
FORMAT(AVG(ListPrice),'c','en-US')

FROM AdventureWorks2012.Production.Product p

WHERE Color is not null

GROUP BY Color   HAVING count(*) > 10

ORDER BY AvgPrice DESC;
```

GO

Color	ProdCnt	AvgPrice
Yellow	36	$959.09
Blue	26	$923.68
Silver	43	$850.31
Black	93	$725.12
Red	38	$1,401.95

-- Equivalent with column aliases on the right

```
SELECT                    Color,

            COUNT(*)
            AS ProdCnt,

            FORMAT(AVG(ListPrice),'c','en-
US')        AS AvgPrice

FROM AdventureWorks2012.Production.Product p

WHERE Color is not null  GROUP BY Color

HAVING count(*) > 10

ORDER BY AvgPrice DESC;

GO
```

SELECT with Search Expression

SELECT statement can have complex expressions for text or numbers as demonstrated in the next T-SQL query for finding the street name in AddressLine1 column.

```
SELECT          AddressID,

                SUBSTRING(AddressLine1,
CHARINDEX(' ', AddressLine1+' ', 1) +1,

                CHARINDEX(' ', AddressLine1+' ',
CHARINDEX(' ', AddressLine1+' ', 1) +1) -

                CHARINDEX(' ', AddressLine1+' ', 1)
-
1)
AS StreetName,

                AddressLine1,

        City

FROM AdventureWorks2012.Person.Address

WHERE ISNUMERIC (LEFT(AddressLine1,1))=1

  AND City = 'Seattle'

ORDER BY AddressLine1;

-- -- (141 row(s) affected)- Partial results.
```

AddressID	StreetName	AddressLine1	City
13079	boulevard	081, boulevard du Montparnasse	Seattle
859	Oak	1050 Oak Street	Seattle
110	Slow	1064 Slow Creek Road	Seattle
113	Ravenwood	1102 Ravenwood	Seattle
95	Bradford	1220 Bradford Way	Seattle
32510	Steven	1349 Steven Way	Seattle
118	Balboa	136 Balboa Court	Seattle
32519	Mazatlan	137 Mazatlan	Seattle
25869	Calle	1386 Calle Verde	Seattle
114	Yorba	1398 Yorba Linda	Seattle
15657	Book	151 Book Ct	Seattle
105	Stillman	1619 Stillman Court	Seattle
18002	Carmel	1635 Carmel Dr	Seattle
19813	Acardia	1787 Acardia Pl.	Seattle
16392	Orchid	1874 Orchid Ct	Seattle

18053	Green	1883 Green View Court	Seattle
13035	Mt.	1887 Mt. Diablo St	Seattle
29864	Valley	1946 Valley Crest Drive	Seattle
13580	Hill	2030 Hill Drive	Seattle
106	San	2144 San Rafael	Seattle

SELECT Statement with Subquery

Two Northwind category images, Beverages & Dairy Products, from the dbo.Categories table.

The following SELECT statement involves a subquery which is called a derived table. It also demonstrates that INNER JOIN can be performed with a GROUP BY subquery as well not only with another table or view.

```
USE Northwind;

SELECT              c.CategoryName
                        AS Category,

                cnum.NoOfProducts
                AS CatProdCnt,

                    p.ProductName
                    AS Product,

                    FORMAT(p.UnitPrice,'c',
'en-US')            AS UnitPrice

 FROM    Categories c

                    INNER JOIN Products p

                                    ON
c.CategoryID = p.CategoryID

                        INNER    JOIN
(          SELECT           c.CategoryID,

        NoOfProducts = count(* )

                                FROM
    Categories c

                                    I
NNER JOIN Products p
```

```
                              ON c.CategoryID = p.CategoryID

                                                              GROUP
BY c.CategoryID

                                                                  )
cnum                                                             --
derived table

                                                              ON
c.CategoryID = cnum.CategoryID

ORDER BY Category, Product;

-- (77 row(s) affected) - Partial results.
```

Category	CatProdCnt	Product	UnitPrice
Dairy Products	10	Mozzarella di Giovanni	$34.80
Dairy Products	10	Queso Cabrales	$21.00
Dairy Products	10	Queso Manchego La Pastora	$38.00
Dairy Products	10	Raclette Courdavault	$55.00

Grains/Cereals	7	Filo Mix	$7.00
Grains/Cereals	7	Gnocchi di nonna Alice	$38.00
Grains/Cereals	7	Gustaf's Knäckebröd	$21.00
Grains/Cereals	7	Ravioli Angelo	$19.50
Grains/Cereals	7	Singaporean Hokkien Fried Mee	$14.00
Grains/Cereals	7	Tunnbröd	$9.00

Creating Delimited String List (CSV) with XML PATH

The XML PATH clause , the text() function and correlated subquery is used to create a comma delimited string within the SELECT columns. Note: it cannot be done using traditional (without XML) SQL single statement, it can be done with multiple SQL statements only. STUFF() string function is applied to replace the leading comma with an empty string

USE AdventureWorks;

```sql
SELECT          Territory          = st.[Name],

                                    SalesYTD
=       FORMAT(floor(SalesYTD),  'c',  'en-US'),  --
currency format

                SalesStaffAssignmentHistory =

                STUFF((SELECT    CONCAT(',  ',
c.FirstName,    SPACE(1),   c.LastName)          AS
[text()]

                        FROM   Person.Contact
c

                        INNER        JOIN
Sales.SalesTerritoryHistory sth

                        ON   c.ContactID   =
sth.SalesPersonID

                        WHERE  sth.TerritoryI
D =   st.TerritoryID

                        ORDER  BY StartDate

                        FOR XML Path ('')), 1,
1, SPACE(0))

FROM   Sales.SalesTerritory st

ORDER  BY SalesYTD DESC;

GO
```

Territory	SalesYTD	SalesStaffAssignmentHistory
Southwest	$8,351,296.00	Shelley Dyck, Jauna Elson
Canada	$6,917,270.00	Carla Eldridge, Michael Emanuel, Gail Erickson
Northwest	$5,767,341.00	Shannon Elliott, Terry Eminhizer, Martha Espinoza
Central	$4,677,108.00	Linda Ecoffey, Maciej Dusza
France	$3,899,045.00	Mark Erickson
Northeast	$3,857,163.00	Maciej Dusza, Linda Ecoffey
United Kingdom	$3,514,865.00	Michael Emanuel
Southeast	$2,851,419.00	Carol Elliott
Germany	$2,481,039.00	Janeth Esteves
Australia	$1,977,474.00	Twanna Evans

Logical Processing Order of the SELECT Statement

The results from the previous step will be available to the next step. The logical processing order for a SELECT statement is the following. Actual processing by the database engine may be different due to performance and other considerations.

1.	FROM
2.	ON
3.	JOIN
4.	WHERE
5.	GROUP BY
6.	WITH CUBE or WITH ROLLUP
7.	HAVING

8.	SELECT
9.	DISTINCT
10.	ORDER BY
11.	TOP

As an example, it is logical to filter with the WHERE clause prior to applying GROUP BY. It is also logical to sort when the final result set is available.

SELECT Color, COUNT(*) AS ColorCount FROM AdventureWorks2012.Production.Product

WHERE Color is not NULL GROUP BY Color ORDER BY ColorCount DESC;

Color	ColorCount
Black	93
Silver	43
Red	38

Yellow	36
Blue	26
Multi	8
Silver/Black	7
White	4
Grey	1

The TOP Clause

The TOP clause filters results according the sorting specified in an ORDER BY clause, otherwise random filtering takes place.

Simple TOP usage to return 10 rows only.

SELECT TOP 10 SalesOrderID, OrderDate, TotalDue

FROM
AdventureWorks2012.Sales.SalesOrderHeader   OR
DER BY TotalDue DESC;

SalesOrderID	OrderDate	TotalDue
51131	2007-07-01 00:00:00.000	187487.825
55282	2007-10-01 00:00:00.000	182018.6272
46616	2006-07-01 00:00:00.000	170512.6689

46981	2006-08-01 00:00:00.000	166537.0808
47395	2006-09-01 00:00:00.000	165028.7482
47369	2006-09-01 00:00:00.000	158056.5449
47355	2006-09-01 00:00:00.000	145741.8553
51822	2007-08-01 00:00:00.000	145454.366
44518	2005-11-01 00:00:00.000	142312.2199
51858	2007-08-01 00:00:00.000	140042.1209

Complex TOP function usage: not known in advance how many rows will be returned due to "TIES".

SELECT   TOP   1   WITH   TIES   coalesce(Color, 'N/A')   AS Color,

            FORMAT(ListPrice,   'c',   'en-US')   AS ListPrice,

        Name
                        AS ProductName,

        ProductID

FROM   AdventureWorks2012.Production.Product

ORDER BY ROW_NUMBER() OVER(PARTITION BY Color ORDER BY ListPrice DESC);

Color	ListPrice	ProductName	ProductID
N/A	$229.49	HL Fork	804
Black	$3,374.99	Mountain-100 Black, 38	775
Red	$3,578.27	Road-150 Red, 62	749
Silver	$3,399.99	Mountain-100 Silver, 38	771
Blue	$2,384.07	Touring-1000 Blue, 46	966
Grey	$125.00	Touring-Panniers, Large	842
Multi	$89.99	Men's Bib-Shorts, S	855
Silver/Black	$80.99	HL Mountain Pedal	937
White	$9.50	Mountain Bike Socks, M	709
Yellow	$2,384.07	Touring-1000 Yellow, 46	954

The DISTINCT Clause to Omit Duplicates

The DISTINCT clause returns only unique results, omitting duplicates in the result set.

USE AdventureWorks2012;

SELECT DISTINCT Color FROM Production.Product

WHERE Color is not NULL

ORDER BY Color;

GO

Color
Black
Blue
Grey
Multi
Red
Silver
Silver/Black
White
Yellow

```sql
SELECT DISTINCT ListPrice

FROM Production.Product

 WHERE ListPrice > 0.0

ORDER BY ListPrice DESC;

GO

-- (102 row(s) affected) - Partial results.
```

ListPrice
3578.27
3399.99
3374.99
2443.35

```sql
-- Using DISTINCT in COUNT - NULL is counted
SELECT                    COUNT(*)
              AS TotalRows,

                               COUNT(DISTINCT
Color)                AS ProductColors,

                               COUNT(DISTINCT
Size)                 AS ProductSizes
```

FROM AdventureWorks2012.Production.Product;

TotalRows	ProductColors	ProductSizes
504	9	18

-

The CASE Conditional Expression

***The CASE conditional expression evaluates to** a **single value of the same data type**, **therefore** it can be used anywhere in a query where a single value is required.*

```
SELECT          CASE ProductLine

                        WHEN 'R' THEN
'Road'

                        WHEN 'M' THEN
'Mountain'

                        WHEN 'T' THEN
'Touring'

                        WHEN 'S' THEN
'Other'

                        ELSE 'Parts'

                END
            AS Category,
```

                              Name
                      AS ProductName,

                      ProductNumber

FROM AdventureWorks2012.Production.Product

ORDER BY ProductName;

GO

-- (504 row(s) affected) - Partial results.

Category	ProductName	ProductNumber
Touring	Touring-3000 Blue, 62	BK-T18U-62
Touring	Touring-3000 Yellow, 44	BK-T18Y-44
Touring	Touring-3000 Yellow, 50	BK-T18Y-50
Touring	Touring-3000 Yellow, 54	BK-T18Y-54
Touring	Touring-3000 Yellow, 58	BK-T18Y-58
Touring	Touring-3000 Yellow, 62	BK-T18Y-62
Touring	Touring-Panniers, Large	PA-T100
Other	Water Bottle - 30 oz.	WB-H098
Mountain	Women's Mountain Shorts, L	SH-W890-L

Query to return different result sets for repeated execution due to newid().

```
SELECT                    TOP               3
CompanyName,        City=CONCAT(City,    ',    ',
Country),           PostalCode,

        [IsNumeric] =    CASE          WHEN
PostalCode like '[0-9][0-9][0-9][0-9][0-9]'

                                       THEN
'5-Digit Numeric'    ELSE 'Other'  END

FROM     Northwind.dbo.Suppliers

ORDER BY NEWID();                           -
- random sort

GO
```

CompanyName	City	PostalCode	IsNumeric
PB Knäckebröd AB	Göteborg, Sweden	S-345 67	Other
Gai pâturage	Annecy, France	74000	5-Digit Numeric
Heli Süßwaren GmbH & Co. KG	Berlin, Germany	10785	5-Digit Numeric

Same query as above expanded with ROW_NUMBER() and another CASE expression column.

```
SELECT          ROW_NUMBER() OVER (ORDER
BY Name)               AS RowNo,

                CASE ProductLine

                    WHEN 'R' THEN 'Road'

                    WHEN 'M' THEN
'Mountain'

                    WHEN 'T' THEN 'Touring'

                    WHEN 'S' THEN 'Other'

                    ELSE 'Parts'

                END
                    AS Category,

                Name
                    AS ProductName,

                CASE WHEN Color is null THEN
'N/A'

                        ELSE    Color
END                         AS Color,

                ProductNumber
```

FROM Production.Product ORDER BY ProductName;

-- (504 row(s) affected) - Partial results.

RowNo	Category	ProductName	Color	ProductNumber
1	Parts	Adjustable Race	N/A	AR-5381
2	Mountain	All-Purpose Bike Stand	N/A	ST-1401
3	Other	AWC Logo Cap	Multi	CA-1098
4	Parts	BB Ball Bearing	N/A	BE-2349
5	Parts	Bearing Ball	N/A	BA-8327
6	Other	Bike Wash - Dissolver	N/A	CL-9009
7	Parts	Blade	N/A	BL-2036
8	Other	Cable Lock	N/A	LO-C100
9	Parts	Chain	Silver	CH-0234
10	Parts	Chain Stays	N/A	CS-2812

Testing PostalCode with ISNUMERIC and generating a flag with CASE expression.

```
    SELECT   TOP (4)
AddressID,   City,    PostalCode
                    AS Zip,
            CASE WHEN
ISNUMERIC(PostalCode) = 1 THEN 'Y'  ELSE
'N'  END                AS IsZipNumeric
    FROM    AdventureWorks2008.Person.Address
ORDER BY NEWID();
```

AddressID	City	Zip	IsZipNumeric
16704	Paris	75008	Y
26320	Grossmont	91941	Y
27705	Matraville	2036	Y
18901	Kirkby	KB9	N

The OVER Clause

The OVER clause defines the partitioning and sorting of a rowset (intermediate result set) preceding the application of an associated window function, such as ranking. Window functions are also dubbed as ranking functions.

USE AdventureWorks2012;

```
-- Query with three different OVER clauses

SELECT            ROW_NUMBER() OVER ( ORDER
BY                               SalesOrderID,
ProductID)                              AS
RowNum

      ,SalesOrderID, ProductID, OrderQty

         ,RANK()      OVER(PARTITION      BY
SalesOrderID      ORDER      BY       OrderQty
DESC)                 AS Ranking

         ,SUM(OrderQty) OVER(PARTITION BY
SalesOrderID)
   AS TotalQty

         ,AVG(OrderQty) OVER(PARTITION BY
SalesOrderID)
   AS AvgQty

         ,COUNT(OrderQty)  OVER(PARTITION
BY SalesOrderID) AS "Count"  -- T-SQL keyword,
use "" or []

         ,MIN(OrderQty) OVER(PARTITION BY
SalesOrderID)
   AS "Min"

         ,MAX(OrderQty) OVER(PARTITION BY
SalesOrderID)
   AS "Max"
```

FROM Sales.SalesOrderDetail

WHERE SalesOrderID BETWEEN 61190 AND 61199 ORDER BY RowNum;

-- (143 row(s) affected) - Partial results.

Row Num	Sales OrderID	Prod uctID	Ord erQt y	Ran kin g	Tot alQt y	Av gQ ty	Co un t	M i n	M a x
1	61190	707	4	13	159	3	40	1	1 7
2	61190	708	3	18	159	3	40	1	1 7
3	61190	711	5	8	159	3	40	1	1 7
4	61190	712	12	2	159	3	40	1	1 7
5	61190	714	3	18	159	3	40	1	1 7
6	61190	715	5	8	159	3	40	1	1 7
7	61190	716	5	8	159	3	40	1	1 7
8	61190	858	4	13	159	3	40	1	1 7

9	61190	859	7	6	159	3	40	1	17
10	61190	864	8	4	159	3	40	1	17
11	61190	865	3	18	159	3	40	1	17
12	61190	870	9	3	159	3	40	1	17
13	61190	876	4	13	159	3	40	1	17
14	61190	877	5	8	159	3	40	1	17
15	61190	880	1	34	159	3	40	1	17
16	61190	881	5	8	159	3	40	1	17
17	61190	883	2	26	159	3	40	1	17
18	61190	884	17	1	159	3	40	1	17
19	61190	885	3	18	159	3	40	1	17
20	61190	886	1	34	159	3	40	1	17
21	61190	889	2	26	159	3	40	1	17

22	61190	892	4	13	159	3	40	1	17
23	61190	893	3	18	159	3	40	1	17
24	61190	895	1	34	159	3	40	1	17

-

FROM Clause: Specifies the Data Source

The FROM clause specifies the source data sets for the query such as tables, views, derived tables and table-valued functions. Typically the tables are JOINed together. The most common JOIN is INNER JOIN which is based on equality between FOREIGN KEY and PRIMARY KEY values in the two tables.

> PERFORMANCE NOTE
> All FOREIGN KEYs should be indexed. PRIMARY KEYs are indexed automatically with unique index.

USE AdventureWorks2012;

GO

SELECT

```sql
    ROW_NUMBER() OVER(ORDER BY SalesYTD
DESC)                                    AS
RowNo,

    ROW_NUMBER() OVER(PARTITION BY PostalCode
ORDER BY SalesYTD DESC)            AS SeqNo,

                    CONCAT(p.FirstName,
SPACE(1),  p.LastName)                   AS
SalesStaff,

                    FORMAT(s.SalesYTD,'c','en-
US')                                     AS
YTDSales,

            City,

            a.PostalCode
                            AS ZipCode

FROM Sales.SalesPerson AS s

    INNER JOIN Person.Person AS p

    ON s.BusinessEntityID = p.BusinessEntityID

    INNER JOIN Person.Address AS a

    ON a.AddressID = p.BusinessEntityID

WHERE          TerritoryID IS NOT NULL    AND
SalesYTD <> 0 ORDER BY ZipCode, SeqNo;
```

Row No	Seq No	SalesStaff	YTDSales	City	ZipCode
1	1	Linda Mitchell	$4,251,368.55	Issaquah	98027
3	2	Michael Blythe	$3,763,178.18	Issaquah	98027
4	3	Jillian Carson	$3,189,418.37	Issaquah	98027
8	4	Tsvi Reiter	$2,315,185.61	Issaquah	98027
12	5	Garrett Vargas	$1,453,719.47	Issaquah	98027
14	6	Pamela Ansman-Wolfe	$1,352,577.13	Issaquah	98027
2	1	Jae Pak	$4,116,871.23	Renton	98055
5	2	Ranjit Varkey Chudukatil	$3,121,616.32	Renton	98055
6	3	José Saraiva	$2,604,540.72	Renton	98055
7	4	Shu Ito	$2,458,535.62	Renton	98055
9	5	Rachel Valdez	$1,827,066.71	Renton	98055

10	6	Tete Mensa-Annan	$1,576,562.20	Renton	98055
11	7	David Campbell	$1,573,012.94	Renton	98055
13	8	Lynn Tsoflias	$1,421,810.92	Renton	98055

The WHERE Clause to Filter Records (Rows)

The WHERE clause filters the rows generated by the query. Only rows satisfying (TRUE) the WHERE clause predicates are returned.

PERFORMANCE NOTE
All columns in WHERE clause should be indexed.

USE AdventureWorks2012;

String equal match predicate - equal is TRUE, not equal is FALSE.

SELECT ProductID, Name, ListPrice, Color

FROM Production.Product WHERE Name = 'Mountain-100 Silver, 38' ;

ProductID	Name	ListPrice	Color
771	Mountain-100 Silver, 38	3399.99	Silver

-- Function equality predicate

SELECT * FROM Sales.SalesOrderHeader WHERE YEAR(OrderDate) = 2008;

-- (13951 row(s) affected)

> PERFORMANCE NOTE
> When a column is used as a parameter in a function (e.g. YEAR(OrderDate)), index (if any) usage is voided.
> Instead of random SEEK, all rows are SCANned in the table. The predicate is not SARGable.

-- String wildcard match predicate

SELECT ProductID, Name, ListPrice, Color

FROM Production.Product WHERE Name LIKE ('%touring%');

-- Integer range predicate

SELECT ProductID, Name, ListPrice, Color

```
FROM  Production.Product  WHERE  ProductID  >=
997 ;
```

```
-- Double string wildcard match predicate
```

```
SELECT ProductID, Name, ListPrice, Color
```

```
FROM  Production.Product  WHERE  Name  LIKE
('%bike%') AND Name LIKE ('%44%');
```

```
-- String list match predicate
```

```
SELECT ProductID, Name, ListPrice, Color  FROM
Production.Product
```

```
WHERE  Name  IN  ('Mountain-100  Silver,  44',
'Mountain-100 Black, 44');
```

The GROUP BY Clause to Aggregate Results

The GROUP BY clause is applied to partition the rows and calculate aggregate values. An extremely powerful way of looking at the data from a summary point of view.

```
SELECT
                    V.Name
                                    AS Vendor,

                    FORMAT(SUM(TotalDue),  'c',
'en-US')                    AS TotalPurchase,

            A.City,
```

```sql
                SP.Name
                    AS State,

            CR.Name
                    AS Country

    FROM Purchasing.Vendor AS V

        INNER JOIN Purchasing.VendorAddress AS VA

                    ON VA.VendorID = V.VendorID

        INNER JOIN Person.Address AS A

                    ON A.AddressID = VA.AddressID

        INNER JOIN Person.StateProvince AS SP

                        ON      SP.StateProvinceID
    =   A.StateProvinceID

        INNER JOIN Person.CountryRegion AS CR

                        ON CR.CountryRegionCode =
    SP.CountryRegionCode

        INNER   JOIN    Purchasing.PurchaseOrderHeader
    POH

                        ON    POH.VendorID    =
    V.VendorID

    GROUP BY  V.Name, A.City, SP.Name, CR.Name
```

ORDER BY SUM(TotalDue) DESC, Vendor; --
TotalPurchase does a string sort instead of numeric

GO

-- (79 row(s) affected) - Partial results.

Vendor	TotalPurchase	City	State	Country
Superior Bicycles	$5,034,266.74	Lynnwood	Washington	United States
Professional Athletic Consultants	$3,379,946.32	Burbank	California	United States
Chicago City Saddles	$3,347,165.20	Daly City	California	United States
Jackson Authority	$2,821,333.52	Long Beach	California	United States
Vision Cycles, Inc.	$2,777,684.91	Glendale	California	United States

Sport Fan Co.	$2,675,889.22	Burien	Washington	United States
Proseware, Inc.	$2,593,901.31	Lebanon	Oregon	United States
Crowley Sport	$2,472,770.05	Chicago	Illinois	United States
Greenwood Athletic Company	$2,472,770.05	Lemon Grove	Arizona	United States
Mitchell Sports	$2,424,284.37	Everett	Washington	United States
First Rate Bicycles	$2,304,231.55	La Mesa	New Mexico	United States
Signature Cycles	$2,236,033.80	Coronado	California	United States

Electroni c Bike Repair & Supplies	$2,154,77 3.37	Tacom a	Washing ton	Unite d State s
Vista Road Bikes	$2,090,85 7.52	Salem	Oregon	Unite d State s
Victory Bikes	$2,052,17 3.62	Issaqu ah	Washing ton	Unite d State s
Bicycle Specialis ts	$1,952,37 5.30	Lake Osweg o	Oregon	Unite d State s

The HAVING Clause to Filter Aggregates

The HAVING clause is similar to the WHERE clause filtering but applies to GROUP BY aggregates.

USE AdventureWorks;

SELECT

        V.Name
           AS Vendor,

          FORMAT(SUM(TotalDue), 'c',
'en-US')   AS TotalPurchase,

```
            A.City,

            SP.Name
        AS State,

            CR.Name
        AS Country

    FROM Purchasing.Vendor AS V

        INNER JOIN Purchasing.VendorAddress AS VA

                    ON VA.VendorID = V.VendorID

        INNER JOIN Person.Address AS A

                    ON A.AddressID = VA.AddressID

        INNER JOIN Person.StateProvince AS SP

                    ON      SP.StateProvinceID
    =    A.StateProvinceID

        INNER JOIN Person.CountryRegion AS CR

                    ON  CR.CountryRegionCode  =
    SP.CountryRegionCode

        INNER  JOIN  Purchasing.PurchaseOrderHeader
    POH

                    ON   POH.VendorID   =
    V.VendorID

    GROUP BY  V.Name, A.City, SP.Name, CR.Name
```

HAVING SUM(TotalDue) < $26000   -- HAVING clause predicate

ORDER BY SUM(TotalDue) DESC, Vendor;

Vendor	TotalPurchase	City	State	Country
Speed Corporation	$25,732.84	Anacortes	Washington	United States
Gardner Touring Cycles	$25,633.64	Altadena	California	United States
National Bike Association	$25,513.90	Sedro Woolley	Washington	United States
Australia Bike Retailer	$25,060.04	Bellingham	Washington	United States
WestAmerica Bicycle Co.	$25,060.04	Houston	Texas	United States
Ready Rentals	$23,635.06	Kirkland	Washington	United States
Morgan Bike	$23,146.99	Albany	New York	United d

Accessories				States
Continental Pro Cycles	$22,960.07	Long Beach	California	United States
American Bicycles and Wheels	$9,641.01	West Covina	California	United States
Litware, Inc.	$8,553.32	Santa Cruz	California	United States
Business Equipment Center	$8,497.80	Everett	Montana	United States
Bloomington Multisport	$8,243.95	West Covina	California	United States
International	$8,061.10	Salt Lake City	Utah	United States
Wide World Importers	$8,025.60	Concord	California	United States
Midwest Sport, Inc.	$7,328.72	Detroit	Michigan	United States

Wood Fitness	$6,947.58	Philadelphia	Pennsylvania	United States
Metro Sport Equipment	$6,324.53	Lebanon	Oregon	United States
Burnett Road Warriors	$5,779.99	Corvallis	Oregon	United States
Lindell	$5,412.57	Lebanon	Oregon	United States
Consumer Cycles	$3,378.17	Torrance	California	United States
Northern Bike Travel	$2,048.42	Anacortes	Washington	United States

Chapter 3 SQL Data Types

In this chapter you will learn the role of data in a database model, how it is defined, its characteristics and the various types that the SQL software supports. There are general data types that are further categorized into different subtypes. It is advisable that you use defined data types to ensure the portability and comprehensibility of the database model.

Data Definition

Data is the stored information in a database that you can manipulate anytime that you want. If you can remember the calling card example in its database model is a collection of customers' names, contact numbers, company addresses, job titles and so on. When rules are provided on how to write and store data, then you need to have a clear understanding of the different *data types*. You need to take into consideration the length or space allocated by the database for every table column and what data values it should contain - whether it is just all letters or all numbers, combination or alphanumeric, graphical, date or time. By defining what data type is stored in each field during the design phase, data entry errors will be prevented. This is the *field definition* process, a form of validation that controls how incorrect data is to be entered into the database.

When a certain database field does not have any data items at all, then the value is unknown or what is called a *null value*. This is completely different from the numeric zero or the blank character value, since zeroes and blanks are still considered definite values. Check out the following scenarios when you might have a null value:

- Even if the data value could possibly exist, you don't know what it is yet.
- The value does not really exist yet.
- The value could be out of range.
- The field is not appropriate for a particular row.

SQL Data Types

These are the general types of SQL data types and their subtypes.

- *Numeric* – The value defined by this data type is either an exact or an approximate number.

8.   Exact Numeric

8.   *INTEGER* – This consists of positive and negative whole numbers without any decimal nor a fractional part. The INTEGER data value ranges from negative 2,147,483,648 to positive

2,147,483,647, with a maximum storage size of four bytes.

9) *SMALLINT* – This replaces integers when you want to save some storage space. However, its precision cannot be larger than that of an integer. Precision in computer programming is the maximum total of significant digits a certain number can have. The SMALLINT data value ranges from negative 32,768 to positive 32,767, with a maximum storage size of two bytes.

7) *BIGINT* – This is the reverse of SMALLINT, in which the minimum precision is the same or greater than that of an INTEGER. The BIGINT data value ranges from negative 9,223,372,036,854,775,808 to positive 9,223,372,036,854,775,807, with a maximum storage size of eight bytes.

Chapter 4 *NUMERIC (p, s)* – This data type contains an integer part and a fractional part that indicates the precision and scale of the data value. Scale is the number of digits reserved in the fractional part of the data value (located at the right side of the decimal point). In NUMERIC (p, s), 'p' specifies the precision while 's' specifies the scale. For example, NUMERIC (6, 3) means that the number has a total of 6 significant digits with 3 digits following the decimal point.

Therefore, its absolute value will only be up to 999.999.

- *DECIMAL (p, s)* – This also has a fractional component where you can specify both the data value's precision and scale, but allows for greater precision. For example, DECIMAL (6, 3) can contain values up to 999.999 but the database will still accept values larger than 999.999 by rounding off the number. Let us say you entered the number 123.4564, the value that will be stored is 123.456. Thus, the precision given specifies the allocated storage size for this data type.

- **Approximate Numeric**
- *REAL (s)* – This is a single-precision, floating-point number where the decimal point can "float" within the said number. This gives a limitless precision and a scale of variable lengths for the data type's decimal value. For example, the values for π (pi) can include 3.1, 3.14 and 3.14159 (each value has its own precision). This data type's precision ranges from 1 up to 21, with a maximum storage size of four bytes.

10. *DOUBLE PRECISION (p, s)* – As what the name suggests, this is a double-precision, floating-point number with a storage capacity of twice the REAL data type. This data type is suitable when you

require more precise numbers, such as in most scientific field of disciplines. This data type's precision ranges from 22 up to 53 digits, with a maximum storage size of eight bytes.

7) *FLOAT (p, s)* – This data type lets you specify the value's precision and the computer decides whether it will be a single or a double-precision number. It will allow both the precision of REAL and DOUBLE PRECISION data types. Such features make it easier to move the database from one computer platform to another.

9)   *String* – Considered as the most commonly used data type, this stores alphanumeric information.

- *CHARACTER (n)* or *CHAR (n)* – Known as a fixed-length string or a constant character, this data type contains strings that have the same length (represented by *'n'*, which is the maximum number of characters allocated for the defined field). For example, setting the column's data type to CHAR (23) means the maximum length of the data to be stored in that field is 23 characters. If its length is less than 23, then the remaining spaces are filled with blanks by SQL. However, this becomes the downside of using fixed-length strings because storage space is totally wasted. On the other hand, if the length is not specified, then SQL assumes a length of just one character. The CHARACTER data type can have a maximum length of 254 characters.

6) *CHARACTER VARYING (n)* or *VARCHAR (n)* – This data type is for entries that have different lengths, but the remaining spaces will not be filled by spaces. This means that the exact number of characters entered will be stored in the database to avoid space wastage. The maximum length for this data type is 32,672 characters with no default value.

• *CHARACTER LARGE OBJECT (CLOB)* – This was introduced in SQL:1999 where the variable-length data type is used, which contains a Unicode, character-based information. Such data is too big to be stored as a CHARACTER type, just like large documents, and the maximum value is up to 2,147,483,647 characters long.

• **Date and Time – This data type handles information associated with dates and times.**

• *DATE* – This provides a storage space for the date's year, month and day values (in that particular order). The value for the year is expressed in four digits (represented by values ranging from 0001 up to 9999), while the month and day values are both represented by any two digits. The format of this data type is: *'yyyy-mm-dd.'*

• *TIME* – This stores and displays time values using an hour-minute-second format (*"HH:MM:SS"*).

• *DATETIME* – This contains both date and time information displayed using the "YYYY-MM-DD HH:MM:SS" format. The range of this data type is from "1000-01-01 00:00:00" to "9999-12-31 23:59:59".

5) *TIMESTAMP* – Similar to the DATETIME data type, this ranges from "1970-01-01 00:00:01" UTC to "2038-01-19 03:14:07" UTC.

• *Boolean* – This data type is used for comparing information and based from the results they can return TRUE, FALSE, or NULL values. If all the conditions for a given query are met, then Boolean value returns TRUE. Otherwise, the value is either FALSE or NULL.

User-Defined Data Type

We will now discuss user-defined data types or simply UDT's. By the name itself, the user defines or specifies the data values based on the existing data types. This allows customization to meet other user requirements and maximize the available storage space. Moreover, programmers enjoy the flexibility they bring in developing database applications. UDT's make it possible when you need to store the same type of data in a column that will also be defined in several tables. The CREATE TYPE statement is used to define UDT's.

For example, if you need to use two different currencies for your database like the US dollar and the UK pound, you can create and define the following UDT's:

CREATE TYPE USDollar AS DECIMAL (9, 2) ;

CREATE TYPE UKPound AS DECIMAL (9, 2) ;

5) Data is the stored information in a database that a user can define and manipulate.

6) There are different general SQL data types, namely numeric, string, date and time, and Boolean.

7) If you want to define more specific data types when designing your database model, you can use the different subtypes under each general SQL data type.

8) UDT's or user-defined data types are customized and created by the user based on the existing data types, which gives flexibility in developing various database applications.

In the next chapter you will learn the common SQL commands that are used to create, manipulate and retrieve data from a database, in an efficient and effective way.

Chapter 4 Cursors: Read Only, Forward Only, Fast Forward, Static, Scroll, Dynamic, Optimistic

Cursors are database objects that are used to iterate over a set of rows and generally perform some additional logical operations or others on each row of fetched data. The process of cursor operation entails following tasks:

- *Declare the variables to be used*
- *Define the Cursor and type of cursor*
- *Populate Cursor with values using SELECT*
- *Open Cursor that was declared & populated above*
  - Fetch the values from Cursor in to declared variables
- *While loop to fetch next row and loop till no longer rows exist*
  - Perform any data processing on that row inside while loop
- *Close Cursor to gracefully un-lock tables in any*
- *Remove Cursor from memory*

However, Cursors are generally not recommended due to row-by-row fetching and processing of data, consumption of memory (due to allocation of temporary table and filling it with the result set) and sometimes locking tables in unpredictable ways. Thus, alternate approaches like using *while* loop needs to be considered before using cursors.

LOCAL/GLOBAL CURSOR

This cursor specifies the scope and whether this scope allows locally to a stored procedure or trigger or even a batch OR if the scope of the cursor is applicable globally for the connection. Cursor is valid only within the scope defined.

FORWARD_ONLY CURSOR

FORWARD_ONLY Cursor specifies that rows can only be scrolled from first to the end row. Thus, this precludes moving to *prior* or *last* row and *fetch next* is only option available. Below is an example of *FORWARD_ONLY Cursor*:

```
--
===============================
==============
-- Author:        Neal Gupta
-- Create date: 12/01/2013
-- Description: Create a Cursor for displaying
customer info
```

```
--
================================
==============
DECLARE
        @CustomerID INT
        ,@FirstName VARCHAR(50)
    ,@LastName VARCHAR(50)
        ,@City VARCHAR(50)
        ,@State VARCHAR(10)
        ,@ZipCode VARCHAR(10)
-- Create a Cursor
DECLARE        curTblCustomer        CURSOR
FORWARD ONLY
FOR
SELECT
        CustomerID, FirstName, LastName, City,
[State], ZipCode
FROM [IMS].[dbo].[TblCustomer]
ORDER BY CustomerID ASC;
-- Open the Cursor
OPEN curTblCustomer
-- Get the first Customer
```

```
FETCH NEXT FROM curTblCustomer INTO
@CustomerID, @FirstName, @LastName, @City,
@State,@ZipCode

PRINT 'Customer Details:'

-- Loop thru all the customers

WHILE @@FETCH_STATUS = 0

        BEGIN

        -- Display customer details

        PRINT           CAST(@CustomerID          AS
        VARCHAR(50)) + ' ' + @FirstName + ' ' +
        @LastName + ' '+ @City + ' '+ @State + '
        '+ @ZipCode
        -- Get the next customer

        FETCH NEXT FROM curTblCustomer INTO
        @CustomerID, @FirstName, @LastName,
        @City, @State, @ZipCode
END

-- Close Cursor

CLOSE curTblCustomer

-- Remove Cursor from memory of temp database

DEALLOCATE curTblCustomer
```

Cursor by default is FORWARD_ONLY, if *STATIC,
KEYSET* or *DYNAMIC* options are not mentioned and
cursor works as a *DYNAMIC* one if these 3 keywords
are not specified.

READ_ONLY CURSOR

This cursor is similar to above *FORWARD_ONLY* cursor, except that updates on the current fetched row cannot be performed.

FAST_FORWARD CURSOR

This cursor is really a combination of *FAST_FORWARD* (#1) and *READ_ONLY* (#2) along with performance optimizations. Since, it is a *fast forward* cursor, it precludes scrolling to prior or last row and being *read only* cursor also, prevents update of current fetched row. However, due to these 2 restrictions, they help SQL server to optimize the overall cursor performance.

```
--
================================
==============
-- Description: Create a FAST_FORWARD Cursor
================================
==============
DECLARE
            @CustomerID INT
            ,@FirstName VARCHAR(50)
      ,@LastName VARCHAR(50)
            ,@City VARCHAR(50)
            ,@State VARCHAR(10)
```

433

```
        ,@ZipCode VARCHAR(10)

-- Create a Cursor

DECLARE curTblCustomer CURSOR FAST_FORWARD

FOR

SELECT

        CustomerID

    ,FirstName
    ,LastName
    ,City
    ,[State]
    ,ZipCode
FROM

        [IMS].[dbo].[TblCustomer]
ORDER BY

        CustomerID ASC;
-- Open the Cursor

OPEN curTblCustomer

-- Get the first Customer

FETCH  NEXT  FROM  curTblCustomer  INTO
@CustomerID, @FirstName, @LastName, @City,
@State, @ZipCode

PRINT 'Customer Details:'

-- Loop thru all the customers

WHILE @@FETCH_STATUS = 0
```

BEGIN

-- Display customer details

PRINT CAST(@CustomerID AS VARCHAR(**50**)) + ' ' + **@FirstName** + ' ' + **@LastName** + ' '+ **@City** + ' '+ **@State** + ' '+ **@ZipCode**
    -- Get the next customer

FETCH NEXT FROM **curTblCustomer** INTO **@CustomerID, @FirstName, @LastName, @City, @State, @ZipCode**
END

-- Close Cursor

CLOSE curTblCustomer

-- Remove Cursor from memory of temp database

DEALLOCATE curTblCustomer

STATIC CURSOR

If a cursor is specified as *STATIC*, SQL server takes a snapshot of the data and places into temporary table in *tempdb* database. So, when the cursor fetches next row, data comes from this temporary table and therefore, if something is modified in the original table, it is not reflected in the temporary table. This makes the performance of cursor faster as compared to dynamic cursor (explained below) since next row of data is already pre-fetched in temp database.

DYNAMIC CURSOR

As the name suggests, when the cursor is scrolling to next row, data for that row is dynamically brought from the original table, and if there was any change, it is reflected in the data fetched as well.

SCROLL CURSOR

This cursor allows scrolling of rows: *FIRST, LAST, PRIOR, NEXT* and if a cursor is not specified as SCROLL, it can only perform *FETCH* next row. If the cursor is *FAST_FORWARD, SCROLL* option cannot be used.

OPTIMISTIC/SCROLL_LOCKS CURSOR

Below is a cursor declaration using some of the above options: *LOCAL, FORWARD_ONLY, STATIC and READ_ONLY*:

DECLARE curTblCustomerOp1 CURSOR

    LOCAL

    FORWARD_ONLY

    STATIC

    READ_ONLY

FOR

-- Rest of SQL remains same as used in FORWARD_ONLY Cursor

Another cursor declaration could use following options: *GLOBAL, SCROLL, DYNAMIC, OPTIMISTIC:*

DECLARE curTblCustomerOp2 CURSOR

    GLOBAL   -- OR USE LOCAL

    SCROLL   -- OR USE FORWARD_ONLY

    DYNAMIC   --   OR   USE FAST_FORWARD/STATIC/KEYSET

    OPTIMISTIC   --   OR   USE READ_ONLY/SCROLL_LOCKS

FOR

-- Rest of SQL remains same as used in FORWARD_ONLY Cursor

NESTED CURSOR

As the name suggest, cursors can be nested, meaning one cursor can have another inner cursor and so on. In below example we will use one nested cursor.

--

==

-- Description: Create a Nested Cursor for displaying Orders

-- and products ordered

```
--
================================
==============

DECLARE

        @OrderID INT

        ,@ProductID INT

        ,@OrderQty INT

        ,@OrderDate DATETIME

        ,@Name VARCHAR(50)

        ,@Manufacturer VARCHAR(50)

        ,@Price DECIMAL(9,2)

PRINT '***** Orders Details *****'

--- First, declare OUTER Cursor

DECLARE curTblOrder CURSOR

        LOCAL

    FORWARD_ONLY

    STATIC

        READ_ONLY

    TYPE_WARNING

FOR

        SELECT

                OrderID
```

```
                    ,ProductID

                    ,OrderQty

                    ,OrderDate

        FROM

                    [IMS].[dbo].[TblOrder]

        ORDER BY

                    OrderID

-- Open OUTER Cursor

OPEN curTblOrder

-- Fetch data from cursor and populate into variables

FETCH NEXT FROM curTblOrder INTO @OrderID,
@ProductID, @OrderQty, @OrderDate

WHILE @@FETCH_STATUS = 0

BEGIN

        PRINT '*** Order: ' + ' ' +
CAST(@OrderID AS VARCHAR(10))

    -- Now, declare INNER Cursor

    DECLARE curTblProduct CURSOR

        FOR

                SELECT Name, Manufacturer,
Price
```

```
                    FROM [IMS].[dbo].[TblProduct]
P

                    WHERE    P.ProductID    =
@ProductID


        -- Open INNER Cursor

    OPEN curTblProduct

    FETCH NEXT FROM curTblProduct INTO @Name,
@Manufacturer, @Price

        -- Loop for INNER Cursor

    WHILE @@FETCH_STATUS = 0

    BEGIN

    PRINT 'Product: ' + @Name + ' ' + @Manufacturer
+ ' ' + CAST(@Price AS VARCHAR(15))

                    FETCH NEXT FROM curTblProduct
INTO @Name, @Manufacturer, @Price

        END

        -- Close INNER Cursor first and deallocate
it from temp database

    CLOSE curTblProduct

    DEALLOCATE curTblProduct

    -- Fetch next Order
```

FETCH NEXT FROM **curTblOrder** INTO **@OrderID**, **@ProductID**, **@OrderQty**, @OrderDate

END

-- Finally, close OUTER Cursor and deallocate it from temp database

CLOSE curTblOrder

DEALLOCATE curTblOrder

FOR UPDATE CURSOR

This cursor allows updating the column values in the fetched row for the specified columns only, however, if the columns are not specified, then, all the columns can be updated for the row under consideration using *WHERE CURRENT OF* clause.

ALTERNATIVE APPROACH

Note that in above examples, we used cursors to demonstrate the functionality of different types of cursor, however, we could have used alternative approach, like using *WHILE* loop and *counter* approach to perform similar task, as was done in #2 above, as below:

```
--
================================================
==============
-- Description: Alternative Approach
```

```
-- using WHILE loop and Counter Method
--
=================================
==============
    DECLARE @Customers TABLE
    RowID INT IDENTITY(1,1) PRIMARY KEY
    ,CustomerID INT
    ,FirstName VARCHAR(50)
    ,LastName VARCHAR(50)
    ,City VARCHAR(50)
    ,[State] VARCHAR(25)
    ,ZipCode VARCHAR(10)
    DECLARE
            @StartCount INT = 1          -- First
Row Count
            ,@EndCount  INT                  --
Total Row Counts
            ,@CustomerID INT
            ,@FirstName VARCHAR(50)
            ,@LastName VARCHAR(50)
            ,@City VARCHAR(50)
            ,@State VARCHAR(50)
            ,@ZipCode VARCHAR(10)
```

```sql
-- Bulk Insert all the customers into temp table: @Customers

INSERT INTO @Customers (CustomerID,FirstName,LastName,City,[State],ZipCode)

SELECT
        CustomerID
        ,FirstName
        ,LastName
        ,City
        ,[State]
        ,ZipCode
FROM
        [IMS].[dbo].[TblCustomer] WITH (NOLOCK)

-- EndCount is set to total of all rows fetched in above SELECT

SELECT @EndCount = @@ROWCOUNT

-- Loop thru all the rows

WHILE @StartCount <= @EndCount
BEGIN
        SELECT
                @CustomerID = CustomerID
```

```sql
        ,@FirstName = FirstName
        ,@LastName = LastName
        ,@City = City
        ,@State = [State]
        ,@ZipCode = ZipCode
    FROM @Customers
    WHERE
        RowID = @StartCount


PRINT 'Fetched Row#: ' + CAST(@StartCount AS
VARCHAR(5)) + ' from TblCustomer table. Details
below: '
        PRINT 'CustomerID = '+
CAST(@CustomerID AS VARCHAR(5)) + '
        FirstName = ' + @FirstName + '
LastName = ' + @LastName + ' City
        = ' + @City + ' State = ' +
@State + ' ZipCode = ' + @ZipCode
        SELECT @StartCount += 1
END
```

Chapter 5 Preparation

To successfully connect to and work with a SQL Server Database from your Windows PC (desktop or notebook), there are several things that must be properly setup or configured. None of these are very complex, but failure to address these items can and will result in either problems, warnings and/or errors. So while this chapter may be brief, the basic concepts (and their mental images) are nonetheless very critical for your success. So it would be wise to read and learn this chapter's material well.

Database Architecture

The SQL Server database itself will most often reside upon a server somewhere within your organization. While you can both run and access the SQL Server database on most PC's these days, the raw performance, tight security and high availability requirements alone generally require a secure, centrally managed database server.

Database Architecture

The critical item of note is that both the client and the server need some supporting SQL Server network library files in order for communication between your application and the database to occur. Because it's not necessary to know anything about

TDS to connect to a SQL Server database, we won't delve any further into the specifics about it.

What is important is you must have those network library files on your PC for database connections to function properly. Since Windows 2000, all versions of Windows have at least a basic set of these network library files already pre-installed. SQL Server 2005 introduced a new set of network files called the SQL Server Native Client which provides additional functionality based on new features that was added to that version of SQL Server. The features are not essential to retrieve data from a SQL Server database but center around security and management functionality such as the ability to handle passwords similar to the way Windows does. However, if you don't use these additional features, chances are you already have everything you need to connect to the SQL Server database.

Database Versions

The SQL Server database, like most software, has different versions – such as SQL Server 2000, 2005, 2008, and 2008 R2. These are simply the marketing names for the initial or base releases. In addition there are numerous patches available, usually called service packs or cumulative updates. If you're experiencing an issue with something not working the way you'd expect it to, you might check with your system administrator or database administrator to see if one of these is needed. But typically they are only required if you installed specific client software from the SQL Server CDs/DVDs.

Connecting

Thus far we've primarily covered terminology and that is a prerequisite for successfully working with your SQL Server databases. Now it's time to perform your very first SQL Server database task – connecting to your database. That may seem like an anticlimactic task but it's the first step in making use of the data within those databases.

Think of creating the database connection like making a phone call. If you don't have the proper equipment, a service plan, the number of whom you're calling and knowledge of how to dial that number, then you cannot initiate a phone call and thus cannot hold a meaningful conversation. The same is true for databases. You must successfully connect before you can retrieve, insert or update your data.

Connecting Via ODBC

A lot of applications connect to SQL Server using a method called ODBC. Either the application will present an interface where you can create your connection or it will ask you for an existing ODBC connection. Chances are that if it presents an interface, the steps will be similar to when you create your own ODBC connection. In fact, a lot of times applications will simply re-use Windows' own tool for managing these connections. So let's look at how to do that.

Control Panel icon

You'll want to click on it and that will bring up the Control Panel. If you're in Classic View, you should see an icon for Administrative Tools. If you're in Category View you'll have to double-click on the Performance and Maintenance icon first. Once you see the Administrative Tools icon, double-click on it and you should have a new list of options. What you're looking for is the icon for Data Sources (ODBC). Double-click on it and it will bring up the tool ODBC Administrator where you'll be able to configure a new ODBC connection.

There are two types of data sources called data set names (i.e. DSN): user and system. User ones can only be seen and used by the current Windows user, whereas system ones can be seen and used by any Windows user on that same PC.

ODBC Admin Main Screen

Here we have a good number of choices, but usually you'll just want the one that says SQL Server. In this example, the full SQL Server tools are installed for several versions of SQL Server, which is why you also see choices for SQL Server Native Client. You likely won't have the SQL Server Native Client choices unless you need them. Simply select SQL Server and click Finish.

SQL Server Data Source

In the event that you'll one day need to connect to a different database server (Oracle, DB2, etc.) generally speaking you will have the most reliable results and fastest performance using the ODBC driver from the database vendor and it likely will be named so you easily recognize it.

Choose the Name and SQL Server

You'll then need to choose how you connect to the SQL Server in the sense of how does SQL Server know who you are. Most of the time, you'll connect using the user account you logged on to Windows with. If you need a special SQL Server login, your system or database administrator should provide it ahead of time, along with the appropriate password.

In either case, make the appropriate selections for the next screen,

Tell SQL Server Who You Are

Next, you'll need to specify any other options for the connection. Here you'll want to check the checkbox to change the default database and then choose the right one from the drop down list. If you should get an error here, it means either the SQL Server you specified in the previous screen is not available, or you mistyped its name, or you don't have permission to connect. If that's the case, go back to the previous screen, check the name of the SQL Server, and if you believe it's right, follow up with your system or database administrator. It could be down or there could be another reason as to why you can't connect to it.

Specify the Database

This is the database I know contains the sales information I want to access. You'll need to know both the server and the database name to get at the data stored on the SQL Server.

Click the Next button to go to the last configuration screen, where you likely won't need to make any changes, then click Finish to create your ODBC connection. You should be presented with a screen like in - be sure to test your connection to make sure everything is fine before clicking OK.

Review Setup

Conclusion

In this chapter we reviewed the basic concepts and processes you need to understand and perform in order to begin successfully working with your SQL Server databases. We also reviewed covered the prerequisite knowledge to tackle the first and most critical database task – connecting. Much like a phone call – we entered the information necessary to dial in to the database and then placed the call.

Chapter 6 Filters

WHERE Clause

WHERE is the most widely used clause. It helps retrieve exactly what you require. The following example table displays the STUDENT STRENGTH in various Engineering courses in a college:

ENGINEERING_STUDENTS

ENGG_ID	ENGG_NAME	STUDENT_STRENGTH
1	Electronics	150
2	Software	250
3	Genetic	75
4	Mechanical	150
5	Biomedical	72
6	Instrumentation	80
7	Chemical	75
8	Civil	60

9	Electronics & Com	250
10	Electrical	60

Now, if you want to know how many courses have over 200 in STUDENT STRENGTH, then you can simplify your search by passing on a simple statement:

SELECT ENGG_NAME, STUDENT_STRENGTH

FROM ENGINEERING_STUDENTS

WHERE STUDENT_STRENGTH > 200;

ENGG_NAME	STUDENT_STRENGTH
Software	250
Electronics & Com	250

HAVING Clause

HAVING is another clause used as a filter in SQL. At this point, it is important to understand the difference between the WHERE and HAVING clauses. WHERE specifies a condition, and only that set of data that passes the condition will be fetched and displayed in the result set. HAVING clause is used to filter grouped or summarized data. If a SELECT query has both WHERE and HAVING clauses, then when WHERE is used to filter rows, the result is aggregated so the HAVING clause can be applied. You will get a better understanding when you see an example.

For an explanation, another table by the name of Dept_Data has been created, and it is defined as follows:

Field	Type	Null	Key	Default	Extra
Dept_ ID	Bigint (20)	NO	PRI	NULL	auto_ increment
HOD	Varchar (35)	NO			
NO_ OF_ Prof	Varchar (35)	YES		NULL	
ENGG_ ID	Smallint (6)	YES	MUL	NULL	

Now, let's have a look at the data available in this table:

Where Dept_ID is set to 100.

Dept_ID	HOD	NO_OF_Prof	ENGG_ID
100	Miley Andrews	7	1
101	Alex Dawson	6	2
102	Victoria Fox	7	3
103	Anne Joseph	5	4
104	Sophia Williams	8	5
105	Olive Brown	4	6
106	Joshua Taylor	6	7
107	Ethan Thomas	5	8

| 108 | Michael Anderson | 8 | 9 |
| 109 | Martin Jones | 5 | 10 |

There are a few simple differences between the WHERE and HAVING clauses. The WHERE clause can be used with SELECT, UPDATE, and DELETE clauses, but the HAVING clause does not enjoy that privilege; it is only used in the SELECT query. The WHERE clause can be used for individual rows, but HAVING is applied on grouped data. If the WHERE and HAVING clauses are used together, then the WHERE clause will be used before the GROUP BY clause, and the HAVING clause will be used after the GROUP BY clause. Whenever WHERE and HAVING clauses are used together in a query, the WHERE clause is applied first on every row to filter the results and ensure a group is created. After that, you will apply the HAVING clause on that group.

Now, based on our previous tables, let's see which departments have more than 5 professors:

SELECT * FROM Dept_Data WHERE NO_OF_Prof > 5;

Look at the WHERE clause here. It will check each and every row to see which record has NO_OF_Prof > 5.

Dept_ID	HOD	NO_OF_Prof	ENGG_ID
100	Miley Andrews	7	1
101	Alex Dawson	6	2
102	Victoria Fox	7	3
104	Sophia Williams	8	5
106	Joshua Taylor	6	7
108	Michael Anderson	8	9

Now, let's find the names of the Engineering courses for the above data:

SELECT e. ENGG_NAME, e.STUDENT_STRENGTH,

d.HOD,d.NO_OF_Prof,d.Dept_ID

FROM ENGINEERING_STUDENTS e, Dept_Data d

WHERE d.NO_OF_Prof > 5

AND e.ENGG_ID = d.ENGG_ID;

The result set will be as follows:

ENGG_NAME	STUDENT_ STRENGTH	HOD	NO_ OF_ Prof	Dept_ID
Electronics	150	Miley Andrews	7	100
Software	250	Alex Dawson	6	101
Genetic	75	Victoria Fox	7	102
Biomedical	72	Sophia Williams	8	104
Chemical	75	Joshua Taylor	6	106
Electronics & Com	250	Michael Anderson	8	108

Next, we GROUP the data as shown below:

SELECT   e.ENGG_NAME,
d.HOD,d.NO_OF_Prof,d.Dept_ID

FROM ENGINEERING_STUDENTS e, Dept_Data d

WHERE d.NO_OF_Prof > 5 AND e.ENGG_ID = d.ENGG_ID

GROUP BY ENGG_NAME;

ENGG_NAME	STUDENT_STRENGTH	HOD	NO_OF_Prof	Dept_ID
Biomedical	72	Sophia Williams	8	104
Chemical	75	Joshua Taylor	6	106
Electronics	150	Miley Andrews	7	100
Electronics & Com	250	Michael Anderson	8	108

Genetic	75	Victoria Fox	7	102
Software	250	Alex Dawson	6	101

Let's see which departments from this group have more than 100 students:

SELECT e. ENGG_NAME, e.STUDENT_STRENGTH,

d.HOD,d.NO_OF_Prof,d.Dept_ID

FROM ENGINEERING_STUDENTS e, Dept_Data d

WHERE d.NO_OF_Prof > 5 AND e.ENGG_ID = d.ENGG_ID
GROUP BY e.ENGG_NAME HAVING e.STUDENT_STRENGTH > 100;

ENGG_NAME	STUDENT_STRENGTH	HOD	NO_OF_Prof	Dept_ID
Electronics	150	Miley Andrews	7	100

Electronics & Com	250	Michael Anderson	8	108
Software	250	Alex Dawson	6	101

Evaluating a Condition

A WHERE clause can evaluate more than one condition where every condition is separated by the AND operator. Let's take a look at the example below:

SELECT e. ENGG_NAME, e.STUDENT_STRENGTH,

d.HOD,d.NO_OF_Prof,d.Dept_ID

FROM ENGINEERING_STUDENTS e, Dept_Data d

WHERE d.NO_OF_Prof > 5 AND

e.ENGG_ID = d.ENGG_ID AND

100 < e.STUDENT_STRENGTH < 250;

ENGG_NAME	STUDENT _ STRENGTH	HOD	NO_OF _ Prof	Dept _ ID
Electronics	150	Miley Andrews	7	100
Software	250	Alex Dawson	6	101
Genetic	75	Victoria Fox	7	102
Biomedical	72	Sophia Williams	8	104
Chemical	75	Joshua Taylor	6	106
Electronics & Com	250	Michael Anderson	8	108

There is one thing you must understand with the WHERE clause. It is only when all conditions become true for a row that it is included in the result set. If even one condition turns out to be false, the row will not be included in the result set.

The result set will be different if you replace any or all AND operators in the above statement with the OR operator. Say you need to find out which department has either fewer than 100 students OR fewer than 5 professors. Have a look at the following statement:

SELECT e. ENGG_NAME,e.STUDENT_STRENGTH,

d.HOD,d.NO_OF_Prof,d.Dept_ID,e.ENGG_ID

FROM ENGINEERING_STUDENTS e, Dept_Data d

WHERE e.ENGG_ID = d.ENGG_ID AND

(e.STUDENT_STRENGTH < 100 OR d.NO_OF_Prof < 5);

ENGG_NAME	STUDENT _STRENGT H	HOD	NO _ OF_ Prof	Dept _ ID
Genetic	75	Victoria Fox	7	102

Biomedical	72	Sophia Williams	8	104
Instrumentation	80	Olive Brown	4	105
Chemical	75	Joshua Taylor	6	106
Civil	60	Ethan Thomas	5	107
Electrical	60	Martin Jones	5	109

In the above statement, notice how the parentheses are placed. You should clearly define how the AND operator exists between two conditions, and how the OR operator exists between two conditions. You will learn more about the usage of parentheses in the upcoming section. For now, please understand how the outcome of the AND/OR operators are evaluated.

AND Operator

Condition	Outcome
Where True AND True	True
Where False AND True	False
Where True AND False	False
Where False AND False	False

OR Operator

Condition	Outcome
Where True OR True	True
Where False OR True	True
Where True OR False	True
Where False OR False	False

Usage of Parentheses

In the last example, we had three conditions, and we put one condition in parentheses. If the parentheses are missing, the results will be wrong and confusing. For a change, let's try and see what happens if this occurs:

SELECT e.ENGG_NAME,e.STUDENT_STRENGTH,

d.HOD,d.NO_OF_Prof,d.Dept_ID,e.ENGG_ID

FROM ENGINEERING_STUDENTS e, DEPT_DATA d

WHERE e.ENGG_ID = d.ENGG_ID AND

e.STUDENT_STRENGTH < 100 OR d.NO_OF_Prof < 5;

ENGG_ NAME	STUDE NT_ STREN GTH	HOD	NO _ OF _ Pr of	Dept_ ID	ENGG _ID
Genetic	75	Victor ia Fox	7	102	3
Biomedical	72	Sophi a Willia ms	8	104	5

Electronics	150	Olive Brown	4	105	1
Software	250	Olive Brown	4	105	2
Genetic	75	Olive Brown	4	105	3
Mechanical	150	Olive Brown	4	105	4
Biomedical	72	Olive Brown	4	105	5
Instrumentation	80	Olive Brown	4	105	6
Chemical	75	Olive Brown	4	105	7

Civil	60	Olive Brown	4	105	8
Electronics & Com	250	Olive Brown	4	105	9
Electrical	60	Olive Brown	4	105	10
Chemical	75	Joshua Taylor	6	106	7
Civil	60	Ethan Thomas	5	107	8
Electrical	60	Martin Jones	5	109	10

One look at the table above and you know the results are all wrong and misleading. The reason is that the instructions are not clear to the data server. Now, think about what we want to accomplish; we want to know which department has fewer than 100 students OR fewer than 5 professors. Now, witness the magic of the parentheses. The parentheses convert three conditions to two, well-defined conditions.

WHERE e.ENGG_ID = d.ENGG_ID AND

(e.STUDENT_STRENGTH < 100 OR d.NO_OF_Prof < 5);

This follows the following format: Condition1 AND (Condition2 OR Condition3).

Now, this is how the condition will be calculated:

Cond1	Cond2	Cond3	Cond2 OR Cond3	Cond1 AND (Cond2 OR Cond3)
T	T	T	T	T
T	T	F	T	T
T	F	T	T	T
T	F	F	F	F

F	T	T	T	F
F	T	F	T	F
F	F	T	T	F
F	F	F	F	F

By putting e.STUDENT_STRENGTH < 100 OR d.NO_OF_Prof < 5 into parentheses, we convert it into one condition, and the first condition will consider the output of the parentheses for the final result. Out of eight possible conditions from the table above, there are only three scenarios where the final condition is True.

The NOT Operator

To understand the usage of the NOT operator, let's replace AND with AND NOT and find out what output we receive:

SELECT e. ENGG_NAME,e.STUDENT_STRENGTH,

d.HOD,d.NO_OF_Prof,d.Dept_ID,e.ENGG_ID

FROM ENGINEERING_STUDENTS e, Dept_Data d

WHERE e.ENGG_ID = d.ENGG_ID AND NOT

(e.STUDENT_STRENGTH < 100 OR d.NO_OF_Prof < 5);

ENGG_NAME	STUDENT_STRENGTH	HOD	NO_OF_Prof	Dept_ID	ENGG_ID
Electronics	150	Miley Andrews	7	100	1
Software	250	Alex Dawson	6	101	2
Mechanical	150	Anne Joseph	5	103	4
Electronics & Com	250	Michael Anderson	8	108	9

Remember that our desired results find which department has fewer than 100 students or fewer than 5 professors. After applying the NOT operator before the parentheses, our results look for either more than 5 professors, or more than 100 students.

Is it possible to obtain the same results while using the NOT statement? Yes! Just replace '>' with '<' and replace OR with AND.

SELECT e.ENGG_NAME,e.STUDENT_STRENGTH,

d.HOD,d.NO_OF_Prof,d.Dept_ID,e.ENGG_ID

FROM ENGINEERING_STUDENTS e, Dept_Data d

WHERE e.ENGG_ID = d.ENGG_ID AND NOT

(e.STUDENT_STRENGTH ≥ 100 AND d.NO_OF_Prof ≥ 5);

ENGG_ NAME	STUDENT_ STRENGTH	HOD	NO_ OF_ Prof	Dept_ ID	ENGG_ ID
Genetic	75	Victoria Fox	7	102	3
Biomedical	72	Sophia Williams	8	104	5

Instrumentation	80	Olive Brown	4	105	6
Chemical	75	Joshua Taylor	6	106	7
Civil	60	Ethan Thomas	5	107	8
Electrical	60	Martin Jones	5	109	10

Here is the output for applying AND NOT:

Cond1	Cond2	Cond3	Cond2 AND Cond3	Cond1 AND NOT (Cond2 AND Cond3)
T	T	T	T	F
T	T	F	F	T
T	F	T	F	T
T	F	F	F	T

F	T	T	T	T
F	T	F	F	T
F	F	T	F	T
F	F	F	F	T

However, use the NOT operator only when required. It can aid in the legibility of the statement, but if you use NOT when it can be avoided, it could unnecessarily complicate things for the developer.

Sequences

A sequence refers to a set of numbers that has been generated in a specified order on demand. These are popular in databases. The reason behind this is that sequences provide an easy way to have a unique value for each row in a specified column. This section explains the use of sequences in SQL.

AUTO_INCREMENT Column

This provides you with the easiest way of creating a sequence in MySQL. You only have to define the column as auto_increment and leave MySQL to take care of the rest. To show how to use this property, we will create a simple table and insert some records into the table.

The following command will help us create the table:

```
CREATE TABLE colleagues

(

    id INT UNSIGNED NOT NULL AUTO_INCREMENT,

    PRIMARY KEY (id),

    name VARCHAR(20) NOT NULL,

    home_city VARCHAR(20) NOT NULL
);
```

The command should create the table successfully, as shown below:

```
mysql> create database tuw
    -> ;
Query OK, 1 row affected (0.05 sec)

mysql> use tuw;
Database changed
mysql> CREATE TABLE colleagues
    ->     (
    ->     id INT UNSIGNED NOT NULL AUTO_INCREMENT,
    ->     PRIMARY KEY (id),
    ->     name VARCHAR(20) NOT NULL,
    ->     home_city VARCHAR(20) NOT NULL
    -> );
Query OK, 0 rows affected (0.30 sec)

mysql>
```

We have created a table named colleagues. This table has 3 columns: id, name, and home_city. The first column is an integer data type while the rest are varchars (variable characters). We have added the auto_increment property to the id column, so the column values will be incremented automatically. When entering data into the table, we don't need to specify the value of this column. It will start at 1 by default then increment the values automatically for each record you insert into the table.

Let us now insert some records into the table:

INSERT INTO colleagues

VALUES (NULL, "John", "New Delhi");

INSERT INTO colleagues

VALUES (NULL, "Joel", "New Jersey");

INSERT INTO colleagues

VALUES (NULL, "Britney", "New York");

INSERT INTO colleagues

VALUES (NULL, "Biggy", "Washington");

The commands should run successfully, as shown below:

Now, we can run the select statement against the table and see its contents:

```
mysql> select * from colleagues;
+----+---------+------------+
| id | name    | home_city  |
+----+---------+------------+
|  1 | John    | New Delhi  |
|  2 | Joel    | New Jersey |
|  3 | Britney | New York   |
|  4 | Biggy   | Washington |
+----+---------+------------+
4 rows in set (0.01 sec)

mysql>
```

We see that the id column has also been populated with values starting from 1. Each time you enter a record, the value of this column is increased by 1. We have successfully created a sequence.

Renumbering a Sequence

You notice that when you delete a record from a sequence such as the one we have created above, the records will not be renumbered. You may not be impressed by this kind of numbering. However, it is possible for you to re-sequence the records. This only involves a single trick, but make sure to check whether the table has a join with another table or not.

If you find you have to re-sequence your records, the best way to do it is by dropping the column and then adding it. Here, we'll show how to drop the id column of the colleagues table.

The table is as follows for now:

```
mysql> select * from colleagues;
+----+---------+------------+
| id | name    | home_city  |
+----+---------+------------+
|  1 | John    | New Delhi  |
|  2 | Joel    | New Jersey |
|  3 | Britney | New York   |
|  4 | Biggy   | Washington |
+----+---------+------------+
4 rows in set (0.01 sec)

mysql>
```

Let us drop the id column by running the following command:

ALTER TABLE colleagues DROP id;

```
mysql> ALTER TABLE colleagues DROP id;
Query OK, 4 rows affected (0.40 sec)
Records: 4  Duplicates: 0  Warnings: 0

mysql>
```

To confirm whether the deletion has taken place, let's take a look at the table data:

```
mysql> select * from colleagues;
+---------+------------+
| name    | home_city  |
+---------+------------+
| John    | New Delhi  |
| Joel    | New Jersey |
| Britney | New York   |
| Biggy   | Washington |
+---------+------------+
4 rows in set (0.00 sec)

mysql>
```

The deletion was successful. We combined the ALTER TABLE and the DROP commands for the deletion of the column. Now, let us re-add the column to the table:

ALTER TABLE colleagues

ADD id INT UNSIGNED NOT NULL AUTO_INCREMENT FIRST,

ADD PRIMARY KEY (id);

479

The command should run as follows:

```
mysql> ALTER TABLE colleagues
    ->      ADD id INT UNSIGNED NOT NULL AUTO_INCREMENT FIRST,
    ->      ADD PRIMARY KEY (id);
Query OK, 0 rows affected (0.76 sec)
Records: 0  Duplicates: 0  Warnings: 0
```

We started with the ALTER TABLE command to specify the name of the table we need to change. The ADD command has then been used to add the column and set it as the primary key for the table. We have also used the auto_increment property in the column definition. We can now query the table to see what has happened:

```
mysql> ALTER TABLE colleagues
    ->      ADD id INT UNSIGNED NOT NULL AUTO_INCREMENT FIRST,
    ->      ADD PRIMARY KEY (id);
Query OK, 0 rows affected (0.76 sec)
Records: 0  Duplicates: 0  Warnings: 0

mysql> select * from colleagues;
+----+---------+------------+
| id | name    | home_city  |
+----+---------+------------+
|  1 | John    | New Delhi  |
|  2 | Joel    | New Jersey |
|  3 | Britney | New York   |
|  4 | Biggy   | Washington |
+----+---------+------------+
4 rows in set (0.00 sec)

mysql>
```

The id column was added successfully. The sequence has also been numbered correctly.

MySQL starts the sequence at index 1 by default. However, it is possible for you to customize this when you are creating the table. You can set the limit or amount of the increment each time a record is created. Like in the table named colleagues, we can alter the table for the auto_increment to be done at intervals of 2. This is achieved through the code below:

ALTER TABLE colleagues AUTO_INCREMENT = 2;

The command should run successfully, as shown below:

```
mysql> ALTER TABLE colleagues AUTO_INCREMENT = 2;
Query OK, 0 rows affected (0.06 sec)
Records: 0  Duplicates: 0  Warnings: 0

mysql>
```

We can specify where the auto_increment will start at the time of the creation of the table. The following example shows this:

CREATE TABLE colleagues2

(

id INT UNSIGNED NOT NULL AUTO_INCREMENT = 10,

PRIMARY KEY (id),

name VARCHAR(20) NOT NULL,

home_city VARCHAR(20) NOT NULL

);

From the above instance, we set the auto_increment property on the id column, and the initial value for the column will be 10.

Chapter 7 14-SQL Subqueries

A sub-query refers to a query embedded inside another query, and this is done in the *WHERE* clause. It is also referred to as an Inner query or Nested query.

We use a sub-query to return the data that will be used in our main query and as a condition for restricting the data we are to retrieve. We can add sub-queries to *SELECT, UPDATE, INSERT,* and DELETE statements and combine them with operators like $=$, $<$, $>$, $<=$, $>=$, *IN, BETWEEN* and many others.

The following are the rules that govern the use of sub-queries:

·   A sub-query must be added within parenthesis.

·   A sub-query should return only one column, meaning that the SELECT * cannot be used within a sub-query unless where the table has only a single column. If your goal is to perform row comparison, you can create a sub-query that will return multiple columns.

·   One can only create sub-queries that return over one row with multiple value operators like IN and NOT IN operators.

·   You cannot use a UNION in a sub-query. You are only allowed to use one SELECT statement.

·   Your SELECT list should not include a reference to values testing to a BLOB, CLOB, ARRAY, or NCLOB.

·   You cannot immediately enclose a sub-query within a set function.

·   You cannot use the BETWEEN operator with a sub-query. However, you can use this operator within a sub-query.

Subqueries with SELECT Statement

In most cases, we use subqueries with the SQL's SELECT statement.

We do this using the syntax given below:

SELECT columnName [, columnName]

FROM   table_1 [, table_2]

WHERE   columnName **OPERATOR**

   (**SELECT** columnName [,columnName]

   FROM table_1 [, table_2]

   [**WHERE**])

Consider the students table with the data given below:

Let us now create a query with a sub-query as shown below:

SELECT *

FROM students

WHERE regno **IN** (**SELECT** regno

FROM students

WHERE age >= 19);

The command should return the result given below:

We have used the following subquery:

SELECT regno

FROM students

WHERE age >= 19;

In the main query, we are using the results of the above subquery to return our final results. This means that the main query will only return the records of students whose age is 19 and above. That is what the above output shows.

Subqueries with INSERT Statement

We can also use Sub-queries with the INSERT statement. What happens, in this case, is that the insert statement will use the data that has been returned by the query to insert it into another table.

It is possible for us to change the data that the sub-query returns using date, character or number functions.

The following syntax shows how we can add a sub-query to the INSERT statement:

INSERT INTO tableName [(column_1 [, column_2])]

    SELECT [*|column_1 [, column_2]

    FROM table_1 [, table_2]

    [**WHERE** A **VALUE OPERATOR**]

Consider a situation in which we have the table students2 which is an exact copy of the **students'** table. First, let us create this table:

CREATE TABLE students2 **LIKE** students**;**

The table doesn't have even a single record. We need to populate it with data from the students' table. We then run the following query to perform this task:

INSERT INTO students2

    SELECT * **FROM** students

    WHERE regno **IN (SELECT** regno

    FROM students)**;**

The code should run successfully as shown below:

We have used the regno column of the table named **students** to select all the records in that table and populate them into the table named **students2**. Let us query the table to see its contents:

It is clear that the table was populated successfully.

 Subqueries with UPDATE Statement

We can combine the update statement with a sub-query. With this, we can update either single or multiple columns in a table.

We can do this using the following syntax:

UPDATE table

SET columnName = newValue

[**WHERE OPERATOR** [**VALUE**]

   (**SELECT** COLUMNNAME

   FROM TABLENAME)

   [**WHERE**)]

We need to show using the students' table. The table has the data given below:

> The table students2 is a copy of the students' table. We need to increase the ages of the students by 1. This means we run the following command:

UPDATE students

   SET age= age + 1

   WHERE regno **IN** (**SELECT** regno **FROM** students2);

The command should run successfully as shown below:

```
mysql> UPDATE students
    ->     SET age= age + 1
    ->     WHERE regno IN (SELECT regno FROM students2 );
Query OK, 5 rows affected (0.08 sec)
Rows matched: 5  Changed: 5  Warnings: 0

mysql>
```

Since the two tables have exactly the same data, all the records in the students' table were matched to the sub-query. This means that all the records were updated. To confirm this, we run a select statement against the students' table:

> The above figure shows that the values of age were increased by 1.

Subqueries with DELETE Statement

We can use sub-queries with the DELETE statement just like the other SQL statements. The following syntax shows how we can do this:

DELETE FROM TABLENAME

[WHERE OPERATOR [VALUE]

(**SELECT** COLUMNNAME

FROM TABLENAME)

[**WHERE**)]

Suppose we need to make a deletion on the students table. The students table has the following data:

The **students2** table is an exact copy of the above table as shown below:

We need to perform a deletion on the students table by running the following command:

DELETE FROM students

   WHERE AGE **IN** (**SELECT** age **FROM** students2

     WHERE AGE < 20);

The command should run successfully as shown below:

The record in which the value of age is below 20 will be deleted. This is because this is what the subqueries return. We can confirm this by running a select statement on the students' table as shown below:

The above output shows that the record was deleted successfully.

Chapter 8 Database Components

Now that you know more about a database's use in the real world and why you may want to learn SQL, we will dive into the components of the database.

These components or items within a database are typically referred to as "objects". These objects can range from tables, to columns, to indexes and even triggers. Essentially, these are all of the pieces of the data puzzle that make up the database itself.

The examples and screenshots used in the following sections are from the AdventureWorks2012 database, which you will be working with later on in this book.

Database Tables

Within the database are tables, which hold the data itself. A table consists of columns that are the headers of the table, like First_Name and Last_Name, for example. There are also rows, which are considered an entry within the table. The point to where the column and row intersect is called a cell.

The cell is where the data is shown, like someone's actual first name and last name. Some cells may not always have data, which is considered NULL in the database. This just means that no data exists in that cell.

In Microsoft's SQL Server, a table can have up to 1,024 columns, but can have any number of rows.

Schemas

A schema is considered a logical container for the tables. It's essentially, a way to group tables together based on the type of data that they hold. It won't affect an end user who interacts with the database, like someone who runs reports. But one who works directly with the database, like a database administrator or a developer, will see the available schemas.

Consider a realistic example of several tables containing data for Sales records. There may be several tables named Sales_Order, Sales_History or Sales_Customer. You can put all of these Sales tables into a "Sales" schema to better identify them when you work directly with the database.

Columns

Remember that you can only have up to 1,024 columns in a given table in SQL Server!

Rows and NULL values

A row is considered an entry in a table. The row will be one line across, and typically have data within each column. Though, in some cases, there may be a NULL value in one or many cells.

Back to our example of names, most people have first and last names, but not everyone has a middle name. In that case, a row would have values in the first and last name columns, but not the middle name column, like shown below.

Primary Keys

A primary key is a constraint on a column that forces every value in that column to be unique. By forcing uniqueness on values in that column, it helps maintain the integrity of the data and helps prevent any future data issues.

A realistic example of a primary key would be an employee ID or a sales record ID. You wouldn't want to have two of the same employee ID's for two different people, nor would you want to have two or more of the same sales record ID's for different sales transactions. That would be a nightmare when trying to store and retrieve data!

You can see in the below example that each value for BusinessEntityID is unique for every person.

Foreign Keys

Another key similar to the primary key is a foreign key. These differ from primary keys by not always being unique and act as a link between two or more tables.

Below is an example of a foreign key that exists in the AdventureWorks2012 database. The foreign key is ProductID in this table (Sales.SalesOrderDetail):

The ProductID in the above table is linking to the ProductID (primary key) in the Production.Product table:

Essentially, foreign keys will check its link to the other table to see if that value exists. If not, then you will end up receiving an error when trying to insert data into the table where the foreign key is.

Constraints

Primary keys and foreign keys are known as constraints in the database. Constraints are "rules" that are set in place as far as the types of data that can be entered. There are several others that are used aside from primary keys and foreign keys that help maintain the integrity of the data.

UNIQUE – enforces all values in that column to be different. An example of this could be applied to the Production.Product table. Each product should be different, since you wouldn't want to store the same product name multiple times.

NOT NULL – ensures that no value in that column is NULL. This could also be applied to the same table as above. In this case, the ProductNumber cannot have a NULL value, as each Product should have its own corresponding ProductNumber.

DEFAULT – sets a default value in a column when a value is not provided. A great example of this would be the ListPrice column. When a value isn't specified when being added to this table, the value will default to 0.00. If this value were to be calculated in another table and be a NULL value (like a sales table where sales from the company are made), then it would be impossible to calculate based on a NULL value since it's not a number. Using a default value of 0.00 is a better approach.

INDEXES – Indexes are constraints that are created on a column that speeds up the retrieval of data. An index will essentially compile all of the values in a column and treat them as unique values, even if they're not. By treating them as unique values, it allows the database engine to improve its search based on that column.

Indexes are best used on columns that:

- Do not have a unique constraint
- Are not a primary key
- Or are not a foreign key

The reason for not applying an index to a column that satisfies any of the above three conditions, is that these are naturally faster for retrieving data since they are constraints.

As an example, an index would be best used on something like a date column in a sales table. You may be filtering certain transaction dates from

January through March as part of your quarterly reports, yet see many purchases on the same day between those months. By treating it as a unique column, even the same or similar values can still be found much quicker by the database engine.

Views

A view is a virtual table that's comprised of one or more columns from one or more tables. It is created using a SQL query and the original code used to create the view is recompiled when a user queries that table.

In addition, any updates to data made in the originating tables (i.e. the tables and columns that make up the view) will be pulled into the view to show current data. This is another reason that views are great for reporting purposes, as you can pull real-time data without touching the origin tables.

For best practices, DO NOT update any data in a view. If you need to update the data for any reason, perform that in the originating table(s).

To expand a little bit on why a view would be used is the following:

1. To hide the raw elements of the database from the end-user so that they only see what they need to. You can also make it more cryptic for the end-user.

2. An alternative to queries that are frequently run in the database, like reporting purposes as an example.

These are only a few reasons as to why you would use a view. However, depending on your situation, there could be other reasons why you would use a view instead of writing a query to directly obtain data from one or more tables.

To better illustrate the concept of a view, the below example has two tables: 'People' and 'Locations'. These two tables are combined into a view that is called 'People and Locations' just for simplicity. These are also joined on a common field, i.e. the LocationID.

Stored Procedures

Stored procedures are pre-compiled SQL syntax that can be used over and over again by executing its name in SQL Server. If there's a certain query that you're running frequently and writing it from scratch or saving the file somewhere and then opening it to be able to run it, then it may be time to consider creating a stored procedure out of that query.

Just like with SQL syntax that you'd write from scratch and passing in a value for your WHERE clause, you can do the same with a stored procedure. You have the ability to pass in certain values to achieve the end result that you're looking for. Though, you don't always have to pass a parameter into a stored procedure.

As an example, let's say that as part of the HR department, you must run a query once a month to verify which employees are salary and non-salary, in compliance with labor laws and company policy.

Instead of opening a file frequently or writing the code from scratch, you can simply call the stored procedure that you saved in the database, to retrieve the information for you. You would just specify the proper value (where 1 is TRUE and 0 is FALSE in this case).

EXEC   **HumanResources.SalariedEmployees @SalariedFlag = 1**

In the result set below, you can see some of the employees who work in a salary type position:

Triggers

A trigger in the database is a stored procedure (pre-compiled code) that will execute when a certain event happens to a table. Generally, these triggers will fire off when data is added, updated or deleted from a table.

Below is an example of a trigger that prints a message when a new department is created in the HumanResources.Department table.

--Creates a notification stating that a new department has been created

--when an INSERT statement is executed against the Department table

> **CREATE TRIGGER** NewDepartment
> **ON** HumanResources.Department
> **AFTER INSERT**
> > **AS RAISERROR** ('A new department has been created.', *10, 9*)

To expand on this a little more, you specify the name of your trigger after CREATE TRIGGER. After ON, you'll specify the table name that this is associated with.

Next, you can specify which type of action will fire this trigger (you may also use UPDATE and/or DELETE), which is known as a DML trigger in this case.

Last, I'm printing a message that a new department has been created and using some number codes in SQL Server for configuration.

To see this trigger in the works, here's the INSERT statement I'm using to create a new department. There are four columns in this table, DepartmentID, Name, GroupName and ModifiedDate. I'm skipping the DepartmentID column in the INSERT statement because a new ID is automatically generated by the database engine.

<u>--Adding a new department to the Department's table</u>

INSERT INTO HumanResources.Department (**Name**, GroupName, ModifiedDate)

VALUES

('Business Analysis', 'Research and Development', GETDATE()) --GETDATE() gets the current date and time, depending on the data type being used in the table

The trigger will prompt a message after the new record has been successfully inserted.

A new department has been created.

(1 row(s) affected)

If I were to run a query against this table, I can see that my department was successfully added as well.

	DepartmentID	Name	GroupName	ModifiedDate
7	7	Production	Manufacturing	2002-06-01 00:00:00.000
8	8	Production Control	Manufacturing	2002-06-01 00:00:00.000
9	9	Human Resources	Executive General and Administration	2002-06-01 00:00:00.000
10	10	Finance	Executive General and Administration	2002-06-01 00:00:00.000
11	11	Information Services	Executive General and Administration	2002-06-01 00:00:00.000
12	12	Document Control	Quality Assurance	2002-06-01 00:00:00.000
13	13	Quality Assurance	Quality Assurance	2002-06-01 00:00:00.000
14	14	Facilities and Maintenance	Executive General and Administration	2002-06-01 00:00:00.000
15	15	Shipping and Receiving	Inventory Management	2002-06-01 00:00:00.000
16	16	Executive	Executive General and Administration	2002-06-01 00:00:00.000
17	17	Business Analysis	Research and Development	2017-12-25 09:34:44.513

Deadlocks in SQL

In most of the cases, multiple users access database applications simultaneously, which means that multiple transactions are being executed on database in parallel. By default when a transaction performs an operation on a database resource such as a table, it locks the resource. During that period, no other transaction can access the locked resource. Deadlocks occur when two or more than two processes try to access resources that are locked by the other processes participating in the deadlock.

Deadlocks are best explained with the help of an example. Consider a scenario where some transactionA has performed an operation on tableA and has acquired lock on the table. Similarly, there is another transaction named transactionB that is executing in parallel and performs some operation on tableB. Now, transactionA wants to perform some operation on tableBwhich is already locked by transactionB. Similarly, transactionB wants to perform an operation on tableA, but it is already locked by transactionA. This results in a deadlock since transactionA is waiting on a resource locked by transactionB, which is waiting on a resource locked by transactionA. In this chapter we shall see a practical example of deadlocks. Then we will see how we can analyze and resolve deadlocks.

Dummy Data Creation

For the sake of this chapter, we will create a dummy database. This database will be used in the deadlock example that we shall in next section. Execute the following script

```
CREATE DATABASE dldb;
GO
  USE dldb;
  CREATE TABLE tableA
(
  id INT IDENTITY PRIMARY KEY,
  patient_name NVARCHAR(50)
)
  INSERT INTO tableA VALUES ('Thomas')
  CREATE TABLE tableB
(
  id INT IDENTITY PRIMARY KEY,
  patient_name NVARCHAR(50)
)
    INSERT INTO table2 VALUES ('Helene')
```

The above script creates database named "dldb". In the database we create two tables: tableA and tableB. We then insert one record each in the both tables.

Practical Example of Deadlock

Let's write a script that creates deadlock. Open two instances of SQL server management studio. To simulate simultaneous data access, we will run our queries in parallel in these two instances.

Now, open the first instances of SSMS, and write the following script. Do not execute this script at the moment.

Instance1 Script

USE dldb;

BEGIN TRANSACTION transactionA

-- First update statement

UPDATE tableA SET patient name = 'Thomas - TransactionA'

WHERE id = 1

-- Go to the second instance and execute

-- first update statement

UPDATE tableB SET patient name = 'Helene - TransactionA'

WHERE id = 1

-- Go to the second instance and execute

-- second update statement

COMMIT TRANSACTION

In the second instance, copy and paste the following script. Again, do not run the Script.

Instance 2 Script

USE dldb;

BEGIN TRANSACTION transactionB

-- First update statement

UPDATE tableB SET patient name = 'Helene - TransactionB'

WHERE id = 1

-- Go to the first instance and execute

-- second update statement

UPDATE tableA SET patient name = 'Thomas - TransactionB'

WHERE id = 1

COMMIT TRANSACTION

Now we have our scripts ready in both the transaction.

Open both the instances of SSMS side by side as shown in the following figure:

To create a deadlock we have to follow step by step approach. Go to the first instance of SQL Server management studio(SSMS) and execute the following lines from the script:

USE dldb;

BEGIN TRANSACTION transactionA

-- First update statement

UPDATE tableA SET patient name = 'Thomas - TransactionA'

WHERE id = 1

In the above script, transactionA updates the tableAby setting the name of the patient with id one to *'Thomas –TransactionA'*. At this point of time, transactionA acquires lock on tableA.

Now, execute the following script from the second instance of SSMS.

USE dldb;

BEGIN TRANSACTION transactionB

-- First update statement

UPDATE tableB SET patient name = 'Helene - TransactionB'

WHERE id = 1

The above script executes transactionB which updates tableB by setting the name of patient with id one to *'Helene – TransactionB'*, acquiring lock on tableB.

Now come back again to first instance of SSMS. Execute the following piece of script:

UPDATE tableB SET patient name = 'Helene - TransactionA'

WHERE id = 1

Here transactionA tries to update tableB which is locked by transactionB. Hence transactionA goes to waiting state.

Go to the second instance of SSMS again and execute the following piece of script.

UPDATE tableA SET patient name = 'Thomas - TransactionB'

   WHERE id = 1

In the above script, transactionB tries to update tableA which is locked by transactionA. Hence transactionA also goes to waiting state.

At this point of time, transactionA is waiting for a resource locked by transactionB. Similarly, transactionB is waiting for the resource locked by TransactionA. Hence deadlock occurs here.

By default, SSMS selects one of the transactions involved in the deadlock as deadlock victim. The transaction selected as deadlock victim is rolled back, allowing the other transaction to complete its execution. You will see that after few second, the transaction in one of the instances will complete its execution while an error will appear in other instance.

In the example that we just saw, transactionA was allowed to complete its execution while transactionB was selected as deadlock victim. Your result can be different. This is shown in the following figure:

You can see the message "1 row affected" in the instance on the left that is running transactionA. On the other hand in the left instance an error is displayed that reads:

> Msg 1205, Level 13, State 51, Line 12
> Transaction (Process ID 54) was deadlocked on lock
> resources with another process and has been chosen

as the deadlock victim. Rerun the transaction.

The error says that the Transaction with process ID 54 was involved in a deadlock and hence chosen as victim of the deadlock.

Deadlock Analysis and Prevention

In the previous section we generated deadlock ourselves, therefore we have information about the processes involved in the deadlock. In the real world scenarios, this is not the case. Multiple users access the database simultaneously, which often results in deadlocks. However, in such cases we cannot tell which transactions and resources are involved in the deadlock. We need a mechanism that allows us to analyze deadlocks in detail so that we can see what transactions and resources are involved and decide how to resolve the deadlocks. One such ways is via SQL Server error logs.

Reading Deadlock info via SQL Server Error Log

The SQL Server provides only little info about the deadlock. You can get detailed information about the deadlock via SQL error log. However to log deadlock information to error log, first you have to use a trace flag 1222. You can turn trace flag 1222 on global as well as session level. To turn on trace flag 1222 on, execute the following script:

DBCC Traceon(1222, -1)

The above script turns trace flag on global level. If you do not pass the second argument, the trace flag is turned on session level. To see if trace flag is actually turned on, execute the following query:

DBCC TraceStatus(1222)

The above statement results in the following output:

TraceFlag	Status	Global	Session
1222	1	1	0

Here status value 1 shows that trace flag 1222 is on. The 1 for Global column implies that trace flag has been turned on globally.

Now, try to generate a deadlock by following the steps that we performed in the last section. The detailed deadlock information will be logged in the error log. To view sql server error log, you need to execute the following stored procedure.

executesp_readerrorlog

The above stored procedure will retrieve detailed error log a snippet of which is shown below:

Your error log might be different depending upon the databases in your database. The information about all the deadlocks in your database starts with log text "deadlock-list". You may need to scroll down a bit to find this row.

Let's now analyze the log information that is retrieved by the deadlock that we just created. Note that your values will be different for each column, but the information remains same.

ProcessInfo	Text
spid13s	deadlock-list
spid13s	deadlock victim=process1fcf951 4ca8
spid13s	process-list
spid13s	process id=process1fcf9514ca8t

	askpriority=0 logused=308 waitresource=KEY: 8:72057594043105280 (8194443284a0) waittime=921 ownerId=388813 transactionname=trans actionBlasttranstarted= 2017-11- 01T15:51:46.547 XDES=0x1fcf8454490 lockMode=X schedulerid=3 kpid=1968 status=suspended spid=57 sbid=0 ecid=0 priority=0 trancount=2 lastbatchstarted=2017- 11-01T15:51:54.380 lastbatchcompleted=20 17-11- 01T15:51:54.377 lastattention=1900-01- 01T00:00:00.377 clientapp=Microsoft SQL Server Management Studio - Query hostname=DESKTOP-

	GLQ5VRA hostpid=968 loginname=DESKTOP-GLQ5VRA\Mani isolationlevel=read committed (2) xactid=388813 currentdb=8 lockTimeout=4294967295 clientoption1=67109078 4 clientoption2=390200
spid13s	executionStack
spid13s	frame procname=adhoc line=2 stmtstart=58 stmtend=164 sqlhandle=0x02000000 14b61731ad79b1eec67 40c98aab3ab91bd31af4 d0000000000000000000 0000000000000000000 000
spid13s	unknown
spid13s	frame procname=adhoc line=2 stmtstart=4 stmtend=142

	sqlhandle=0x02000000 80129b021f70641be5a 5e43a1ca1ef67e9721c9 7000000000000000000 0000000000000000000 000
spid13s	unknown
spid13s	inputbuf
spid13s	UPDATE tableA SET patient_name = 'Thomas - TransactionB'
spid13s	WHERE id = 1
spid13s	process id=process1fcf9515468 taskpriority=0 logused=308 waitresource=KEY: 8:72057594043170816 (8194443284a0) waittime=4588 ownerId=388767 transactionname=trans actionAlasttranstarted= 2017-11-01T15:51:44.383 XDES=0x1fcf8428490 lockMode=X

	schedulerid=3 kpid=11000 status=suspended spid=54 sbid=0 ecid=0 priority=0 trancount=2 lastbatchstarted=2017- 11-01T15:51:50.710 lastbatchcompleted=20 17-11- 01T15:51:50.710 lastattention=1900-01- 01T00:00:00.710 clientapp=Microsoft SQL Server Management Studio - Query hostname=DESKTOP- GLQ5VRA hostpid=1140 loginname=DESKTOP- GLQ5VRA\Mani isolationlevel=read committed (2) xactid=388767 currentdb=8 lockTimeout=42949672 95 clientoption1=6710907 84 clientoption2=390200

spid13s	executionStack
spid13s	frame procname=adhoc line=1 stmtstart=58 stmtend=164 sqlhandle=0x02000000 ec86cd1dbe1cd7fc9723 7a12abb461f1fc27e278 00000000000000000000 00000000000000000000 00
spid13s	unknown
spid13s	frame procname=adhoc line=1 stmtend=138 sqlhandle=0x02000000 3a45a10eb863d6370a5 f99368760983cacbf489 5000000000000000000 00000000000000000000 000
spid13s	unknown
spid13s	inputbuf
spid13s	UPDATE tableB SET patient_name = 'Helene - TransactionA'

spid13s	WHERE id = 1
spid13s	resource-list
spid13s	keylockhobtid=720575 94043105280 dbid=8 objectname=dldb.dbo.t ableAindexname=PK__t ableA__3213E83F1C2C 4D64 id=lock1fd004bd600 mode=X associatedObjectId=72 057594043105280
spid13s	owner-list
spid13s	owner id=process1fcf9515468 mode=X
spid13s	waiter-list
spid13s	waiter id=process1fcf9514ca8 mode=X requestType=wait
spid13s	keylockhobtid=720575 94043170816 dbid=8 objectname=dldb.dbo.t ableBindexname=PK__t ableB__3213E83FFE08

	D6AB id=lock1fd004c2200 mode=X associatedObjectId=72 057594043170816
spid13s	owner-list
spid13s	owner id=process1fcf9514ca8 mode=X
spid13s	waiter-list
spid13s	waiter id=process1fcf9515468 mode=X requestType=wait

The deadlock information logged by the SQL server error log has three main parts.

1-___The deadlock Victim

2-___Process List

The process list is the list of all the processes involved in a deadlock. In the deadlock that we generated, two processes were involved. In the processes list you can see details of both of these processes. The id of the first process is highlighted in red whereas the id of the second process is highlighted in green. Notice that in the process list, the first process is the process that has been selected as deadlock victim too.

Apart from process id, there you can also see other information about the processes. For instance, you can find login information of the process, the isolation level of the process etc. You can see the script that the process was trying to run. For instance if you look at the first process in the process list, you can find that it was trying to update the patient_name column of the table tableA, when the deadlock occurred.

3-___Resource List

The resource list contains information about the resources that were involved in the deadlock. In our example, tableA and tableB were the only two resources involved in the deadlock. You can both of these tables highlighted in blue in the resource list of the log in the table above.

Some tips for Deadlock Avoidance

From the error log we can get detailed information about the deadlock. However we can minimize the chance of deadlock occurrence if we follow these tips:

- *Execute transactions in a single batch and keep them short*

- *Release resources automatically after a certain time period*
- *Sequential resource sharing*
- Not allowing user to interact with the application when transactions are being executed.

This chapter presented a brief overview to deadlocks. In the next chapter, we shall see another extremely useful concept, i.e. Cursors.

Chapter 9 How to Manage Database Objects

This chapter will discuss database objects: their nature, behaviors, storage requirements, and interrelatedness. Basically, databases objects are the backbone of relational databases. You use these objects to store data (i.e. they are logical units found inside a database). For this reason, these objects are also called back-end databases.

What is a Database Object?

Database objects are the defined objects within a database utilized to save or retrieve information. Here are several examples of database objects: views, clusters, tables, indexes, synonyms, and sequences.

The Schema

A schema is a set of database objects linked to a certain database user. This user, known as the "schema owner," owns the set of objects linked to his/her username. Simply put, any person who generates an object has just generated his/her own schema. That means users have control over database objects that are generated, deleted, and manipulated.

Let's assume that you received login credentials (i.e. username and password) from a database administrator. The username is PERSON1. Let's say you accessed the database and created a table named EMPLOYEES_TBL. In the database's records, the file's actual name is PERSON1.EMPLOYEES_TBL. The table's "schema name" is PERSON1, which is also the creator/owner of that table.

When accessing a schema that you own, you are not required to use the schema name. That means you have two ways of accessing the imaginary file given above. These are:

- PERSON1.EMPLOYEES_TBL

- EMPLOYEES_TBL

As you can see, the second option involves fewer characters. This is the reason why schema owners prefer this method of accessing their files. If other users want to view the file, however, they must include the schema in their database query.

The screenshot below shows two schemas within a database.

Tables – The Main Tool for Storing Data

Modern database users consider tables as the main storage tool. In general, a table is formed by row/s and column/s. Tables take up space within a database and may be temporary or permanent.

Fields/Columns

Fields, referred to as columns when working with a relational database, are parts of a table where a particular data type is assigned to. You should name a field so that it matches the data type it will be used with. You may specify fields as NULL (i.e. nothing should be entered) or NOT NULL (i.e. something needs to be entered).

Each table should have at least one field. Fields are the elements inside a table that store certain kinds of data (e.g. names, addresses, phone numbers, etc.). For instance, you'll find a "customer name" column when checking a database table for customer information.

Rows

Rows are records of data within a table. For instance, a row in a customer database table might hold the name, fax number, and identification number of a certain customer. Rows are composed of fields that hold information from a single record in the table.

SQL Statement – CREATE TABLE

"CREATE TABLE" is an SQL statement used to generate a table. Even though you can create tables quickly and easily, you should spend time and effort in planning the structures of your new table. That means you have to do some research and planning before issuing this SQL statement.

Here are some of the questions you should answer when creating tables:

- What kind of data am I working on?
- What name should I choose for this table?
- What column will form the main key?
- What names should be assigned to the fields/columns?
- What type of data can be assigned to those columns?
- Which columns can be empty?
- What is the maximum length for every column?

Once you have answered these questions, using the CREATE TABLE command becomes simple.

Here's the syntax to generate a new table:

The final character of that statement is a semicolon. Almost all SQL implementations use certain characters to terminate statements or submit statements to the server. MySQL and Oracle use semicolons to perform these functions. Transact-SQL, on the other hand, utilizes the "GO" command. To make this book consistent, statements will be terminated or submitted using a semicolon.

The STORAGE Clause

Some SQL implementations offer STORAGE clauses. These clauses help you in assigning the table sizes. That means you can use them while creating tables. MySQL uses the following syntax for its STORAGE clause:

The Naming Conventions

When naming database objects, particularly columns and tables, you should choose names that reflect the data they will be used for. For instance, you may use the name EMPLOYEES_TBL for a table used to hold employee information. You need to name columns using the same principle. A column used to store the phone number of employees may be named PHONE_NUMBER.

SQL Command - ALTER TABLE

You can use ALTER TABLE, a powerful SQL command, to modify existing database tables. You may add fields, remove columns, change field definitions, include or exclude constraints, and, in certain SQL implementations, change the table's STORAGE values. Here's the syntax for this command:

Altering the Elements of a Database Table

A column's "attributes" refer to the laws and behaviors of data inside that column. You may change a column's attributes using ALTER TABLE. Here, the term "attributes" refers to:

- The type of data assigned to a column.
- The scale, length, or precision of a column.
- Whether you can enter NULL values into a column.

In the screenshot below, ALTER TABLE is used on the EMPLOYEE_TBL to change the attributes of a column named EMP_ID:

If you are using MySQL, you'll get the following statement:

Adding Columns to a Database Table

You must remember certain rules when adding columns to existing database tables. One of the rules is this: You can't add a NOT NULL column if the table has data in it. Basically, you should use NOT NULL to indicate that the column should hold some value for each data row within the table. If you'll add a NOT NULL column, you will go against this new constraint if the current data rows don't have specific values for the added column.

Modifying Fields/Columns

Here are the rules you should follow when altering existing columns:

- You can always increase a column's length.

- You can decrease a column's length only if the highest value for the column is lower than or equal to the desired length.
- You can always increase the quantity of digits for numeric data types.
- You can only decrease the quantity of digits for numeric data types if the value of the largest quantity of digits in the column is lower than or equal to the desired quantity of digits.
- You can increase or decrease the quantity of decimal places for numeric data types.
- You can easily change the data type of any column.

Important Note: Be extremely careful when changing or dropping tables. You might lose valuable information if you will commit typing or logical mistakes while executing these SQL statements.

How to Create New Tables from Existing Ones

You may duplicate an existing table using these SQL statements: (1) CREATE TABLE and (2) SELECT. After executing these statements, you'll get a new table whose column definitions are identical to that of the old one. This feature is customizable: you may copy all of the columns or just the ones you need. The columns generated using this pair of statements will assume the size needed to store the information. Here's the main syntax for generating a table from an existing one:

This syntax involves a new keyword (i.e. SELECT). This keyword can help you perform database queries. In modern database systems, SELECT can help you generate tables using search results.

How to Drop Tables

You can drop tables easily. If you used the RESTRICT statement and referenced the table using a view/constraint, the DROP command will give you an error message. If you used CASCASE, however, DROP will succeed and all constraints and/or views will be dropped. The syntax for dropping a table is:

Important Note: When dropping a database table, specify the owner or schema name of the table you are working on. This is important since dropping the wrong table can result to loss of data. If you can access multiple database accounts, make sure that you are logged in to the right account prior to dropping any table.

The Integrity Constraints

You can use integrity constraints to ensure the consistency and accuracy of data within a database. In general, database users handle integrity concerns through a concept called "Referential Integrity." In this section, you'll learn about the integrity constraints that you can use in SQL.

Primary Key

A primary key is used to determine columns that make data rows unique. You can form primary keys using one or more columns. For instance, either the product's name or an assigned reference number can serve as a primary key for a product table. The goal is to provide each record with a unique detail or primary key. In general, you can assign a primary key during table creation.

In the example below, the table's primary key is the column named EMP_ID.

You can assign primary keys this way while creating a new table. In this example, the table's primary key is an implicit condition. As an alternative, you may specify primary keys as explicit conditions while creating a table. Here's an example:

In the example given above, the primary key is given after the comma list.

If you need to form a primary key using multiple columns, you use this method:

Unique Column Constraint

Unique column constraints are similar to primary keys: the column should have a unique value for each row. While you need to place a primary key in a single column, you may place unique constraints on different columns. Here's an example:

In the example above, EMP_ID serves as the primary key. That means the column for employee identification numbers is being used to guarantee the uniqueness of each record. Users often reference primary key columns for database queries, especially when merging tables. The EMP_PHONE column has a unique value, which means each employee has a unique phone number.

Foreign Key

You can use this key while working on parent and child tables. Foreign keys are columns in a child table that points to a primary key inside the parent table. This type of key serves as the primary tool in enforcing referential integrity within a database. You may use a foreign key column to reference a primary key from a different table.

In the example below, you'll learn how to create a foreign key:

Here, EMP_ID serves as a foreign key for a table named EMPLOYEE_PAY_TBL. This key points to the EMP_ID section of another table (i.e. the EMPLOYEE_TBL table). With this key, the database administrator can make sure that each EMP_ID inside the EMPLOYEE_PAY_TBL has a corresponding entry in EMPLOYEE_TBL. SQL practitioners call this the "parent/child relationship."

Study the following figure. This will help you to understand the relationship between child tables and parent tables.

How to Drop Constraints

You can use the option "DROP CONSTAINT" to drop the constraints (e.g. primary key, foreign key, unique column, etc.) you applied for your tables. For instance, if you want to remove the primary key in a table named "EMPLOYEES", you may use this command:

Some SQL implementations offer shortcuts for removing constraints. Oracle, for instance, uses this command to drop a primary key constraint:

On the other hand, certain SQL implementations allow users to deactivate constraints. Rather than dropping constraints permanently, you may disable them temporarily. This way, you can reactivate the constraints you will need in the future.

Chapter 10 Database Advance Topics

In this chapter you will be introduced to some advance topics in SQL that goes beyond basic database transactions. Even if this section only includes an overview of cursors, triggers and errors, such knowledge could possibly help you extend the features of your SQL implementations.

Cursors

Generally, SQL commands manipulate database objects using set-based operations. This means that transactions are performed on a group or block of data. A cursor, on the other hand, processes data from a table one row at a time. It is created using a compound a statement and destroyed upon exit. The standard syntax for declaring a cursor is (which may differ for every implementation):

DECLARE CURSOR CURSOR_NAME
IS {SELECT_STATEMENT}

You can perform operations on a cursor only after it has been declared or defined.

- Open a Cursor

Once declared, you perform an OPEN operation to access the cursor and then execute the specified SELECT statement. The results of the SELECT query will be saved in a certain area in the memory. The standard syntax for opening a cursor is:

OPEN **CURSOR_NAME**;

- Fetch Data from a Cursor

The FETCH statement is performed if you want to retrieve the query results or the data from the cursor. The standard syntax for fetching data is:

FETCH NEXT FROM **CURSOR_NAME** [INTO **FETCH_LIST**]

In SQL programming, the optional statement inside the square brackets will let you assign the data retrieved into a certain variable.

- Close a Cursor

There is a corresponding CLOSE statement to be executed when you open a particular cursor. Once the cursor is closed, all the names and resources used will be deallocated. Thus, the cursor is no longer available for the program to use. The standard syntax for closing a cursor is:

CLOSE **CURSOR_NAME**

Triggers

There are instances when you want certain SQL operations or transactions to occur after performing some specific actions. This scenario describes an SQL statement that triggers another SQL statement to take place. Essentially, a trigger is an SQL procedure that is compiled in the database that execute certain transactions based on other transactions that have previously occurred. Such triggers can be performed before or after the execution of DML statements (INSERT, DELETE and UPDATE). In addition, triggers can validate data integrity, maintain data consistency, undo transactions, log operations, modify and read data values in different databases.

- Create a Trigger

The standard syntax for creating a trigger is:

CREATE TRIGGER **TRIGGER_NAME**
    TRIGGER_ACTION_TIMETRIGGER_EVENT
ON TABLE_NAME
[REFERENCING
OLD_OR_NEW_VALUE_ALIAS_LIST**]**
TRIGGERED_ACTION

TRIGGER_NAME - the unique identifying name for this object

TRIGGER_ACTION_TIMETRIGGER_EVENT - the specified time that the set of triggered actions will occur (whether before or after the triggering event).

TABLE_NAME – the table for which the DML statements have been specified

TRIGGERED_ACTION – specifies the actions to be performed once an event is triggered

Once a trigger has been created, it cannot be altered anymore. You can just either re-create or replace it.

How a trigger works depends what conditions you specify – whether it will fire at once when a DML statement is performed or it will fire multiple times for every table row affected by the DML statement. You can also include a threshold value or a Boolean condition, that when such condition is met will trigger a course of action.

- Drop a Trigger

The basic syntax for dropping a trigger is the same as dropping a table or a view:

DROP TRIGGER TRIGGER_NAME;

Errors

An error-free design or implementation is one of the ultimate goals in any programming language. You can commit errors by simply not following naming conventions, improperly writing the programming codes (syntax or typo errors like a missing apostrophe or parenthesis) or even when the data entered does not match the data type defined.

To make things easier, SQL has devised a way to return error information so that programmers will be aware of what is going on and be able to undertake the appropriate actions to correct the situation. Some of these error-handling mechanisms are the status parameter SQLSTATE and the WHENEVER clause.

- SQLSTATE

The status parameter or host variable SQLSTATE is an error-handling tool that includes a wide selection of anomalous condition. It is a string that consists of five characters (uppercase letters from A to Z and numerals from 0 to 9), where the first two characters refer to the class code while the next three is the subclass code. The class code identifies the status after an SQL statement has been completed – whether it is successful or not (if not successful, then one of the major types of error conditions are returned). Supplementary information about the execution of the SQL statement is also indicated in the subclass code.

The SQLSTATE is updated after every operation. If the value is '00000' (five zeroes), it means that the execution was successful and you can proceed to the next operation. If it contains a five-character string other than '00000', then you have to check your programming lines to rectify the error committed. There are numerous ways on how to handle a certain SQL error, depending on the class code and subclass code specified in the SQLSTATE.

- WHENEVER Clause

The WHENEVER clause error-handling mechanism focuses on execution exceptions. With this, an error is acknowledged and gives the programmer the option to correct it. This is better than not being able to do something if an error occurs. If you cannot rectify or reverse the error that was committed, then you can just gracefully terminate the application program.

WHENEVER **CONDITION ACTION;**

> **CONDITION** – value can either be SQLERROR (returns TRUE if SQLSTATE class code is other than 00, 01 or 02) or NOT FOUND (returns TRUE if SQLSTATE is 02000)
>
> **ACTION** – value can either be CONTINUE (execution of the program is continued normally) or GOTO address (execution of a designated program address)

In this chapter you have learnt the primary role of cursors, how triggers work and the importance of handling errors in SQL programming. Learning these advance topics is one step closer in maximizing the potentials of your SQL implementations.

Chapter 11 Clauses and Queries

In this chapter we'll be dealing with clauses and queries. A query, is, simply put, a set of instructions you give in order to change a table within a database. The ones we will be looking at in this chapter are primarily the UPDATE and DELETE queries.

While you should have learned about other queries prior to reading this book, these two are the building blocks of any SQL developer worth their salt.

Both of these queries are very self-explanatory. The UPDATE query will take the information currently within a table, and change it to whatever you desire. The DELETE query is quite like an UPDATE query just with "null" instead of what you wanted to change it to. It will delete any entries that you wish.

It is important to note that while these queries are extremely important, they're also inefficient. You'll learn later on that there are much more efficient ways to do what these queries do, and at a much larger scale.

With that being said, they are still a must-learn for budding developers. They help you learn the fundamental blocks that advanced SQL is based on. After all, every business owner has heard horror stories of developers that only know higher-level material, and low-level techniques become their downfall.

These queries will primarily be useful in debugging and lower-level positions. Otherwise, they're only useful for manually editing smaller tables, at which point you might as well use Excel instead of SQL.

On the other side of the coin, we have the TOP query. The TOP query, rather than actually changing the information inside a table, shows you only specific entries from a table. To be precise, the TOP query will show you the topmost N or topmost N % of a given table.

This is especially useful if you're using SQL for maths or science, in which case it can make recurring certain functions very easy.

Besides that, this chapter will also cover the LIKE and ORDER BY clauses. The LIKE clause is meant to compare different objects/strings while the ORDER BY clause will sort a table in ascending or descending order, as you feel fit.

These are two extremely powerful tools that you'll use throughout your career as a SQL developer, so let's dive right in!

UPDATE & DELETE Query

The UPDATE query in SQL is mainly intended to be used when modifying the records that are already in a table. What's worth noting here is that if you use the WHERE clause together with the UPDATE query, only the rows you selected with the WHERE clause will be updated. If you don't do this, then every row inside the table will be equally affected.

The Syntax for an UPDATE query within a WHERE clause is:

UPDATE name_of_table

SET column01 = value01, column02=value02..., columnN = valueN

WHERE[your_condition];

When using the UPDATE query, you'll be able to combine any N number of conditions by using the two operators you should be familiar with already: the AND and OR operators.

Take this for example:

In the following table, there are customer records listed, and you're trying to update the record.

You can combine N number of conditions using the AND or the OR operators.

```
+--+----------+-----+----------+----------+
| ID | NAME     | AGE | ADDRESS  | SALARY   |
+--+----------+-----+----------+----------+
| 1 | Ilija     | 19 | Uruguay   | 1500.00 |
| 2 | Frank     | 52 | France    | 200.00 |
```

```
| 3 | Jim       | 53 | Serbia     | 8040.00 |

| 4 | Martinia| 54 | Amsterdam| 9410.00 |

| 5 | Jaffar    | 66 | Podgorica  | 55200.00 |

| 6 | Tim       | 33 | Prune      | 1200.00 |

| 7 | Kit       | 24 | England    | 700.00 |

+--+----------+-----+-----------+----------+
```

Let's say you want to update the address of the customer with the ID number 2, you would do it as such:

SQL> UPDATE CUSTOMER

SET ADDRESS = 'Tom_St'

WHERE ID = 2;

Now, the CUSTOMERS table would have the following records −

```
+--+----------+-----+-----------+----------+
| ID | NAME     | AGE | ADDRESS   | SALARY   |
+--+----------+-----+-----------+----------+
| 1 | Ilija     | 19 | Uruguay    | 1500.00 |

| 2 | Frank     | 52 | Tom_St     | 200.00 |

| 3 | Jim       | 53 | Serbia     | 8040.00 |

| 4 | Martinia| 54 | Amsterdam| 9410.00 |

| 5 | Jaffar    | 66 | Podgorica  | 55200.00 |
```

```
| 6 | Tim         | 33 | Prune      | 1200.00 |

| 7 | Kit         | 24 | England    | 700.00  |

+--+----------+-----+----------+----------+
```

Now, if instead, let's say you want to change the salaries and addresses of all your customers, then you won't need to use the WHERE clause. The UPDATE query will handle it all by itself. This can sometimes save quite a bit of time, let's look at the following example:

SQL> UPDATE CUSTOMER

SET ADDRESS = 'Tom_St', SALARY = 1000.00;

Now, CUSTOMERS table would have the following records —

```
+--+----------+-----+----------+----------+
| ID | NAME     | AGE | ADDRESS  | SALARY   |
+--+----------+-----+----------+----------+
| 1 | Ilija    | 19 | Tom_St    | 1000.00 |
| 2 | Frank    | 52 | Tom_St    | 1000.00 |
| 3 | Jim      | 53 | Tom_St    | 1000.00 |
| 4 | Martinia | 54 | Tom_St | 1000.00 |
| 5 | Jaffar   | 66 | Tom_St    | 1000.00 |
| 6 | Tim      | 33 | Tom_St    | 1000.00 |
| 7 | Kit      | 24 | Tom_st    | 1000.00 |
```

+--+----------+-----+-----------+----------+

If you can't really tell where this would be useful, don't worry. There are countless examples from around the corporate world. This will let you replace any given thing in a matter of minutes. While it might not seem practical in a table with 7 people in it, imagine you're Microsoft and instead of 4 columns and 7 rows, you have 50 columns and 7000 rows, that isn't very practical to do by hand now is it?

Now let's take a look at the DELETE query. You can probably imagine what it does. It helps you delete certain records from a table. Now, obviously you don't want your whole table gone, so you should probably use the WHERE clause together with it, so you don't accidentally end up deleting, well, everything. When you use the WHERE clause with the DELETE query, only what you've selected will be deleted. Kind of like clicking on a file and pressing delete on your keyboard.

Let's turn our eyes to the syntax a bit, let's use the customers example again for it.

DELETE FROM name_of_table

WHERE [your_condition];

Similarly to the UPDATE query, you can use this in conjunction with the OR and AND operators to get more complex and precise results. Let's look at the past example we used:

```
+--+----------+-----+-----------+----------+
| ID | NAME | AGE | ADDRESS   | SALARY   |
+--+----------+-----+-----------+----------+
| 1 | Ilija     | 19 | Tom_St   | 1000.00 |
| 2 | Frank     | 52 | Tom_St      | 1000.00 |
| 3 | Jim       | 53 | Tom_St       | 1000.00 |
| 4 | Martinia| 54 | Tom_St | 1000.00 |
| 5 | Jaffar    | 66 | Tom_St   | 1000.00 |
| 6 | Tim       | 33 | Tom_St      | 1000.00 |
| 7 | Kit       | 24 | Tom_st    | 1000.00 |
+--+----------+-----+-----------+----------+
```

Let's say you want to erase a customer. Maybe they stopped shopping at your locale? Moved to a different state? Whatever reason it may be, this is how you could do it, let's say the customer's number is 7.

SQL> DELETE FROM CUSTOMER

WHERE ID = 7;

As you can see, this is quite similar to the UPDATE query, and they really are similar. If you need some help in thinking about the DELETE query, think about it as an UPDATE query that updates with empty spaces (this isn't entirely accurate, but it helps).

Now the customers table would look like this:

```
+--+----------+-----+-----------+----------+
| ID | NAME | AGE | ADDRESS  | SALARY  |
+--+----------+-----+-----------+----------+
|  1 | Ilija       | 19 | Tom_St  | 1000.00 |
|  2 | Frank    | 52 | Tom_St  | 1000.00 |
|  3 | Jim       | 53 | Tom_St  | 1000.00 |
|  4 | Martinia| 54 | Tom_St | 1000.00 |
|  5 | Jaffar   | 66 | Tom_St  | 1000.00 |
|  6 | Tim       | 33 | Tom_St  | 1000.00 |
+--+----------+-----+-----------+----------+
```

As you can see, all that changed is the 7th column is now empty. If you've been wondering how it would look if you hadn't used the WHERE operator, this is how:

```
+--+----------+-----+-----------+----------+
+--+----------+-----+-----------+----------+
```

That's right! Using the DELETE query without a WHERE operator results in an empty table.

Now, hopefully you won't be using the DELETE query too much wherever you end up working, but it can be useful for a variety of things. For example, when your company is moving servers, or simply purging outdated entries.

Like & Order by Clause

The LIKE clause is utilized when you want to compare two different values. This is done using wildcard operators such as the percent sign and the underscore. Now, while these are the only wildcard operators which are used with the LIKE clause, you'll encounter many more throughout this book.

First, the percentage symbol (%) serves to represent 0, 1 or N characters. Meanwhile the underscore (_) is used to represent only a single digit or symbol. You can also choose to combine these two when it suits you.

The syntax for using the percentage and underscore signs is:

1. - SELECT FROM name_of_table

   WHERE column LIKE '%NNNN%'

2. - SELECT FROM name_of_table

   WHERE column LIKE 'NNNN%'

3. - SELECT FROM name_of_table

   WHERE column LIKE 'NNNN_'

4. - SELECT FROM name_of_table

   WHERE column LIKE '_NNNN'

5. - SELECT FROM name_of_table

   WHERE column LIKE '_NNNN_'

So, to summarize, it doesn't matter whether you put the underscore or percentage symbol on one side of the "NNNN" or on both, as long as they're present.

NNNN here can be any string or numerical value, and you can combine any N conditions by utilizing the OR and AND operators.

When it comes to the ORDER BY clause, that is usually utilized when you need to sort the data ascendingly or descendingly. This will be done by basing it off of 1-N columns. Keep in mind though, that some databases have an ORDER BY clause set as ascending by default.

When it comes to the syntax for the ORDER BY clause, it's a bit more complex than those we've looked at so far, so make sure to pay good attention to it. The syntax is:

SELECT list-column

FROM name_of_table

[WHERE your condition]

[ORDER BY column01, column02, .. column0N] [ASC | DESC];

Keep in mind you can use more than a single column with the ORDER BY clause. It's possible to manipulate and access any N columns at the same time. It's important to ascertain that whichever column you're currently sorting is the column that should be in the list-column.

Let us consider the previous customer example once again:

ID	NAME	AGE	ADDRESS	SALARY
1	Ilija	19	Tom_St	1500.00
2	Frank	52	Tom_St	1300.00
3	Jim	53	Tom_St	1200.00
4	Martinia	54	Tom_St	1900.00
5	Jaffar	66	Tom_St	1000.00
6	Tim	33	Tom_St	1000.00
7	Kit	24	Tom_st	1000.00

You might want to sort your customers in ascending order by their names and salary. You might want to do this so you can know which ones pay the most and which pay the least, so you can later make informed decisions about this, you would do it as follows:

SQL> SELECT * FROM CUSTOMER

ORDER BY NAME, SALARY;

If you did this, you would get a result where Jaffar is first, Jim 2nd and so on. Although it would also take salary into consideration, so the list may not be precisely as you would expect.

On the other hand, if you simply wanted to sort by name, that would look like:

SQL> SELECT * FROM CUSTOMER

ORDER BY NAME;

The ORDER BY clause is extremely important to remember, as sorting and order play a heavy hand in many programs.

TOP

The TOP clause in SQL does just what it says on the tin. It will output the top N or N percent of entries from a given table. This can make it useful when organizing data, as most of the time you won't need every single data point.

An important thing to notice here is that not all databases use the TOP clause. MySQL will use LIMIT in its place, doing functionally the same thing as a TOP clause does in regular SQL. Oracle also uses the ROWNUM command to do the exact same thing.

All in all, just remember to check which database you're using before using the TOP clause, as one of its relatives may be more appropriate.

The essential syntax for the TOP clause, with a necessary SELECT statement, is:

SELECT TOP number|percent name_of_column(s)

FROM name_of_table

WHERE [your_condition]

Returning back to the familiar customer example, here's how you would separate the top 3 from the following table:

```
+--+----------+-----+-----------+----------+
| ID | NAME     | AGE | ADDRESS   | SALARY   |
+--+----------+-----+-----------+----------+
|  1 | Ilija    |  19 | Uruguay   |  1500.00 |
|  2 | Frank    |  52 | France    |   200.00 |
|  3 | Jim      |  53 | Serbia    |  8040.00 |
|  4 | Martinia|  54 | Amsterdam|  9410.00 |
|  5 | Jaffar   |  66 | Podgorica |  55200.00 |
|  6 | Tim      |  33 | Prune     |  1200.00 |
|  7 | Kit      |  24 | England   |   700.00 |
+--+----------+-----+-----------+----------+
```

SQL> SELECT TOP 3 * FROM CUSTOMERS;

The output of this would be:

```
+--+----------+-----+-----------+----------+
```

```
| ID | NAME    | AGE | ADDRESS   | SALARY   |
+--+----------+-----+-----------+----------+
| 1 | Ilija    | 19 | Urugu    | 1500.00 |
| 2 | Frank    | 52 | France   | 200.00 |
| 3 | Jim      | 53 | Serbia   | 8040.00 |
+--+----------+-----+-----------+----------+
```

Now, the TOP clause isn't used very often in business. With that being said, it can sometimes be useful when it comes to mathematics and sciences. Many mathematical functions rely on finding the first X numbers of a sequence and doing something to them. You could separate these using a TOP clause with ease.

While it isn't the most useful clause, it is nonetheless necessary to learn in order to progress as an SQL developer.

Conclusion

With this, we have come to the end of this book. I thank you once again for choosing this book.

In today's world, there is a lot of data that is made available to you. If you own a business or want to start a business, you must know how to take care of the data you collect and use that information to improve the functioning of the business. You should also learn to store the information in one location, to ensure that you can access it whenever necessary. Whether you are trying to hold on to the personal information of your customers in one place or you are more interested in putting the sales information in an easy to look at way, you need to have a database that is easy to use.

In this guidebook, we are going to spend some time talking about SQL and how you can use it in a manner that will help you to deal with all your data management needs. SQL is a simple language that can help you analyze your data regardless of the type of business you run. We are going to cover some of the basic information you need to make this system work for you.

There is so much that you can learn about when it comes to SQL and using this system to make your business more successful. This guidebook is going to help you to get started so that you can organize and access your data any time you want to.

COMPUTER PROGRAMMING JAVASCRIPT:

Introduction

If there is anything, I want you to hold at the end of this programming guide for JavaScript is the fact that:

- JavaScript is the HTML and web language
- *It is easy to Learn*

If you can do that, then at the end, you will smile your way to programming for the web. However, your speed in learning JavaScript and other programming language is very dependent on you. If you find yourself struggling, don't feel demoralized rather take a break and reread the material after you have settled down. Remember, this chapter gives you the basics of JavaScript as a beginner to familiarize yourself with the language.

Variables in JavaScript

```
var exam = 50;

var test = 12;

var score = exam * test;
```

In the example above, exam, test, and score are variables given values with the value stored. We can perform various operations in JavaScript including multiplication, subtraction, addition, subtraction, and division. Variables and values can be declared as a number, string, or letter.

```
var name = "insert your name";

var number = '45';
```

From the example, you can enclose string with a single or double quote because they work exactly the same way.

JavaScript Identifiers

Every variable in JavaScript must have a unique name, which is used to identify it. These unique names are called identifiers. Identifiers have certain rules, which include:

- Every identifier must begin with a letter
- They can contain digits (0-9), letters (a-z), dollar signs ($), and underscores (_)
- Reserved words are not accepted
- Variable names are case sensitive
- *An identifier can begin with a dollar sign or underscore.*

Scope of JavaScript Variable

JavaScript allows two types of variable scope, which includes global and local variable scope. A variable is said to be global if it is declared outside the function body. With this, every statement has access to the variable within the same document. However, a local variable scope has its scope within the function. With this, the variable is only available to statements within the same function.

Basic JavaScript on the Browser side

When you hear about JavaScript on the browser side, it refers to the client-side, which means the code is run on the machine of the client – the browser. The browser-side components comprise of JavaScript, JavaScript libraries, CSS, images, HMTL, and whatever files downloaded to the browser.

Browser-Side JavaScript Features

JavaScript is important for the web as it is likely to use it to write programs that execute arbitrary computations. You have the opportunity of writing simple scripts such as the search for prime numbers or Fibonacci numbers. However, in the context of web browser and the Web, JavaScript enables programmers to program with the capability of computing sales tax, based on the information provided by the users through an HTML form.

The truth about JavaScript language is in the document-based objects and browser that the language is compatible with. This may sound complex, however, I will explain the significant capabilities of JavaScript on the browser side along with the objects it supports.

- *Controls the Browser* – There are various JavaScript objects that permit the control of the browser behavior. Furthermore, the Window object support means of popping up dialog boxes that display messages for the users. Additionally, users can also input messages. Besides this, JavaScript doesn't provide a method that gives users the opportunity to directly create and manipulate frames inside the browser window. Notwithstanding, you can take advantage of the ability to make HTML animatedly by creating the particular frame layout you want.
- *Interact with HTML Forms* – another significant part of the JavaScript on the browser side is its capability to work together with HTML forms. The ability comes because of the form element and its objects, which contains Text, submit, select, reset, radio, hidden, password, and text area objects. With these elements, you can write and read the values of the elements in the form.

- Interact with Users – *JavaScript has another feature, which is its ability to define event handlers. Most times, users initiate these events. For instance, when someone moves the mouse through a hyperlink, clicks the submit button, or enters a value. The capability to handle such events is important because programming with graphic interfaces requires an event-driven model.*

In addition to these aforementioned features, JavaScript on the browser side has other capabilities such as:

- Changing the displayed image by using the <img> tag to generate an animation effect and image rollover
- It has a window.setTimeout () method, which allows some block of random source code to be performed in the future within a split of a second
- It streamlines the procedure of working and computing with times and dates

JavaScript Framework

Take a moment and consider creating a web application and websites like constructing a house. In building a house, you can decide to create every material you need to start the house from scratch before building without any plans. This will be time-consuming and won't make much sense. One thing you may likely do is to buy pre-manufactured materials such as bricks, woods, countertops, etc. before assembling them based on the blueprint you have.

Coding is like taking it upon yourself to build a house. When you begin coding a website, you can code all areas of the site from scratch without. However, there are certain website features, which gives your website more sense by applying a template. Assuming you want to buy a wheel, it will make to look for one that you can reinvent. This is where JavaScript Frameworks come to the scene.

JavaScript Framework is a collection of JavaScript code libraries, which gives website developers pre-written JavaScript codes to use for their routine programming tasks and features.

You can also refer to it as an application framework, which is written in JavaScript where the developers can manipulate the functions of these codes and reuse them for their own convenience. They are more adaptable for website designing, which is why many developers use them in building websites.

Top JavaScript Framework

Vue.js

This is one of the JavaScript frameworks, which was created to make the user interface development more organized. Created by Evan You, it is the perfect JavaScript framework for beginners because it's quite easy to understand. Furthermore, it focuses on view layers. With Vue.js, you don't need Babel. A Babel is a transpiler with the responsibility of converting JavaScript codes to the old version of ES5 that can run in all browsers. All templates in the Vue.js framework are valid HTML, which makes their integration easier. If you want to develop lightweight apps as a beginner, it is best to start with Vue.js.

Next.js

Another important JavaScript Framework is the Next.js framework, which is an additional tool for server-side rendering. The framework allows developers to simplify the developing process similar to the Vue.js framework.

The features of this JavaScript Framework include page-based client-side routing and automatic splitting of codes. The framework also comes with a full CSS support, which makes styling of the user's interface easier for beginners and professionals.

Ember.js

This framework, which was created a few years ago, is among the most sought JavaScript framework in the web industry. Famous companies such as LinkedIn, Heroku, and Kickstarter use the Ember.js framework in the design of their websites. It also comes with regular updates and offers a complete feature for users. Unlike the Vue.js framework, it is effective for developers who want to develop complex web applications. The focus of this framework is on scalability, which allows developers to use it for both web and mobile projects.

Angular

Google released this JavaScript Framework in 2010 with regular updates and improvements taking place. It is one of the most sought after the framework for many developers because it simplifies the development of websites and apps. For other developers, it is because of its ability to create dynamic web apps.

Chapter 1.   Use of a Global Variable as a Cache

In cases where a small app is to be created and in which one will incur an overhead when trying to integrate the app with a third-party mechanism, these can easily be handled inside the Node.js app, and this should be executed in the mode for a single thread.

In this mode, that is, the single threaded mode, a single application is executed at a time, and this is responsible for handling all of the requests sent to it. This is similar to what happens with desktop allocations. Other web apps developed by use of other programming languages for web development such as PHP, Ruby, and Python do not function in this manner. A global variable can be defined in this case, and this will become accessible to all of the requests that we make. This needs to be considered with a lot of concern.

For this mechanism to be achieved, one can create global variables of the necessary type and then a manipulation mechanism should be added inside this function. This will make it persist inside all of our requests.

Consider the code given below, which shows how this can be done effectively:

```javascript
'use strict';

//this should be the cache for the js file

var  cache = {};

exports.someMethod = function(data){

/*The business logic should be added here*/

//setting the cache

cache[key] = val;

//retrieving the cache

cVal = cache[key];

//deleting the cache

delete cache[key];

/*The business logic should be added here*/
```

Logging without the use of a third-part Library

Whenever we want to print temporary information, we use the *"console.log"* so as to log in to the system. In the deployment stage, there are good libraries which can be used for this purpose. Some people hate the idea of using third-party libraries so as to log into their node.js app. However, this has been solved by the provision of an alternative. With the native support, one can be availed with a very decent mechanism for logging into their node.js app.

The Node.js's console object provides us with different levels of logging. These need to be used in the way they were designed to be used, otherwise, you will have trouble in using them. When you want to execute your node app, you should specify a logfile in which you will need to have everything written. This can be done as shown in the command given below:

$node app.js > mylogfile.log

After executing the above command, you will be set. The information about logging will be kept in the above file, and you will be in a position to view it later when you want to gain insight into some useful or critical information. It is also good for security purposes.

Whenever we want to print something on our console terminal, we should use the format given below:

console.log("The value of my variable should be:"+xyz);

This should only work for items which are single valued. If it was a json object, then we could have used *"console.log(xyz)."* This shows that the + operator does not work in this case.

About the use of "*"

It is recommended that this should not be used in a production dependency. Most people use it in their package.json file so as to specify the version or to use the "*" so that they can always have the latest package with them. One should have all of their packages updated to the latest version, since it might have some bug fixes, several improvements, and even new features added to it. However, this is only good for those whose product is in the development stage but has not reached the production stage.

In case of compatibility errors, fixing it will be easy. This is shown in the code given below:

//other of this:

"dependencies": {

"clustered-node": "*"

//use the following

"dependencies": {

"clustered-node": "~0.0.10"

For those who use such notations in a production environment, this is very risky. This is because one will not know when and which package might break and crash the application, which is possible. This is why it should only be used in the development phase, but once the product gets into the production environment, you should switch to dependencies which are based on a specific version. This should be done during the deployment phase of the product.

Asynchronous looping

Whenever we use the AsyncJS/underscoreJS in asynchronous flow looping/control, we get very useful and essential support. For those who know more about the callback concept, they can use it in a very native manner. If you are not interested in using this library in a simple task, then use the mechanism given in the code below. Here is the code:

```
var iterate = function(items, it){

console.log("Now handling: "+it);

//async methods

someAsyncMethod(parameterss,          function
callback(){

if(items.length <= it)return;

return iterate(items, ++it);

})

};

var items = [5, 6, 7, 8];

iterate(items, 0);
```

Chapter 2. The Basics of JavaScript Function and Scope

Let's see now, normally when we are talking about a 'function' what's the first thing that comes to your mind? Obviously an activity right?

The functions in JavaScript also work in a similar manner. Functions are blocks of codes which are required to be executed over and over again by the program. A Function is used to perform a particular task. A Function can contain any number of arguments and statements; they can even have none. Depending on how the structure is coded, it may or may not return any value to the user.

A Function is declared in the following manner:

Function name(   ) { /*code blocks to be executed*/}

To start the Function, we start with the function keyword, and then we add the *name,* and parentheses. To finish the function, we place the code blocks to be executed in a curvy brackets.

You can also put the function in a named variable-

var jam = function() {/* code blocks to be executed*/}

Below are few examples of how you can execute a function-

i)   **This is the example of the most basic function**

```
varsayHello = function(person, greeting) {

var text = greeting + ` , `+ person;

console.log(text);

};

Say Hello (` Jessica` , ` Hello`);
```

ii)   **This is the example of a function that returns a value**

```
var greet = function (person, greeting)

{

var writing = greeting + ` , ` + person ;

return function () {console.log(text); };

}

console.log(greet('Richard' ,' Hello"));
```

iii)   **Sometimes, you might want to use a nested function. (Note: A nested function is a function within another function.)**

```
varsayHi = function( person, greeting) {
```

```
var text = greeting + ',' + person;

return function() {console.log (text);}

};

var greeting = greet( ' Richard' , 'Hello');
greeting();
```

Self-Executing Anonymous Function
Programmers have always been looking for the most advanced and clever methods available to improve their programming experience and ways to make it more accessible and easier for them. This resulted in the creation of the*Self-Executing Anonymous function*.

The core purpose of the self-executing anonymous function is to create a JavaScript function and then immediately execute it upon its conception.

This makes it much easier for a programmer who isworking on large scale programs. Likewise, it will help you to code without creating a messy global namespace.

A basic Self-Executing Anonymous Function Would be-

It is very important that you understand how to use this type of function if you plan on programming complex code in JavaScript. Using the Self-Executing Anonymous Function can produce some great code that is easy to use. As an example, the

JQuery library is designed to make using JavaScript on websites much easier. It does this by wrapping the entire library in one large self-executing function.

Typeof Operator

You might run into a situation where you need to determine the type of variable that you are working in JavaScript. You won't have call Sherlock Holmes to find that! Instead, you can simply use the 'typeof' operator to determine the type of any specific value. In other words, the typeof operator is used to evaluate the type of the operand.

EX-

Varmyvar=0

alert(typeofmyvar) *//alerts "number"*
Number isn't the only type of operand that can be detected. It can also be: string, Boolean, object, null, and not defined.

Scope

Scope is the accessibility of a variable.
A good understanding of Scope is necessary when it comes to debugging because it allow you to know what variable from which code block is causing the problem.

The simple rule here is that whenever you declare a variable inside a scope, it will only be recognized by the statements that are inside that scope; the statements that are outside the scope will not acknowledge its existence and so that variable will not work.

Another way to look at this is to imagine your entire code as a hotel with specific functions and sections of code as hotel rooms. The hotel rooms represent the private scopes of the code, while the common areas represent the global scope. A person in one hotel room cannot see or use what is in another hotel room. Staff who work in the hotel (and the global scope) also don't have access to private hotel rooms unless they have specific permission. Meanwhile, guests can go through the common areas and make use of any object there.

Thus, you can see how scope can affect how your code runs. If you need two different functions to access the same variable, you need to ensure that they both have access to it. One key way to ensure that the necessary variables have access to is to make your variables globally accessible.

There are two possible alternatives if you want your variables to become globally accessible.

The first thing you can do is to declare the variable outside the scope of your given piece of code, this will allow any functions in your program to be able to call it and recognize it.

The other thing you can do is to declare the variables inside your scope without using the word var. If the same variable was not defined at the beginning of the code outside the scope of the piece of code in question, then the variable will act similarly to a global one.

Ex-

```
var foo = 'hello';

var talkHello = function() {

console.log(foo);

};

talkHello(); // logs 'hello'

console.log(foo); // also logs 'hello'
```

As you can see, the variable foo is declared outside of the function talkHello. That means that foo is a global variable and any function will be able to access it, so when the function talkHello calls it, it is accessible.

The following example is contradictory to the first example. This shows that a code block that was written outside the scope is not being able to recognize the variable.

```
var talkHello = function() {

var doo = 'hello';

console.log(doo);

};
```

talkHello(); // logs 'hello'

console.log(doo); // gives an empty log.

In this example, the variable doo is called inside the function talkHello. This creates a private variable that is only accessible to the function, hence when the command console.log(doo) attempts to access it, it returns a null value.

Some Common Mistakes to Avoid

☐ Always remember that a variable is only accessible by the functions within a specific scope, outside of that scope the variable is invalid.

Practice

☐ Explain what a scope is and how the variables are affected by it.

☐ Write a simple program to illustrate the functionalities of a:-

a) Simple Function

b) A Function with returnable value

c) A function passed as a parameter (Argument)

☐ Explain the concept of a Self-Executing Anonymous Function and give an example.

Chapter 3. Loop Constructs

Looping is another fundamental programming construct that most programming languages support. Fundamentally, looping is used to execute the same set of statements iteratively until a condition remains true. JavaScript supports four types of looping constructs.

While Loop

The most basic loop construct is the while loop. This type of a loop executes the set of statements inside the while loop until the expression for the while is true. As soon as the expression becomes false, the while loop execution terminates. The syntax for implementation of while is given below –

while (expression){

//Statements of the while block

}

Sample implementation of the while loop is given below –

<html>

<body>

<script type="text/javascript">

```
<!--

var c = 0;

document.write("Loop begins...");

while (c < 5){

document.write("Value  of  c:  "  +  c  +  "<br
/>");

c++;

}

document.write("Loop Terminates!");

//-->

</script>

<p>Change the values of the looping variable to see
how things change</p>

</body>

</html>
```

The output of the code upon execution is shown in
the image given below.

Do...While Loop

Another looping construct is the do...while loop. The
condition's validity is checked at the end of the loop.
So, this loop is that it executes at least once. This
type of a loop executes the set of statements inside
the do...while loop until the expression for the while

is true. As soon as the expression becomes false, the while loop execution terminates. The syntax for implementation of while is given below –

do{

//Statements of the while block

}while (expression)

Sample implementation of the do...while loop is given below –

```
<html>

<body>

<script type="text/javascript">

<!--

var c = 0;

document.write("Loop begins...");

do{

document.write("Value of c: " + c + "<br />");

c++;

} while (c < 5)

document.write("Loop Terminates!");

//-->

</script>
```

<p>Change the values of the looping variable to see how things change</p>

</body>

</html>

The output of the code upon execution is shown in the image given below.

For Loop

The most commonly used looping construct is the 'for' loop. The for loop integrates the looping variable initialization, condition checking and looping variable update in the for statement. The syntax for implementation of while is given below –

for(init; expression; update){

//Statements of the for block

}

Here, init is the initialization statement and expression is the condition, which is to be tested. Lastly, the update is the expression that updates the looping variable. Sample implementation of the while loop is given below –

<html>

<body>

<script type="text/javascript">

```
<!--

var c;

document.write("Loop begins...");

for(c=0; c<5; c++){

document.write("Value of c: " + c + "<br
/>");

}

document.write("Loop Terminates!");

//-->
```

</script>

<p>Change the values of the looping variable to see how things change</p>

</body>

</html>

The output of the code upon execution is shown in the image given below.

For...In Loop

This loop is typically used with objects. The loop uses a variable of the object and loops through until the value of the property associated with the object variable is exhausted. In other words, this loop works around object properties. The syntax for the implementation of the for...in loop is as follows –

```
for (variable in object){

//Statements inside the for...in loop block

}
```

Sample implementation to demonstrate the working of the for...in loop is given below.

```
<html>

<body>

<script type="text/javascript">

<!--

var demoObject;

document.write("Properties of the Object: <br /> ");

for (demoObject in navigation) {

document.write(demoObject);

document.write("<br />");

}

document.write ("Loop Terminated!");

//-->

</script>

<p>Change the object to see how the result changes</p>

</body>
```

</html>

Controlling the Loop

Although, once the loop starts, it terminates only when the expression stated for condition holds false, there are certain ways in which the developer can control the loop. There may be situation where you might want to terminate the loop in between execution if a special case occurs or you may want to start a new iteration on the occurrence of a scenario. In order to control and implement all these conditions, JavaScript has provided continue and break statements.

Break Statement

Whenever this keyword is encountered in a JavaScript code, the loop immediately terminates and execution is shifted to the statement that comes right after the closing bracket of the loop. In order to understand the working of break statement, let us take an example,

```
<html>

<body>

 <script type="text/javascript">

<!--

var a = 5;
```

```javascript
document.write("Loop          Begins...<br          />
");
while (a < 30)          {
if (a == 5){
break;
}
a = a + 1;
document.write( a + "<br />");
}
document.write("Loop terminates!<br /> ");
//-->
</script>
```

```html
<p>Change the value of a to see how the loop execution is modified</p>
</body>
</html>
```

The output of the code is shown in the image given below.

Continue Statement

When this statement is encountered in a loop, the rest of the loop statements are ignored and the control is shifted to the next iteration of the loop.

With that said, it is important to understand that the next iteration is execution only if the loop condition is found true. In case, the loop expression is found false, loop execution is terminated.

The sample code given below demonstrates the use of continue statement.

```
<html>

<body>

<script type="text/javascript">

<!--

var a = 0;

document.write("Loop        begins<br        />
");

while (a < 9){

a = a + 1;

if (a == 4){

continue; // skip rest of the loop body

}

document.write( a + "<br />");

}

document.write("Loop terminates!<br /> ");

//-->
```

```
</script>
```

<p>Change the value of a to see how the result changes!</p>

```
</body>
```

```
</html>
```

The output generated after execution of this code is illustrated in the image shown below.

Labels for Controlling Loop Flow

While the break and continue statements can redirect flow of control around the boundaries of the loop construct, they cannot be used to transfer control to precise statements. This is made possible in JavaScript with the use of labels. A label is simply an identifier followed by colon, which is placed before the statement or code block. The following code demonstrates the use of labels.

```
<html>
```

```
<body>
```

```
<script type="text/javascript">
```

```
<!--
```

```
document.write("Loop begins!<br /> ");
```

```
loop1: for (var i = 0; i < 3; i++) {
```

```
document.write("Loop1:    "   +   i   +   "<br
/>");
```

```
loop2: for (var j = 0; j < 3; j++) {

if (j > 3 ) break ; // Quit the innermost loop

if (i == 2) break loop1; // Do the same thing

if (i == 4) break loop2; // Quit the outer loop

document.write("Loop2: " + j + " <br />");

}

}

document.write("Loop terminates!<br /> ");

//-->

</script>

</body>

</html>
```

The output of the code has been illustrated in the image given below.

Chapter 4.   An Introduction to ES6

Some of the key features of ES6 are:

Arrows - Arrows is a function shorthand using the `=>` syntax. It is syntactically similar to the related feature in C#, Java 8 and CoffeeScript.

Classes - There is support for classes, inheritance, super calls, instances and static methods.

Template strings - Template strings are used for constructing strings.

Modules - There is language-level support for component definition modules.

Data structures - There is support for Maps, Sets, WeakMaps and WeakSets.

Most modern browsers have support for ES6. If you want to try out ES6 code, there are a few online editors that can help you do so. Below are two of my favourites. Both of them provide the next generation of JavaScript compilers.

https://jsbin.com

https://babeljs.io/

Let's now look at some simple examples of ES6 JavaScript code. In these examples we are going to use JS Bin to enter and run the code.

Example 55: The following program is a simple example of ES6 scripting.

```
let num1=5;
        console.log(num1);
```

The following should be noted about the above program:

The 'let' command is used to assign values to variables.

We then output the value of the variable using the 'console.log' command.

With this program, the output is as follows:

5

We can also declare constants using the 'const' keyword. Let's look at an example of this.

Example 56: The next program is an example of ES6 scripting using constants.

```
const num=6;
let num1=5;
        console.log(num);
        console.log(num1);
```

With this program, the output is as follows:

6

5

We can also define functions in ES6. Let's look at a simple example.

Example 57: The program below is an example of ES6 scripting using functions.

```
var start=function()

        {
const num=6;

let num1=5;

        console.log(num);
        console.log(num1);
        }
        start();
```

With this program, the output is as follows:

6

5

Decision Making and Loops

ES6 has support for the following Decision Making and Loop commands.

If statement - This is used to evaluate an expression and then execute statements accordingly.

If...else statement - This is used to evaluate an expression and then execute statements accordingly. Then execute another set of statements if the Boolean expression evaluates to false.

Nested if statements - This is useful to test multiple conditions.

Switch...case statement - This evaluates an expression, matches the expression's value to a case clause, and executes the statements associated with that case.

For loop - Here a set of statements are executed 'n' number of times.

While loop - Here a set of statements are executed until a condition remains true.

Do...while loop - Here a set of statements are executed until a condition remains true. The difference from the while loop is that one execution of the statements will always occur.

Let's look at some examples of these statements.

Example 58: The following program is an example of loops (if else) in ES6.

```
var start=function()
        {
const num=6;

let num1=5;

  if(num<7){
console.log("The value is less than 7");}

  else{
console.log("The value is greater than 7");

  }

        }
        start();
```

With this program, the output is as follows:

"The value is less than 7"

587

Example 59: The next program is an example of loops (for loop) in ES6.

```
var start=function()
        {
  for(x=0;x<5;x++)
   {
     console.log(x);
   }
        }
        start();
```

With this program, the output is as follows:

0

1

2

3

4

Example 60: This program is an example of loops (while loop) in ES6.

```
var start=function()
        {
  let x=0;
  while(x<5)
   {
```

```
    console.log(x);
    x++;
  }
 }
 start();
```

With this program, the output is as follows:

0

1

2

3

4

Classes

ES6 also has the support for classes. A class can be defined as follows:

```
class classname
 {
 constructor(parameters)
 {
//Assign values to the properties
 }
// More methods
 }
```

Where:

'classname' is the name assigned to the class.

We have a constructor that is called when an object is created.

The constructor can take in parameters. These parameters can be used to assign values to the properties of the class.

We can then have more methods defined in the class.

Let's look at an example of a simple class in ES6.

Example 61: The following program shows how to use classes in ES6.

```
var start=function()
         {
  class Rectangle
    {
       constructor(height, width) {
      this.height = height;
      this.width = width;
    }
       Display()
       {
         console.log(this.height);
         console.log(this.width);
       }
     }
  var newrect=new Rectangle(3,4);
  newrect.Display();
```

```
        }
        start();
```

The following things can be noted about the above program:

First we define a class called 'Rectangle'.

It accepts 2 parameters, namely 'height' and 'width'.

This can be used to define the properties of 'height' and 'width' for the class.

We then create a 'Display' method that can be used to display the properties of the class.

With this program, the output is as follows:

3

4

Collections

ES6 also has the support for collections, such as the map collection. As an example, if we want to set the value of a map collection, we would use the 'set' method as shown below:

```
mapname.set(key,value);
```

Where:

- 'mapname' is the name of the map.
- 'key' is the key assigned to the element.

- 'value' is the value associated with that key.

Let's look at an example of using maps with ES6.

Example 62: The program below shows how to use maps in ES6.

```
var start=function()
        {
var map = new Map();

map.set('keyA','valueA');

map.set('keyB','valueB');

map.set('keyC','valueC');

console.log(map.get("keyB"));

        }
        start();
```

With this program, the output is as follows:

valueB

Chapter 5. Form

Form takes information from the web page visitors and sends it to a back-end application such as PHP script, CGI or ASP Script. HTML forms are used to collect data from visitors on a site. Forms are important for membership registration on a website, online shopping, or a job application form. For instance, during user registration, information such as email address, name, credit card, and so on would be collected. Then required processing would be performed on the sent data based on the specific logic contained in the back-end application. There are different available form elements such as the text area fields, radio buttons, drop-down menus, checkboxes, etc.

Form structure

<form>

HTML form is created with the <form> element. This tag must carry the action attribute at all times and would occasionally have an id and method attribute too.

Action

An action attribute is required for every <form> element. The value of the action attribute is the URL it contains for the page on the server which retrieves the information contained in the submitted form.

Method

Forms go to the back-end application in two ways. They "get" or "post".

Get

The GET method enables value from the form to return to the end of the specified URL in the action attribute. The GET method is perfect for data collection from the web server. The technique ensures parameter stores in the browser cache. There are limits of the quantity of information this method can send. Do not use the GET method while dealing with sensitive information such as passwords or credit card numbers because of the process that displays in the browser's address bar is visible to everyone.

Post

The POST method sends values through the HTTP headers. The POST method is perfect when the form contains sensitive information such as passwords and when visitors need to upload files. Parameters do not get saved in web server cache or browser history. The POST method is safer than the GET method.

Id

This value specifies a unique identity for an HTML form from other elements on the page.

Text input

The <input> tag enables the creation of different form controls. The type of attribute value determines the type of input created.

type="text"

With the type attribute value of the text, it creates a single line of text.

Name

When information is entered into a form by the user, the server demands to know what value the control

594

data holds. For instance, in a login form, the server wants to know which declares the username and the password. Each form control needs the name attribute, and the attribute value recognizes the form control which is sent together with the information entered into the server.

Max length

The max length attribute can be used to determine the number of characters entered into a text field. The value of the max length attribute is the number of characters that it holds.

Password input

type="password"

The <input> tag of type "password" creates a way for users to input a password safely. The element presents a one-line plain text editor control replacing characters with a symbol such as the ("*") or a dot (" • ") which cannot be read and keeps the text secured.

Name

This attribute specifies the name of the password input which is transferred to the server including the password visitors enter.

```
<body>

<form action="http://www.alabiansolutions.com/login.php">

<p>Username:

<input type="text" name="username" size="15"maxlength="30" />

</p>
```

```
<p>Password:
<input     type="password"     name="password"
size="15"maxlength="30" />
</p>
</form>
</body>
```

Textarea

A multi-line input is created with the <textarea> element. The <textarea> is not an empty element compared to other input elements, therefore, it should contain an opening and closing tag. Texts that surface between the opening <textarea> and closing </textarea> elements will be displayed in the text box when the page is loaded.

```
<form action="process.php">
<p>What did you think of this gig? </p>
<textarea name="comment"></textarea>
</form>
```

Radio Button

The <input type="radio"> element represents a radio button. It is used to create several selectable options.

Name

To be treated as a group, the value of the name attribute must correspond with the radio group because selecting any other radio button in the same group deselects the first selected button. A lot of radio groups can be created on a page as long as each has its name.

Value

The value attribute indicates the unique value connected with each selected option. Values of each button in a group should be different so the server can recognise the selected option.

Checked

The checked attribute specifies the selected value when the page loads. This attribute should be used by one radio button in a group.

<body>

Pizza Size:

<label>

<input type="radio" name="size" value="small"/>Small</label>

<label>

<input type="radio" name="size" value="medium"/>Medium

</label>

<label>

<input type="radio" name="size" value="large"/>Large

</label>

</body>

Checkbox

Checkbox is used to select and deselect one or more options.

type="checkbox"

Users are permitted to select or deselect one or more options in response to a question.

Name

This attribute is transferred to the server alongside the value of the option(s) selected by the user. The name attribute value must remain the same for all buttons when users have to respond to questions with options for answers in the checkboxes form.

Value

When a checkbox is checked, this attribute specifies the value sent to the server.

Checked

The checked attribute specifies the box that should be checked when the page is being loaded.

<body>

Pizza Toppings:

<label>

<input type="checkbox" value="bacon" />Bacon

</label>

<label>

<input type="checkbox" value="extra cheese" />Extra Cheese

</label>

<label>

<input type="checkbox" value="extra cheese" />Onion

</label>

```
</body>
```

Dropdown list box

A select Box, also known as the Drop-down list box enables the user to choose one option from a drop-down list. A drop-down list box is created with the <select> tag, and it consists of two or more <option> tags.

Name

The name attribute shows the form control name, which is being sent to the server together with the value selected by the user.

<option>

This element is used to indicate the options for a visitor. The text in-between the opening <option> and closing </option> elements will be displayed to the visitor in a drop-down box.

Value

The <option> tag utilises the value attribute to specify the value sent to the server together with the control name when the option is selected.

Selected

This attribute is used to specify the option that should be automatically selected when the page loads.

```
<body>

<label>Phones:

<select name="devices">

     <option value="techno">Sony</option>

   <option value="infinix">Infinix</option>
```

```
                                    <option
value="samsung">Samsung</option>

        <option    value="sony"   selected>Choose   a
device</option>

</select>

</label>

</body>
```

File input box

The file input box is used to enable users to upload a file on a web page. A file could be an image, audio, PDF or video.

```
type="file"
```

This input produces a box, a text input lookalike accompanied with a browse button. When the browse button is selected, a window pops up which enables users to select a file from their computer in order to be uploaded on the site.

```
<form action=" process.php" method="post">

<p>Upload your songs in MP3 format:</p>

<input type="file" name="user-song" /><br />

<input type="submit" value="Upload" />

</form>
```

```
type="submit"
```

This attribute is used when a user needs to submit a form.

```
<body>

<form action="process.php" method="post">
```

```html
<p>Subscribe to our email list:</p>
<input type="text" name="email" value="email" />
<input type="submit" value="subscribe" />
</form>
</body>
```

Name

It can use a name attribute although it's not necessary.

Value

The value attribute is used to influence the appearance of the text on a button. It is advisable to designate the words that appear on a button because buttons default value on some browsers is "Submit query" and this can be inappropriate for forms.

Reset button

type="reset"

This button is used to erase all inputs by the user.

```html
<input type="reset" value="Reset" />
```

Image button

An image can be used for the submit button. The type attribute must be given the value of the image. The SRC attribute can also be provided

```html
<form action="http://www.websitename.com/subscribe.php">
<p>Subscribe to our email list:</p>
<input type="text" name="email" />
```

```
<input      type="image"      src="subscribe.png"
width="100" height="20"
```

```
alt="Subscribe" />
```

```
</form>
```

Button Tag

The <button> tag specifies a button that can be clicked. Texts, content, or images can be inserted into the <button> element. The buttons created with the <input> element is different from buttons created with the <button> tag. The <button> element attribute type should always be specified.

```
<button type="submit">Click Me! </button>
```

Fieldset Element

Longer forms benefit a lot from the <fieldset> element. It is used to group form controls that are related together.

```
<form method="post">
```

```
<fieldset>
```

```
    <legend>Contact Details</legend>
```

```
<label>Address:<br>
```

```
                    <input           type="text"
name="text"><br>
```

```
    </label>
```

```
    <label>Phone Number:<br>
```

```
 <input type="number" name="number"><br>
```

```
    </label>
```

```
<label>Email:<br>
```

```
<input type="email" name="email"><br>
    </label>
</fieldset>
</form>
```

Legend element

The <legend> element appears immediately after the opening <fieldset> tag and consists of a caption which identifies the motive of that form control group.

```
<form method="post">
 <fieldset>
<legend>Contact Details</legend>
<label>Address:<br>
<input type="text" name="text"><br>
</label>
<label>Phone Number:<br>
<input type="number" name="number"><br>
</label>
<label>Email:<br>
                    <input          type="email" name="email"><br>
</label>
 </fieldset>
</form>
```

Label element

The label tag can be used to caption a form control so that users would know what should be entered into the area.

```html
<form >
        <label for="male">Male</label>
<input type="radio" name="gender" id="male" value="male"><br>
        <label for="female">Female</label>
 <input type="radio" name="gender" id="female" value="female"><br>
        <label for="other">Other</label>
 <input type="radio" name="gender" id="other" value="other"><br><br>
 <input type="submit" value="Submit">
</form>
```

Chapter 6. Iframe and Multimedia

Iframe

The <iframe> element can be used to embed web pages into your web page.

Iframe embeds: Google Map

Google map can be embedded into your webpage using the iframe tag.

<iframe

src="https://www.google.com/maps/embed?pb=!1m18!1m12!1m3!1d3963.341775346873!

2d3.3422253148425853!3d6.604381995223933!2m3!1f0!2f0!3f0!3m2!1i1024!2i768!4f1

3.1!3m3!1m2!1s0x103b8d7c33eb87b3%3A0xfc23c9556f669273!2sWebsite+Name!5e0!3m2!1sen!2sng!4v1516009132030" width="600" height="450"

frameborder="0"   style="border:0" allowfullscreen></iframe>

Iframe embeds: YouTube

<body>

<iframe width="450" height="400"

src="https://www.youtube.com/embed/MhPGaOTiK0A"

frameborder="0" allowfullscreen></iframe>

</body>

Multimedia in HTML5

HTML5 enables users to embed video or audio using the native HTML tags. The browser will give users control to play the file if it supports it. Both audio and video tags are new features and can be used on the recent version of browsers. Popular video formats are .mp4, .m4v, Flash Video {.flv}, Audio Video Interleave {.avi} etc.

The video element:

A video player can be embedded using the video element for a specific video file. Those attributes are used to customize the player: preload, loop, auto play, poster, auto and controls.

Preload

The preload attribute instructs the browser on what action to take when the page loads. one of these three values can occur:

None: The video should not load automatically when the page loads until the user clicks play.

Auto: when the page loads the browser should download the video.

Metadata: this means that information such as first frame, size, track list and duration should be received by the browser.

Src

The path to the video is specified by this attribute.

Poster

This attribute enables users to direct an image to be displayed while the video downloads or until the user decides to play the video.

Width, height

The size of the player is specified with these attributes.

Controls

This attribute specifies that the browser should provide its own controls for playback when used.

Autoplay

This attribute indicates that the file should play automatically when used.

Loop

This attribute specifies that the video should start playing again from the beginning the moment it ends when utilized.

Multiple video formats

HTML5 enables users state multiple sources for audio and video elements so that browsers can use any one that works for them.

```
<video      poster="images/calvin.jpg"      controls
preload="none" width="450" height="420">

<source src="calvin.mp4" type="video/mp4" />

<source src="calvin.webm" type="video/webm" />

<source src="calvin.ogv" type="video/ogv" />

<p>Calvin Harris music video</p>

</video>
```

The audio element

Embedding an audio player into a page for a particular audio file is done using the audio element. Different attributes can be used to customize the player, attributes such as auto play, controls, loop and preload.

Autoplay

This is a boolean attribute. If utilized, the audio will play automatically and continue without stopping.

Loop

The loop attribute is also a boolean attribute, and it states that the audio will restart over and over again every time the audio ends.

```
<body>

<audio      src="avicii.mp3"      controls="true"
autobuffer="true"></audio>

</body>
```

Control

Audio controls are inserted using the control attribute, and it includes controls like pause, play, and volume. The <source> element enables the user to indicate alternative audio files that the browser could choose from. The browser would recognize the first organized format. Texts between the <audio> and </audio> elements will be displayed in browsers that do not recognize the <audio> element.

<audio src="audio/test-audio.ogg" controls autoplay>

    <p>This browser does not support our audio format. </p>

</audio>

Multiple audio formats

<audio controls autoplay>

<source src="audio/test-audio.ogg" />

<source src="audio/test-audio.mp3" />

<p>This browser does not support our audio format. </p>

</audio>

Chapter 7. The Document Object Model

The document object refers to your whole HTML page. After you load an object into the web browser, it immediately becomes a document object, which is the root element representing the html document. It comes with both properties and methods. The document object helps us add content to the web pages.

It is an object of the window, which means that having:

window.document

Is the same as having?

document

DOM Methods

DOM methods are the actions that you can perform on the html elements. The **DOM** properties are the values of the **HTML** elements which one can set or change. The following are the document object methods:

1. write("string")- it writes a string to a document.
2. writeln("string")- it writes a string to a document with a new line character.
3. getElementById()- gives the element with the specified id.
4. getElementsByName()-gives all the elements with the specified name.

5. getElementsByTagName()-gives all the elements with the specified tag name.
6. getElementsByClassName()-gives all the elements with the specified class name.

Accessing Field Values

The DOM is a good way of getting the values of an input field. Many are the times you will need to get input from a user. This can be done using the following property:

document.formname.name.value

Where:

- document- is the html document representing our root element.
- form name- is the name of the form with the fields.
- field name- is the name of the input text.
- value- is a property which returns the value of input text.

Consider the following example:

```
<html>

<body>

<script type="text/javascript">

    function readValue(){

                                                var name=document.memberform.memberName.value;

        alert("Hi: "+name);

    }

</script>
```

```
<form name="memberform">

    Enter        Name:<input        type="text"
name="memberName"/>

    <input    type="button"    onclick="readValue()"
value="Click Here"/>

</form>
```

```
</body>
```

```
</html>
```

When you run the code, it will give you the following simple form:

Just enter your name in the input field and click the Click Here button. See what happens.

You will get an alert box with your name and some text appended to it:

We simply created a simple form with an input text field. The method READVALUE() helps us get the value that we enter into the field. Consider the following line:

```
var
name=document.memberform.memberName.value;
```

The MEMBERNAME is the name given to the text field in the form, and these must match, otherwise, you will not the right results.

getElementById()

Other than the name, we can also get the element by its id. This can be done using the DOCUMENT.GETELEMENTBYID() method. However, the input text field should be given an id.

For example:

```html
<html>
<body>
<script type="text/javascript">
    function computeSquare(){
    var x=document.getElementById("integer").value;
    alert(x * x);
    }
    </script>
    <form>

    Enter an Integer:<input type="text" id="integer"
name="myNumber"/><br/>

    <input type="button" value="Compute Square"
onclick="computeSquare()"/>

    </form>
</body>
</html>
```

The code should give you the following simple form upon execution:

Enter a number in the input field and click the Compute Square button.

This should return the square of the number in a popup box as shown below:

In the example, we have defined the COMPUTESQUARE() method which helps us get the square of a number entered in the input text field. Consider the following line:

var x=^{document}.getElementById(*"integer"*).value;

In the line, we have used the GETELEMENTBYID() method which takes the id of the input text field as the argument. The method helps us get the value typed in the input text field using its id.

getElementsByName()

The DOCUMENT.GETELEMENTSBYNAME() method can help us get an element by its name. The method has the syntax given below:

^{document}.getElementsByName(*"name"*)

The name is needed.

Example:

<html>

<body>

<script type=*"text/javascript"*>

   function getNumber()

   {

                                           var options=^{document}.getElementsByName(*"option"*);

       ^{alert}("Total Options:"+*options.length*);

   }

   </script>

   <^{form}>

     Yes:<input type=*"radio"* name=*"option"* value=*"yes"*>

No:<input   type=*"radio"*   name=*"option"* value=*"no"*>

<input   type=*"button"*   onclick=*"getNumber()"* value=*"Available Options"*>

</form>

</body>

</html>

Upon execution, the code returns the following:

Click the Available Options button and see what happens. A popup window will be shown as follows:

We have created two radio buttons with options YES and NO. Note that these two input types have been given the same name, that is, OPTION.

Consider the following line:

var options=document.getElementsByName(*"option"*);

The line helps us count the number of elements with the name OPTION. This should be **2** as shown in the output.

getElementsByTagName()

The   DOCUMENT.GETELEMENTSBYTAGNAME() property returns the elements with the tag name which is specified. It takes the syntax given below:

document.getElementsByTagName(*"name"*)

For example:

<html>

<body>

```
<script type="text/javascript">
function allparagraphs(){
var pgs=document.getElementsByTagName("p");
        alert("Total paragraphs are: "+pgs.length);
}
</script>
    <p>This is a paragraph</p>
    <p>This is a paragraph</p>
    <p>This is a paragraph</p>
    <p>This is a paragraph</p>
<button                 onclick="allparagraphs()">Total Paragraphs</button>
</body>
</html>
```

The code returns the following upon execution:
Click the Total Paragraphs button and see what happens.
You will see the following popup:

This means that the code was able to count the number of paragraphs that we have.

The main logic lies in the following line:

```
var pgs=document.getElementsByTagName("p");
```

We have passed the tag **"p"** as the argument to our method, and the tag represents a paragraph. There are three elements with the tag **"p"**, so the output should be **4** paragraphs.

Here is another example:

```html
< html>
<body>
<script type="text/javascript">
function countheader2(){
var h2count=document.getElementsByTagName("h2");
        alert("Total    count    for    h2    tags:
        "+h2count.length);
}
function countheader3(){
var h3count=document.getElementsByTagName("h3");
        alert("Total    count    for    h3    tags:
        "+h3count.length);
}
</script>
<h2>A h2 tag</h2>
<h2>A h2 tag</h2>
<h2>A h2 tag</h2>
<h2>A h2 tag</h2>
<h3>A h3 tag</h3>
<h3>A h3 tag</h3>
<h3>A h3 tag</h3>
<h3>A h3 tag</h3>
<h3>A h3 tag</h3>
```

```
<button onclick="countheader2()">Total h2</button>
<button onclick="countheader3()">Total h3</button>
```

</body>

</html>

The code returns the following output upon execution:

We have a total of **4 h2** tags and a total of **5 h3** tags. Click the Total **h2** button and see what happens.

You should get the following popup box:

Click the Total **h3** button and see what happens.

You should get the following popup box:

innerHTML

This property can be used for addition of a dynamic content to an html page. It is used on html pages when there is a need to generate a dynamic content like comment form, registration form, etc.

 Consider the following example:

<html>

<body>

<script type="text/javascript" >

function displayform() {

     var   data="Username:
<input type='text' name='name'>
Comment:
<textarea rows='6'

```
                cols='45'></textarea><br><input
                type='submit' value='Contact us'>";
document.getElementById('area').innerHTML=data;

  }

</script>

<form name="form1">

<input      type="button"      value="Contact      us"
onclick="displayform()">

<div id="area"></div>

</form>

</body>

</html>
```

The code returns the following button upon execution:

Click the button and see what happens. You will get the following:

What we have done is that we are creating a contact us form after the user has clicked a button. Note that the html form has been generated within a div that we have created and given it the name AREA. To identify the position, we have called the DOCUMENT.GETELEMENTBYID() method.

innerText

We can use this property to add a dynamic property into an HTML page. Note that when this property is used, your text is interpreted as a normal text rather than as html content. A good application of this is when you need to write the strength of a password based on its length, write a validation message etc.

For example:

```html
<html>
<body>
<script type="text/javascript" >
function validatePass() {
var message;
if(document.form1.userPass.value.length>5){
message="good";
}
else{
message="poor";
}
document.getElementById('area').innerText=message;
}
</script>
<form name="form1">
<input type="password" value="" name="userPass" onkeyup="validatePass()">
Strength:<span id="area"> Pasword strength </span>
</form>
</body>
</html>
```

The code returns the following upon execution:

Just begin to type the password and see what happens to the text on the right of the input field as you type. If you type less than 5 characters for the password, the message will change to poor as shown below:

Continue to type the password until you have more than 5 characters. You will see the message change to good as shown below:

That is how powerful this property is.

Animations

With JavaScript, we can animate elements. We can use JavaScript to move elements such as **<img />**, **<div>** etc. on a page depending on an equation. The following are the common methods used for animations in JavaScript:

1. <u>setTimeout(method, time)- this method will call the METHOD after someTIME in milliseconds.</u>
2. setInterval (method, time)- the method will call the METHOD after TIME milliseconds.

With JavaScript, one can set some attributes of the **DOM** object such its position on the screen. The position of the object can be set using TOP and LEFT attributes.

This is demonstrated below:

<u>// Set the distance from the left edge of the screen.</u>

object.style.left = distance measures in points or pixels;

or

<u>// Set the distance from the top edge of screen.</u>

object.style.top = distance measures in points or pixels;

Manual Animation

In the following example, we will be animating the image towards the right:

```html
<html>

<body>

<script type="text/javascript">

        var image = null;

        function init(){

        image = document.getElementById('myImage');

        image.style.position= 'relative';

        image.style.left = '0px';

        }

        function moveImage(){

        image.style.left = parseInt(image.style.left) + 10
+ 'px';

        }

        window.onload =init;

    </script>

    </head>

    <body>

    <form>
```

```
<img id="myImage" src="house.jpg" />
```

```
<p>Click the button to move the image</p>
```

```
<input    type="button"    value="Move    Image"
onclick="moveImage();" />
```

```
</form>
```

```
</body>
```

```
</html>
```

You should use the correct name of your image in the following line:

```
<img id="myImage" src="house.jpg" />
```

In my case, I have a .jpg image named HOUSE. When I run the code, it returns the following:

Click the **"Move Image"** button. The image should move to the right with each click. This is shown below:

Consider the following line in the script:

```
image = document.getElementById('myImage');
```

We are getting the image using its **ID**, then it is assigned to the IMAGE variable. The INIT() method helps us set the initial position of the image on the window. The method will be called when the window is being loaded. The MOVEIMAGE() function will move the image towards the right by **10 pixels** after every click. To move the image towards the left, the value should be set as negative. The animation, in this case, is manual as we have to click a button.

Automated Animation

To automate the process of animating an element, we can use the SETTIMEOUT() function provided by JavaScript.

Example:

```html
<script type="text/javascript">
        var image = null;
        var animate ;
        function init(){
                image = document.getElementById('myImage');
                image.style.position= 'relative';
                image.style.left = '0px';
        }
        function animateImage(){
                image.style.left = parseInt(image.style.left) + 10 + 'px';
                animate = setTimeout(animateImage,20);
        }
        function stopAnimation(){
                clearTimeout(animate);
                image.style.left = '0px';
        }
        window.onload =init;
    </script>
    </head>
    <body>
```

624

```
<form>
      <img id="myImage" src="house.jpg " />

      <p>Click the Animate button to launch
animation</p>

      <input type="button" value="Animate"
onclick="animateImage();" />

      <input type="button" value="Stop"
onclick="stopAnimation();" />

      </form>
```

The code returns the following upon execution:

Click the "Animate" **button. The animation should start. When you click the Stop button, the animation will stop.**

The ANIMATEIMAGE() method is calling the SETTIMEOUT method which sets the position of the image after every 20 milliseconds. This will result in the animation of the image. The STOPANIMATION() method helps in clearing the timer which is set by the SETTIMEOUT() method. The object, which is the image, is set back to its initial position.

Rollover

We can use a mouse image to rollover an image in JavaScript. Once you move the mouse over the image, it will change to another image.

Example:

```
<html>
```

```
<body>
```

```
<script type="text/javascript">
```

```
if(document.images){

    var img1 = new Image();

    img1.src = "ps.jpg";

    var img2 = new Image();

    img2.src = "house.jpg";

    }

  </script>

 </head>

 <body>

  <p>Move mouse over to rollover</p>

<a                                  href="#"
onMouseOver="document.img.src=img2.src;"

onMouseOut="document.img.src=img1.src;">

  <img name="img" src="nicsam.jpg" />

  </a>

</body>

</html>
```

We have used the IF statement to check whether the image exists or not. We have the used the IMAGE() constructor so as to preload some new object named IMG1. The same has also been done to preload the second image, IMG2. The SRC is given the name of the image stored externally. The # helps to disable the link so that a URL is not opened once it is clicked. The method ONMOUSEOVER is called once the mouse cursor is moved over the image. The ONMOUSEOUT method will be called once the mouse cursor is moved out of the image.

Chapter 8. Clauses

GROUP BY clause

The GROUP BY clause gathers in all the rows that have data in the specified columns. It will also allow the aggregate functions we talked about earlier to be performed on the columns as well. The best way to explain this is with an example:

- SELECT column1,
- SUM(column2)
- FROM "list-of-tables"
- GROUP BY "column-list";

GROUP BY clause syntax:

Let's assume that you want to retrieve data on the maximum salaries paid for each separate department. Your statement would look like this:

- SELECT max(salary), dept.
- FROM employee
- GROUP BY dept;

This statement is going to show the highest salary in each unique department by name. In short, the name of the person in each department who earns the most will be displayed along with their salary and the department they work in.

HAVING clause

The HAVING clause is the one that lets you specify conditions on rows for each specific group, in other words, certain rows to be selected based on the specific conditions you input. The HAVING clause should always follow the GROUP BY clause if you are using it:

HAVING clause syntax:

- SELECT column1,
- SUM(column2)
- FROM "list-of-tables"
- GROUP BY "column-list"
- HAVING "condition";

The HAVING clause is best shown in an example so let's assume that you have a table that contains the names of your employees, the department they work in, their salary and their age. Let's say you want to find the average salary for each employee in each separate department, you would enter:

- **SELECT DEPT.,
  AVG(SALARY)**

- **FROM employee**
- **GROUP BY dept;**

But, let's now assume that you only want to calculate the average and display it if their salary is more than $20,000. Your statement would look like this:

- **SELECT DEPT,
  AVG(SALARY)**

- **FROM employee**
- **GROUP BY dept**

- **HAVING AVG(SALARY)
  > 20000;**

ORDER BY clause

The ORDER BY clause is optional and it lets you display your query results in an order that is sorted

– either ascending or descending – based on whichever columns you choose to order the data by. *ORDER BY* clause syntax:

- SELECT column1, SUM(column2) FROM "list-of-tables" ORDER BY "column-list" [ASC | DESC];
- [ ] = optional

This statement is going to show the employee ID, department, their name, age and salary from the table you specify – in this case, the employee_info table – where the department is equal to SALES. The results will be listed in ascending order, sorted by salary:

- ASC = Ascending Order - default
- DESC = Descending Order
- For example:
- SELECT employee id, dept, name, age, salary FROM employee info WHERE dept = 'Sales' ORDER BY salary;

If you want to order data from multiple columns, each column name must be separated with a comma:

- SELECT employee_id, dept, name, age, salary
- FROM employee_info
- WHERE dept = 'Sales'
- ORDER BY salary, age DESC;

Chapter 9. Operators, Data Types and Other Priorities

JavaScript Calculations

All programming languages allow you to perform calculations. You can use JS, in a sense, as a replacement pocket calculator. For example, enter the following:

```
"use strict";

console.log(3 + 4);
```

***Listing 5* accompanying_files/03/examples/c alc.js**

As expected, you get *7* as your result.

You can see a few key JS concepts just in this very small, simple example. *3 + 4* is an EXPRESSION. Expressions are one of the most important concepts in JS. Expressions characteristically have a RETURN VALUE — in this case, the number *7*.

In turn, you can use return values in different places in your code, e. g. as an argument to a function call. Or to put this another way, JavaScript replaces expressions by their (return) values.

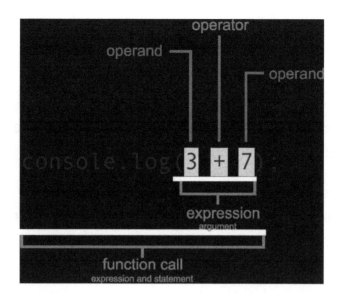

Expressions

Expressions in Firefox Web Console

You can also enter expressions directly into Firefox Web Console. Try entering *3 + 4* in the input line (next to the double arrow ") ().

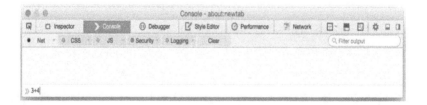

Entering expressions directly in console — input

After you confirm your input with Return, the console will immediately display the return value ().

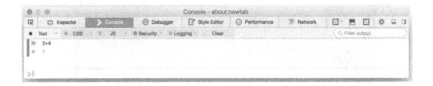

Entering expressions directly in console — output

FYI, you can also use Shift-Return to input a multi-line statement, i. e. a single statement which runs over multiple lines. The entire statement is executed only after you hit return.

Alternatively, you can also select parts of expressions in Scratchpad and examine these using **Inspect** (Ctrl-I / Cmd-I). As you see in , Scratchpad displays the result of *4 * 2* as *value: 8* in the side panel to the right.

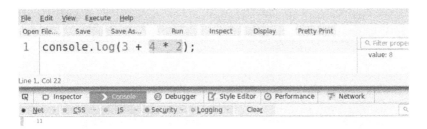

Inspect a selected (partial) expression in Scratchpad

Notation

From now on, we'll often point out a value returned by some expression or which appears at the console.

To do this, we'll insert a comment in the code and show the value in front of a => — the so-called FAT ARROW.

Example

3 + 4 // => 7

console.log(3 + 4 * 2); //=> 11

JavaScript as a Pocket Calculator: Arithmetic Operators

In addition to multiplication and addition operators, JS has corresponding operators for the arithmetic operations of **subtraction, division** and **modulus**. All of these operators fall under the group of so-called ARITHMETIC OPERATORS:

Symbol	Operation
+	Addition
-	Subtraction
*	Multiplication
/	Division

%	Modulus — remainder of an integer division
**	Exponentiation (ECMAScript 2016+)

Table *Arithmetic operators*

Example

3. *5 + 4* returns *9*

4. *5 - 4* returns *1*

5. *5 * 4* returns *20*

6. *5 / 4* returns *1.25*

7. *10 % 3* returns *1* since 10 - 3 * 3 = 1.

8. *5 ** 4* returns *625* since 5 * 5 * 5 * 5 = 625 .

Exercise 3: 2000 Seconds

How many minutes and remainder seconds are there in 2000 seconds? Use *console.log* to print out the answer.

Tips: The easiest way to solve this exercise is to use the modulus operator. Right now, we haven't taught you how to remove decimal places; we'll come back to that later.

Characters and Strings

Have you noticed anything about how numbers and text are coded differently? The *"Hello world"* at the beginning of the previous lesson was written out in quotation marks, while numbers were not. A text element is written out within quotation marks, and actually involves stringing or linking individual characters together — giving us the programming term STRING to indicate such text.

Two Types of Quotation Marks

You may use both single quotes or double quotes to delimit a string, but the marks at the beginning and at the end of the string must be the same.

Example

"Some text string" is allowed

'Some text string' is also allowed

"Some text string' is invalid

Most JS developers consistently use double quotes, and only use single quotes in exceptional cases, e. g. when they need to use double quotes within a string to indicate literal wording.

Coding Guidelines

You should normally use double quotes to delimit strings.

Determining Length

Sometimes you need to know how long a string is — i. e. how many characters are in it. As you do more and more development, you'll come across many situations where length is important.

For example, blogs, lists of products, and similar items sometimes provide a text preview which only shows part of the entire text. Before generating this preview, the length of the entire text item must first be measured to see whether the text actually needs to be shortened.

So at this point, we'd like to introduce you to the string property LENGTH. You can have a string return this property by typing **.length** after the string.

```
"length matters - sometimes".length // => 26
```

Then pack your statement into a *console.log* so you can see the response you need on the console:

```
"use strict";

console.log("length matters -
sometimes".length);
```

Listing 6 accompanying_files/03/examples/l ength.js

Exercise 4: Lucky Numbers & Name Codes

Do you know about lucky numbers and code names? Here's an interesting way to come up with a name code:

> Multiply the length of your first name (including your middle name(s) if you want) by the length of your last name and print out the result in the console. (Just to let you know, these are the numbers we got: 40 and 30.)

Literals: They Say What They Mean

Now that you've been introduced to strings and numbers, there's another important concept we need to tell you about: Basically, any value — whether a string or a number — which is specified literally in your code is known as a (you guessed it) *literal*. Literals always have a fixed value.

Examples

6. 42

7. "house"

8. "green"

9. 5.47

10. 1998

11. "Please enter your name"

Number & String Data Types

JavaScript literals have a so-called DATA TYPE. As the term implies, a data type specifies what kind of data the literal represents, and in turn its possible values.

Up to this point, we've used the following data types:

Data Type	Permissible Values / Meaning	Example of Literal
String	Any text	"Hello"
Number	Any positive or negative number	246.5

Table *String & number data types*

JavaScript encodes strings in so-called UTF-16 character format [ECMA-262]. An encoding format is responsible for how characters are represented digitally. UTF-16 makes it possible for you to use a wide variety of special characters as well as specific letters from different languages (e. g. German umlauts, accented French characters, etc.).

The value range for numbers is also limited. However, as long as you don't carry out any astronomical calculations, you should be safe.

It's easy to find out the data type of a literal — just use the JavaScript operator *typeof*. *typeof* returns a string which tells you the literal's data type.

Examples

```
"use strict";

console.log(typeof 3764);        // => number

console.log(typeof "beautiful JS");  // => string

console.log(typeof 27.31);       // => number
```

Listing 7 **accompanying_files/03/examples/type.js**

Exercise 5: Hmmm...So What are You Really?

What is the data type of the following literal?

"42"

Chapter 10. Document Object Model (DOM)

The document object is an object that is created by the browser for each new HTML page. When it is created, JavaScript allow us access to a number of properties and methods of this object that can affect the document in various ways, such as managing or changing information. As a matter of fact we have been continuously using a method of this object, document.write(), in order to display content in a web page. Nevertheless, before exploring properties and methods we will first take a look at the Document Object Model (DOM).

Fundamental DOM Concepts

We are aware that when the web browser receives an HTML file it displays it as a web page on the screen with all of the accompanying files like images and CSS styles. Nevertheless, the browser also creates a model of that web document based on its HTML structure. This means that all the tags, their attributes and the order in which they appear is remembered by the browser. This representation is called the Document Object Model (DOM) and it is used to provide information to JavaScript how to communicate with the web page elements. Additionally, the DOM provides tools which can be used to navigate or modify the HTML code.

The Document Object Model is a standard defined by the World Wide Web Consortium (W3C) that is used by most browser developers. To better understand the DOM, let us first take a look at a very simple web page:

```
<!doctype html>

<html>

<head>

<meta charset="utf-8">

<title>Party Schedule</title>

<style type="text/css">

.current {

color:red;

}

.finished {

color:green;

}

</style>

</head>

<body>

<h1 id="partytitle">Party Plan</h1>

<ul id="partyplan">

  <li id="phase1">20:00 - Home warm-up</li>
```

```
<li id="phase2">22:00 - Joe's Bar</li>

<li id="phase3">00:00 - Nightclub 54</li>

</ul>

</body>

</html>
```

On a web page, tags wrap around other tags. The <html> tag wraps around the <head> and <body> tags. The <head> tag wraps around tags such as <title>, <meta> and <script>. The <body> wraps around all content tags such as <p>, <h1> through <h6>, <ul>, <table> and so on.

This relationship between tags can be represented with a tree structure where the <html> tag acts as the root of the tree, while other tags represent different tree branch structures dependent on the tag hierarchy within the document. In addition to tags, a web browser also memorizes the attributes of the tag as well as the textual content within the tag. In the DOM each of these items, tags, attributes and text, are treated as individual units which are called nodes.

Image 26. Tree structure of an HTML document

In the tree structure for our basic HTML page the <html> element acts as a root element, while the <head> and <body> elements are nodes. In defining this relationship we can also refer to <html> as the parent node, and the <head> and <body> elements as child notes. In turn, both the

<head> and <body> elements contain child nodes and so on. When we reach an item that contains no other child node we terminate the tree structure at that node, also known as a leaf node.

Selecting Document Elements

With the DOM structure in place, JavaScript can access the elements within the document in several different ways, dependent on whether we want to select individual or multiple elements. In all approaches we first have to locate the node representing the element we need to access and subsequently use the content, child elements and attributes of that node.

Selecting Individual Elements

To select individual elements we most commonly use the getElementById() method. This method will let us select an element with a particular ID attribute applied to its HTML tag. This method is the most efficient way to access an element if we follow the presumption that the ID attribute is unique for every element within the page. In the following example we will access the element whose ID attribute has the value 'phase1':

var firststop =
document.getElementById("phase1");

By using the getElementById() method on the document object means that we are searching for the element with this ID anywhere on the page. Once the 'phase1' element is assessed, which in our case is the first <h1> element, the reference to this node is stored in the firststop variable and we can use JavaScript to make changes. As an example we will assign the attribute class with the value 'current' to this element. We will include this code in a <script> tag in the <head> section of our document.

```
var firststop =
document.getElementById("phase1");

firststop.className = "current";
```

Image 27. Changing the style of a page element

> *Note:* In some browsers we have to either put the <script> tag before the closing </body> tag or in an external .js file in order for the code in this chapter to work.

If we want to collect the text from a node, we can use the textContent property. More importantly, we can also use the textContent property to change the content of the node. In the following example we will first select the element that has the value 'partytitle' in its id attribute and assign it to the title variable. Then we will effectively change the text of this element by changing the textContent property of the title variable. Let us add the following lines to our JavaScript code:

```
var title = document.getElementById("partytitle");

title.textContent = "Party Schedule";
```

Image 28. Changing the content of a page element

Selecting Group Elements

While sometimes selecting an individual element will be sufficient, other times we may need to select a group of elements. For example, we might need to select all <li> tags on a page, or all elements that share a class attribute. In these cases JavaScript offers the following two methods:

- *getElementsByTagName()* – a method which will let us select every instance of a particular tag.
- *getElementsByClassName( )* – a method that retrieves all elements that share a particular class name.

Selecting a group of elements means that the method will return more than one node. This collection of nodes is known as a NodeList and will be stored in an array-like item. Each node will be given an index number, starting with 0, while the order of the nodes will be the same order in which they appear on the page. Although NodeLists look like arrays and behave like arrays, semantically they are a type of object called a collection. As an object, a collection has its own properties and methods which are rather useful when dealing with a NodeList.

The following example will select all <li> elements and assign their node references to the schedule variable.

```
var schedule =
document.getElementsByTagName("li");
```

If we want to access each element separately, we can use an array syntax. For example:

var item1 = schedule[0];

var item2 = schedule[1];

var item3 = schedule[2];

However, when we select a group of items we usually want to interact with the whole group. As an example, let us assign the class attribute with the "finished" value to all <li> elements. For this purpose we can use a loop to go through each element in the NodeList.

```
var schedule =
document.getElementsByTagName("li");
for (var i = 0; i < schedule.length; i++) {
schedule[i].className = "finished";
}
```

Image 29. Changing the class attribute for all <li> elements

Similarly to working with arrays, when working with collections we can use the length property to determine the size of the collection. We can then use this information in a for loop in order to effectively go through every NodeList item and assign the "finished" class attribute.

We can use exactly the same logic for the getElementsByClassName() method. We will get a NodeList stored in a collection with each node having an index number. Like with the getElementByTagName() method, we can access individual items and manage the collection through its object properties and methods.

Traveling Through the DOM

When we use any of the previously discussed methods to select an element node, we can also select other elements in relation to this elements. This type of relative selection is considered as an element property.

previousSibling & nextSibling

The previousSibling and nextSibling properties refer to adjacent elements on the same DOM level. For example, if we select the second <li> element with the id value "phase2", the "phase1" <li> element would be considered a previousSibling, while the "phase3" <li> element would be nextSibling. In the case where there is no sibling, (ex. the "phase1" element has no previousSibling), the value of this property remains null.

In the following example we select the <li> element which has "phase2" as a value for its id attribute and we change the class attribute for both the selected element and its previous sibling.

var secondstop = document.getElementById("phase2");

var prevstop=secondstop.previousSibling;

secondstop.className = "current";

prevstop.className = "finished";

Parents & Children

We can also travel to different levels of the DOM hierarchy using the selected element as a starting point. If we want to move one level up we can use the parentNode property. For example, if we have the second <li> element selected we can refer to its parent element, the <ul> element, with the following syntax:

```
var secondstop =
document.getElementById("phase2");
```

```
var upperelement = secondstop.parentNode;
```

Alternatively, if we want to move one level down, we can use either the firstChild or the lastChild property. In the following example we have selected the <ul> element with "partyplan" as a value for its id attribute. Using the firstChild property we refer to the first <li> element of this list, while with the lastChild property we refer to the last <li> element of this list.

```
var plan = document.getElementById("partyplan");
```

```
var child1 = plan.firstChild;
```

```
var child2 = plan.lastChild;
```

Adding and Managing Content

Until this point we discussed how to find elements in the DOM. The more interesting aspect are the approaches to managing content within the DOM.

Changing HTML

We already talked about the textContent property, but this property retrieves only text values and ignores the subsequent HTML structure. If we want to edit the page HTML we have to use the innerHTML property. This property can be used on any element node and it is capable of both retrieving and editing content.

**var liContent =
document.getElementById("phase1").innerH
TML;**

When retrieving the HTML from the <li> element with "phase1" as a value for its id attribute, innerHTML captures the whole content of the element, text and markup, as a string variable. If we apply the same syntax for the <ul> element, the innerHTML property will capture all of the <li> items.

We can also use the innerHTML property to change the content of the element. If this content contains additional markup, these new elements will be processed and added to the DOM tree. For example, let us add the <em> tag to the first <li> item in the party list:

```
var firstStop = document.getElementById("phase1");

firstStop.innerHTML = "<em>20:00 - Home warm-up</em>";
```

Image 30. Adding an <em> element with content to the first list item

DOM Manipulation

A more direct technique to managing document content is to use DOM manipulation. This is a 3-step process that uses the following methods:

- *createElement()* - The process begins by creating a new element node with the createElement() method. This element node is stored in a variable and it is not yet a part of the DOM.

- *createTextNode()* - The process continues by creating a new text node with the createTextNode() method. Like in the previous step, this text node is stored in a variable and it is not a part of the document.

- *appendChild()* - The final step is adding the created element to the DOM tree with the appendChild() method. The element will be added as a child to an existing element. The same method can be used to add the text node to the element node.

As an example let us create a new element that we will add to the existing party list. We will use the createElement() method and add this element to the newPlan variable.

var newPlan = document.createElement("li");

Following, we will create a new text node and add its content as a value to the newPlanText variable.

var newPlanText = document.createTextNode("04:00 - Back to home");

We can now assign the content of the text node to the newPlan element by using the appendChild() method.

newPlan.appendChild(newPlanText);

Finally, we would like to add this element to the list. We will use the getElementById() method to select the list through its "partyplan" id, and apply the appendChild() method to attach the newPlan element to the list.

document.getElementById("partyplan").appendChild(newPlan);

The complete syntax is as follows:

```
var newPlan = document.createElement("li");

var newPlanText =
document.createTextNode("04:00 - Back to
home");
newPlan.appendChild(newPlanText);
document.getElementById("partyplan").appendChil
d(newPlan);
```
   Image 31. Adding a new <li> element

Using a similar process we can also use DOM manipulation to remove an element from the page. As an example let us remove the <h1> element which acts as the main page heading. We will first select the element through its id attribute with "partytitle" as its value and store that element node in a variable.

**var removeHeading =
document.getElementById("partytitle");**

Next, we will need to find the parent element which acts as a container for the <h1> element, which in this case is the <body> element. We can either select this element directly, or use the parentNode property of the previously selected element. In either case we will need to store the parent element in another variable.

```
var containerForHeading =
removeHeading.parendNode;
```

Finally, we will use the removeChild() method on the parent element in order to discard the element that we want removed from the page.

```
containerForHeading.removeChild(removeHeading)
;
```

The complete syntax is as follows:

```
var removeHeading =
document.getElementById("partytitle");

var containerForHeading =
removeHeading.parentNode;

containerForHeading.removeChild(removeHe
ading);
```

Image 32. Removed heading

Chapter 11. Events (Not the Kind You Celebrate)

If you can finish the new chat feature by tonight, we'll throw an office party to celebrate its release. Nothing fancy, just some drinks, good music and a little something to eat ...

The chat code is now stored in a separate JavaScript file and is also a little cleaner. But Marty's not completely happy, there's still something missing...

Of course, visitors to the website shouldn't have to program JS to highlight chat members — highlighting should change automatically based on the input in the search box.

In order for that to happen, the code needs to react to user input. Your browser provides so-called EVENTS for just that purpose (no, we don't mean events like weddings or parties — unfortunately).

Browser Events

Any exertion of influence by a user, no matter how small, is considered by your browser to be an event. An event can be almost anything, including:

6) <u>clicking on a button</u>

7) <u>moving your mouse over an image</u>

8) <u>releasing an input key</u>

9) <u>leaving an input field using your mouse or by tabbing</u>

10)   <u>finger gestures on a touch screen, e. g. zoom</u>

There're also events which aren't triggered directly by users, and are triggered instead through occurrences like network requests or files which have finished loading. But first, we'll concentrate only on those events directly related to user behavior.

Dealing With Events as They Come Up: Event Handlers

<u>Preliminary Measures</u>

First, try a small experiment in your console. The event you're interested in is a user releasing a key while typing in an input field. Look in the chat HTML document and you'll find the input field (<u>INPUT</u>

element) within a DIV element with the ID
member_search:

```
<div
id
member_search
<input
type
text
placeholder
...Find a member...
/>
</div>
```

First, let's select the field using $('#MEMBER SEARCH INPUT'). You'll get back the INPUT element as a return value in the console. Move your cursor over the element in the console and you'll see that it's the right field.

Now, we'll bind an event to that field. To do this, we'll use the method ADDEVENTLISTENER. That method is available on almost every HTML element object.

$('#member search input').addEventListener(...);

ADDEVENTLISTENER requires two arguments. The first argument is the EVENT TYPE, in the form of a string. The event type we should use in this case is 'KEYUP', or releasing a key.

$('#member search input').addEventListener('keyup', ...);

ADDEVENTLISTENER's second argument must be a function — this will be executed by your browser when the specified event occurs. In this case, we'll just use a simple function to make sure the process is working:

() => alert(1)

FYI, the function you register on an event is called an EVENT LISTENER or EVENT HANDLER, and it's responsible for processing the event you specify.

And now our statement is complete — let's test it out in the console:

$('#member search input').addEventListener('keyup', () => alert(1));

If you go to the member search input box and type in a character, an alert box with the alert 1 will appear as soon as you release the key. Of course, this function isn't very useful yet. And maybe clicking away alert boxes is making you a little irritated — but at least now you know how event handlers work. Mission accomplished!

Putting Everything Together

Now comes the tough part — you need to combine your existing code for highlighting and for event registration into one complete program.

Delete the call HIGHTLIGHTCHATMEMBERS('ERT'); from your JS file. Instead, your KEYUP event should now trigger the function call:

$('#member_search input')

  .addEventListener('keyup', () =>

  hightlightChatMembers('ert'));

And actually, as soon as you type a key in the search box, the highlighting changes. However, instead of permanently highlighting the string 'ERT', we want to use the actual input. But how can we do that?

Once again, we'll need to use the input element object. We can retrieve it by using the selector $('#MEMBER_SEARCH_INPUT'), then query it for the value input by the user. We'll find that value in the property VALUE, i. e. $('#MEMBER_SEARCH INPUT').VALUE. You'll learn more about VALUE and other properties in **lesson 6**.

Putting it all together, we get the following statement:

$('#member_search input')

 .addEventListener('keyup', () =>

 hightlightChatMembers($('#member_search input').value));

Which then gives us the following overall code:

1

"use strict";

2

3

4

```
const highlightChatMembersBy =
partOfMemberName => {
5
    chatMembers()
6
        .filter(member =>
7
            doesMemberMatch(partOfMemberName,
member))
8
        .forEach(highlight);
9
};
10

11

const doesMemberMatch = (partOfMemberName,
memberElement) =>
12
    memberElement.innerHTML.toLowerCase()
```

```
13
        .includes(partOfMemberName.toLowerCase());
14
15
  const chatMembers = () => $$("#chat members
li");
16
  const highlight = el =>
el.classList.add("highlighted");
17
18
  const $ =
document.querySelector.bind(document);
19
  const $$ =
document.querySelectorAll.bind(document);
20
  NodeList.prototype. proto = Array.prototype;
21
22
```

```
    $("#member_search_input")

23

    .addEventListener("keyup", () =>

24

    highlightChatMembersBy($("#member_search
input").value));

25
```

Listing 16 accompanying_files/05/examples/highlig
ht_chat_members_1_event/highlight_chat_membe
rs.js

Enter different strings and experiment a little with
your current implementation. What do you notice?

Guard Clauses: Protection for Your Functions

*Oops — I just found a bug. If I search for a chat
member, suddenly* all *of them are highlighted.*

*Could you fix that? As it is, we can't possibly put the
highlight feature online.*

Okay, here's the problem — although the program
is highlighting the matching members, it's not

removing that highlighting again when the search string is updated.

Instead of going through the trouble to find out what highlighting we need to remove, it'd be a lot simpler just to remove all highlighting, then highlight only those chat members who match the search. To do this, we'll need some additional code which removes the corresponding CSS class from all members:

```
const removeHighlightsFromAllChatMembers = () =>
 chatMembers().forEach(removeHighlight);
const removeHighlight = el => el.classList.remove('highlighted');
```

FYI, it's not a problem that a few LI elements with chat members don't have the class *highlighted* at all — in that case, nothing will be removed.

Order the two functions according to their level of detail. In addition, we still need to add a call to the new function REMOVEHIGHLIGHTSFROMALLCHATMEMBERS. To do this, we recommend you create a higher-level function called

UPDATEHIGHLIGHTINGOFCHATMEMBERS, which first removes all highlights (REMOVEHIGHLIGHTSFROMALLCHATMEMBERS) then marks the matching chat members (HIGHTLIGHTCHATMEMBERSBY):

```
const updateHighlightingOfChatMembers = partOfMemberName => {

 removeHighlightsFromAllChatMembers();

 hightlightChatMembersBy(partOfMemberName);

};
```

Now we just need to add the new function UPDATEHIGHLIGHTINGOFCHATMEMBERS to the event handler in place of the function HIGHTLIGHTCHATMEMBERSBY, which was only responsible for highlighting. We then get the following code:

1

```
"use strict";
```

2

3

4

```
const updateHighlightingOfChatMembers =
partOfMemberName => {
```

5

```
    removeHighlightsFromAllChatMembers();
```

6

```
    highlightChatMembersBy(partOfMemberName);
```

7

```
};
```

8

9

```
const removeHighlightsFromAllChatMembers = ()
=>
```

10

```
    chatMembers().forEach(removeHighlight);
```

11

12

```
const highlightChatMembersBy =
partOfMemberName => {
```

13

```
        chatMembers()
14
        .filter(member =>
15
        doesMemberMatch(partOfMemberName, member))
16
        .forEach(highlight);
17
};
18
19
const doesMemberMatch = (partOfMemberName, memberElement) =>
20
    memberElement.innerHTML.toLowerCase()
21
        .includes(partOfMemberName.toLowerCase());
22
```

```
23
  const chatMembers = () => $$("#chat_members
li");
24
  const      highlight      =      el      =>
el.classList.add("highlighted");
25
  const    removeHighlight    =    el    =>
el.classList.remove("highlighted");
26
27
  const                $                =
document.querySelector.bind(document);
28
  const                $$                =
document.querySelectorAll.bind(document);
29
  NodeList.prototype.  proto   = Array.prototype;
30
31
```

```
  $("#member_search_input")
```

32

```
  .addEventListener("keyup", () =>
```

33


```
updateHighlightingOfChatMembers($("#member_s
earch_input").value));
```

34

Listing 17 accompanying_files/05/examples/highlig ht_chat_members_2_remove/highlight_chat_mem bers.js

The code from **listing 17** works ... almost. It works except for the small glitch that all members are selected in case of blank input. But the empty string occurs in every string!

We can suppress this behavior just by adding code at the beginning of the function HIGHTLIGHTCHATMEMBERSBY to check whether PARTOFMEMBERNAME is empty. In case of an empty string, the function just needs to refuse to work. Add a RETURN to make the function exit prematurely.

```
if (partOfMemberName === "") return;
```

Code like this, which runs before the main body of a function is actually executed to make sure the values of the arguments passed to the function make sense, are called <u>guard clauses</u>or just GUARDS. They protect functions from invalid input values.

```
const hightlightChatMembersBy = partOfMemberName => {
  if (partOfMemberName === "") return;
  chatMembers()
    .filter(member => doesMemberMatch(partOfMemberName, member))
    .forEach(highlight);
};
```

Listing 18 The function highlightChatMembersBy with a guard

The code from **listing 18** finally behaves like it should. But before you run to Marty to bring him the good news, let's take a little time to add a couple of improvements. Your maintenance programmer will thank you for that someday!

Making a Stunning Entrance Using init

The event registration code is still just kind of out there, with no motivation — it would be better to put it into its own function. This will give us a number of advantages — the code will be reusable and it'll also have its own name, making it easier to identify. In addition, putting the code into a separate function will provide us advantages in terms of things we haven't yet covered in this class — e. g. the code will be easier to test.

A good function name might be *registerEvents*, or even just *init*. If we wanted to, we could get even more specific and name the function *registerEventsForChatMemberHighlighting*.
However, given the context (i. e. our entire file is geared for a specific task) the generic *init* is perfectly acceptable.

The name *init* stands for initialization. It's a function which calls all other functions, acting as an entry point into the rest of the code in the program. We could essentially name the function anything we wanted to, but *init* has already been established as the name for such functions. Other programmers can read the function name and understand immediately what we mean by it.

Based on our newspaper metaphor, INIT's function definition belongs at the beginning of your code. However, the call to INIT() can be made only after all other function have been defined.

```
1
"use strict";

2

3

4
const init = () => $("#member search input")

5
   .addEventListener("keyup", () =>

6

updateHighlightingOfChatMembers($("#member search input").value));
```

```
7

8

const    updateHighlightingOfChatMembers    =
partOfMemberName => {

9

    removeHighlightsFromAllChatMembers();

10

    hightlightChatMembersBy(partOfMemberName);

11

};

12

13

const removeHighlightsFromAllChatMembers = ()
=>

14

    chatMembers().forEach(removeHighlight);

15

16
```

```
16  const hightlightChatMembersBy = partOfMemberName => {
17    if (partOfMemberName === "") return;
18    chatMembers()
19      .filter(member =>
20        doesMemberMatch(partOfMemberName, member))
21      .forEach(highlight);
22  };
23
24  const doesMemberMatch = (partOfMemberName, memberElement) =>
```

```
25    memberElement.innerHTML.toLowerCase()

26      .includes(partOfMemberName.toLowerCase());

27

28  const chatMembers = () => $$("#chat_members li");

29  const highlight = el => el.classList.add("highlighted");

30  const removeHighlight = el => el.classList.remove("highlighted");

31

32  const $ = document.querySelector.bind(document);
```

33

```
const                    $$                    =
document.querySelectorAll.bind(document);
```

34

```
NodeList.prototype.  proto   = Array.prototype;
```

35

36

```
init();
```

37

Listing 19 accompanying_files/05/examples/highlig
ht_chat_members_3_init/highlight_chat_members.
js

Take a Look Behind the Facade With the Event
Object

The fact that our current code can use some
improvements will become clear once we take a
closer look at event registration.

```
$('#member search input')

  .addEventListener('keyup', () =>
```

```
   hightlightChatMembers($('#member search
input').value));
```

The function we'll register as our event handler here is:

```
() => hightlightChatMembers($('#member search
input').value);
```

The interesting thing to note here is that the function, when it's called by the event, is automatically passed the event as an argument. So we just need to implement a parameter to capture the event:

```
event                                              =>
hightlightChatMembers($('#member search
input').value);
```

What can we do with the EVENT? One thing would be to print it out to the console to see what it contains:

```
event => {

  console.log(event);

  hightlightChatMembers($('#member search
input').value);
```

If you type the letter **a**, the console will show:

keyup { target: <input>, key: "a", charCode: 0, keyCode: 65 }

If you click on *keyup*, you'll see that EVENT is a JS object of "type"[1]KEYBOARDEVENT. Keyboard events have a number of very interesting properties — the table below shows you just a few:

1 In reality, JS doesn't have specific object types. It would be more correct to say that *keyup* is a JS object which has the KEYBOARDEVENT object in its prototype chain. We're using the term *type* here for purposes of simplification. It's only to show that all objects of the same "type" also have the same properties.

Property	Content
type	keyup
code	KeyA
key	a

timeStamp	[timestamp, i. e. when the event occurred]
target	[element which triggered the event]
ctrlKey	false [was the Ctrl key pressed?]
altKey	false [was the Alt key pressed?]

Events have many other properties, but just the few we've listed above show you that an event object contains all the information which comes into play when an event occurs, e. g.:

- What type of event is it? *keyup*

- What key was released? *a*

- When was the event triggered?

- From where was the event triggered?

Your event handler can then put this information to use. TARGET is the property which is of primary interest to us in our current program. TARGET contains the input field we intend to use, which we'd otherwise select by using $('#MEMBER SEARCH INPUT'). Therefore, we could also register our event handler as follows:

event => hightlightChatMembers(event.target.value);

Doing so gives us a number of concrete advantages. In all cases, it's more efficient, since your browser doesn't have to find the element object again — it's already in TARGET. But a much more important advantage is better maintainability. If our selector for finding the input field should change (e. g. because of a change to the HTML structure), we won't have to worry about also changing the event handler. It always refers to the current TARGET, no matter how we found the element and registered the event on it.

1

"use strict";

2

3

4

 const init = () => $("#member search input")

```
5
    .addEventListener("keyup", event =>

6

updateHighlightingOfChatMembers(event.target.val
ue));

7

8

  const    updateHighlightingOfChatMembers    =
partOfMemberName => {

9

   removeHighlightsFromAllChatMembers();

10

   hightlightChatMembersBy(partOfMemberName);

11

  };

12

13

  const removeHighlightsFromAllChatMembers = ()
=>
```

```
14
    chatMembers().forEach(removeHighlight);
15
16
const        hightlightChatMembersBy        =
partOfMemberName => {
17
    if (partOfMemberName === "") return;
18
    chatMembers()
19
      .filter(member =>
20
        doesMemberMatch(partOfMemberName,
member))
21
      .forEach(highlight);
22
};
```

```
23

24

  const doesMemberMatch = (partOfMemberName,
memberElement) =>

25

    memberElement.innerHTML.toLowerCase()

26

    .includes(partOfMemberName.toLowerCase());

27

28

  const chatMembers = () => $$("#chat_members
li");

29

  const        highlight        =        el        =>
el.classList.add("highlighted");

30

  const    removeHighlight    =    el    =>
el.classList.remove("highlighted");

31

32
```

```
const                    $              =
document.querySelector.bind(document);
```

33

```
const                    $$             =
document.querySelectorAll.bind(document);
```

34

```
NodeList.prototype.  proto  = Array.prototype;
```

35

36

```
init();
```

37

Listing 20 accompanying_files/05/examples/highlig ht_chat_members_4_target/highlight_chat_membe rs.js

FYI, we can abbreviate EVENT as E. Normally abbreviations are considered "bad" and should be avoided, but in this case it's okay. The single letter E is a common abbreviation for EVENT and is acceptable as long as its scope (range over which a variable exists) is limited to a very small function.

Now we're ready! You can finally show Marty the improved feature, and he's so happy about it he throws another party — here's to hoping it'll be an unforgettable event!

Chapter 12. A Storing Information in Variables

Learning to use Variables

In this chapter we are going to discuss variables. Variables are important elements of any programming language, and Javascript is no exception.

Variables are memory allocations used to hold values. They are called variables because their value may vary over time throughout the execution of the program.

You can use variables to hold text values (also known as alphabetic or string values) such as a person's name, company name or any other text content in your program. Variables may also hold numerical values.

To show you how variables are used, let's start with an HTML document page. For this example, we will use an HTML 4.01 document. To insert Javascript, a script tag is used with attributes set as follows:

<script   language="javascript" type="text/javascript">

All Javascript commands must be placed within the script element. The first Javascript element that must be identified is the variable to be used. We need to name the variable and declare it.

When you declare a variable in Javascript, you use the *var* statement followed by the name of the variable. It is ideal that the name of the variable is something that describes what the variable represents. The variable name can be any alphanumeric set of characters, and should be treated as case sensitive. No punctuation marks or special characters are allowed, except for underscore.

An example of a variable declaration is:

var userName;

It's not required to use the var statement when declaring a variable in Javascript, however, it is a good idea always to do so. Consistently using var when declaring variables avoids difficulties with variable scope.

We'll be discussing variable scope later in the course, but the short explanation is that there are variables that are only used within a certain segment of your program, such as a function. Variables can be declared so that their value is only retrievable within that scope.

Now that we have declared our variable, we can assign it a value. This is called *variable assignment*. When we set the initial value of the variable, it is known as *initialization*. Once you have declared your variable, you no longer need to use the var statement. All you need is the name of the variable followed by the equal sign and the value of the variable. In this example, our variable initialization is:

userName="Mark Lassoff";

The value assigned in the above example is a string, also known as text, which is why it was enclosed with quotes. If you are assigning a numerical value to a variable, you do not need to enclose the value with quotes. For example:

age = 39;

A shortcut method for simultaneously declaring and initializing variables is to combine declaration and initialization on the same line. This is a more efficient way of initializing and declaring a variable. Declaring and initializing a variableConcurrently is as follows:

var userName="Mark Lassoff";

We can now display the variable's value. To display the value of the variable you can use the *document.write()* command, followed by the name of the variable in parentheses. The command syntax is:

document.write(userName);

When you want to display the variable's value, you do not need to put quotes around the variable name (like you would if you were outputting text). Instead you simply write the variable name in the parentheses. If it is the actual string value you want to print, then surrounding the string value with quotes is a must. For example:

document.write ("Austin, Texas");

This will display Austin, Texas.

We can also change the value of a variable during the program's execution. Suppose you have displayed the first value assigned to your variable. You then assign another value to the same variable name and then have it displayed. The second value assigned to *userName* replaces the initial value.

So far, we have been assigning values to our variable with the equal sign. However, the equal sign does not mean "equal to" in the context of Javascript. In Javascript, the equal sign is known as the *assignment operator*. The assignment operator merely assigns a value to the variable.

We will discuss more operators and their functions in greater detail later on. The way we read the variable initialization in the previous example is that the variable *userName* was assigned the value Mark Lassoff. The value being in quotes indicates it as a string value.

When a number is assigned as the value of a variable, it is referred to as a *numeric variable*. This is an example of declaring and assigning a numeric variable:

var userAge= 37;

In the next section, we will use numeric variables to perform some arithmetic operations.

The complete example code listing for the above discussion is presented here, followed by a screenshot of the expected output when viewed in the browser.

Code Listing: Declaring and Assigning Variables

```
<!DOCTYPE HTML PUBLIC "-//W3C//DTD HTML 4.01//EN"
    "http://www.w3.org/TR/html4/strict.dtd" >
<html lang="en">
<head>
</head>
<body>
    <script language="javascript"
        type="text/javascript">
    //var userName="Mark Lassoff";
        var     userName;              //Variable Declaration
        userName="Mark     Lassoff";       //Variables Initialization
            document.write(userName);          //No quotes:  Output value of variables
        userName="Brett Lassoff"; // = Known as the assignment operator
```

```
document.write("<br/>");

document.write(userName);

document.write("<br/>");

    var userAge = 37;        //Combined
initialization/declaration

document.write(userAge);

  </script>

</body>

</html>
```

This is how the output appears in the browser. Notice how the names and age were displayed on separate lines. This was made possible by using the break *
* tags, along with the *document.write()* command.

Questions for Review

1. In Javascript, what statement do you use to declare a variable?

a. variable

b. declare

c. var

d. dar

2. What happens if you don't put quotes around a variable's string assigned value?

a. The script outputs the value of the variable.

b. You get an HTML error.

c. The script will not assign the variable correctly.

d. Nothing will happen.

3. Which of the following is known as the assignment operator in Javascript?

a. The + sign

b. The = sign

c. The – sign

d. The @ sign

4. Which is an example of combined initialization/declaration?

a. var Size

b. Size = 0

c. var Size; Size = 0;

d. var Size = 0;

5. Why is it important to use the var statement every time you declare a variable?

a. You will have trouble with variable scope if you don't.

b. Variables won't work without being declared.

c. It's confusing without it.

d. You shouldn't use it.

Lab Activity

1) Create a Javascript code that will display the following output:

2) The program must have two variables. The first variable will hold the values for the adult animals, *adultAnimalName*, while the second variable will hold the values for the young animal, *youngAnimalName.*

3) Assign one value to each of the variables. Have these two variable values displayed using *document.write().*

4) Use the following values for your program:

adultAnimalName	youngAnimalName
Horse	Pony
Goat	Kid
Dog	Puppy

Lab Activity Solution: Code Listing

```
<!DOCTYPE HTML PUBLIC "-//W3C//DTD HTML 4.01//EN"
"http://www.w3.org/TR/html4/strict.dtd"
>
<html lang="en">
<head>
</head>
<body>
        <script                language="javascript" type="text/javascript">
    var adultAnimalName;
    var youngAnimalName;
    adultAnimalName = "Horse";
    youngAnimalName = "Pony";
    document.write(adultAnimalName);
        document.write(":");
    document.write(youngAnimalName);
    document.write("<br/>");
    adultAnimalName = "Goat";
    youngAnimalName = "Kid";
    document.write(adultAnimalName);
        document.write(":");
```

```
document.write(youngAnimalName);

document.write("<br/>");

adultAnimalName = "Dog";

youngAnimalName = "Puppy";

document.write(adultAnimalName);

    document.write(":");

document.write(youngAnimalName);

document.write("<br/>");

    </script>

</body>

</html>
```

Variable Operators

In this section we are going to discuss variable operators. Once again, start with an HTML 4.01 file, and make sure you include a <script> tag to indicate to the browser that we are using Javascript.

First, we need to declare two variables as *operandOne* and *operandTwo*. These two variables will be assigned the values 125 and 15.371, respectively.

Note that they are two distinct value types. The variable *operandOne* holds the *integer number* 125, while the variable *operandTwo* contains the *floating point number* 15.371. A floating point number is capable of holding numbers with decimal points.

```
operandOne = 125;

operandTwo = 15.371;
```

In other programming languages, you would normally have to declare the specific variable type—you have to tell the program if you are using an integer or a floating point number. However, Javascript automatically understands what variable type you are creating the moment you assign its value. There is no need to explicitly specify which type of variable you are using.

With our variables defined and initialized, we can have them displayed as output using the *document.write()* command. Since you are instructing that the program's output be whatever the variable contains, you do not need quotation marks. Let us display the two values on two different lines. The code should be written as follows:

```
document.write (operandOne);

document.write ("<br/>");

document.write (operandTwo);
```

We can also perform arithmetic operations with our variables. To add the two numbers together, we use the addition operator "+". If we want the sum of the two variables displayed, then our code should be:

```
document.write("The sum is " + (operandOne + operandTwo));
```

The addition operator is used twice in this example. The plus (+) sign has two purposes in Javascript—it can be used as a *string concatenation operator,* and also as an *addition operator.* When we write *operandOne + operandTwo,* we are using it to add the two variables.

Concatenation, on the other hand, is also an important operation in any programming language. In Javascript, concatenation joins two strings or values together. In the context of this example, we are concatenating (placing next to each other) the string value "The sum is" to the sum of the two variables. The addition operation is placed within its own parentheses so the program understands that it is a separate operation from the concatenation.

Here is a list of the variable operators you can use and how they function:

Operator	Symbol	**Function**
Addition	+	Adds variables together and concatenates strings and other values.
Subtraction	-	Subtracts the value of one variable from another.

Multiplication	*	Multiplies variables.
Division	/	Divides one variable from another.
Modulus	%	Outputs the remainder of the division operation.
Increment	++	Adds one to the value of the variable.
Decrement	--	Subtracts one from the value of the variable.

The increment and decrement operators function by increasing and decreasing, respectively, the value of the variable by one.

There are two ways to use the increment and decrement operators. When the operator is placed after the variable, it is called a *postfix operator*. This means that the mathematical expression is evaluated and then the increment takes place.

The following code listing provides examples on how each variable operator is used.

Code Listing: Variable Operators
```
<!DOCTYPE HTML PUBLIC "-//W3C//DTD HTML 4.01//EN"
```

```
"http://www.w3.org/TR/html4/strict.dtd"
>
<html lang="en">
<head>
</head>
<body>
        <script              language="javascript"
type="text/javascript">
    var operandOne;

    var operandTwo;

    operandOne = 125;      //Integer

    operandTwo = 15.371;      //Floating Point
Number

    document.write(operandOne);

    document.write("<br/>");

    document.write(operandTwo);

    document.write("<br/>");

    document.write("Addition " + (operandOne +
operandTwo));

    document.write("<br/>");

    document.write("Subtraction " + (operandOne
- operandTwo));

    document.write("<br/>");
```

```
        document.write("Multiplication      "      +
(operandOne * operandTwo));

    document.write("<br/>");

        document.write("Division        "        +
(operandOne/operandTwo));

    document.write("<br/>");

    document.write("10 % 3 " + (10 % 3));

    document.write("<br/>");

    document.write("11 % 3 " + (11 % 3));

    operandOne++;      //Increment Operator Add
One to the variable;

    operandTwo--;      //Decrementing One from
the variable

    document.write("<br/>");

    document.write(operandOne);

    document.write("<br/>");

    document.write(operandTwo);

    /*

        variable++      <--- PostFix  Increment
Operator

        ++variable      <--- PreFix  Increment
Operator

        PostFix- The rest of the mathematical
expression is evaluated and then
```

the increment takes place

PreFix- The increment takes place and then the rest of the expression

is evaluated

```
*/
var teamCity;

var teamName;

teamCity ="New York";

teamName= "Yankees";

var  fullTeamInfo  =  teamCity  +  "  "  + teamName;

document.write("<br/>");

document.write(fullTeamInfo);
```
    </script>

</body>

</html>

In order to better understand how concatenation works, an example of concatenating two string variables and outputting them is demonstrated within the previous code. We have created a new variable called *fullTeamInfo* and concatenated the two variables *teamCity* and *teamName*. We also concatenated a space within the quotation marks so the two variable strings are spaced properly. The output "New York Yankees" is the result.

This is a screenshot of the output shown in the browser. Here all possible use of concatenation is shown; all four mathematical operations are also demonstrated including the modulus operator.

Questions for Review

1. What does the "+" symbol mean when you place it next to a numerical variable?

a. Add the values together.

b. Take away the values.

c. Concatenate the values.

d. Divide the values.

2. What does the "+" symbol mean when you place it between two string values?

a. Add the values together.

b. Take away the values.

c. Concatenate the values.

d. Divide the values.

3. What does the % operator do?

a. Gives you the sum of division.

b. Gives you the remainder after division.

c. Gives you the multiplication sum.

d. Gives you the subtraction sum.

4. Which is the increment operator?

a. −

b. *

c. ++

d. #

5. How does a prefix increment operator function?

a. It adds one to the variable.

b. The rest of the mathematical expression is evaluated and the increment takes place.

c. It subtracts one from the variable.

d. The increment takes place and then the rest of the expression is evaluated.

1) Create an HTML 4.01 document. In the document body, add script tags with the appropriate attributes to add Javascript code.

2) Declare the following variables (but do not initialize yet):

   firstName
   lastName
   age
   city
   favoriteFood

3) Initialize the variables with information about you. (Your first name, last name, age, etc.)

4) Create a variable called *operand1* and use combined initialization and assignment to assign it an initial value of 1555.

5) Create a variable called *operand2* and use combined initialization and assignment to assign it an initial value of 96.255.

6) Demonstrate your knowledge of the mathematical operators with *operand1* and *operand2* by adding, subtracting, multiplying, and dividing the two values. Format your output as follows:

1555 + 96.255 = 1651.255

The line of code that would produce this output is:

document.write(*operand1* + " + " + *operand2* + " = " + (*operand1*+*operand2*));

7) Demonstrate the use of increment operator with *operand1* and decrement operators with *operand2*. Display the results.

```html
<!DOCTYPE HTML PUBLIC "-//W3C//DTD HTML 4.01//EN"
  "http://www.w3.org/TR/html4/strict.dtd"
  >
<html lang="en">
<head>
</head>
<body>
        <script          language="javascript"
type="text/javascript">
    var firstName;

    var lastName;

    var age;

    var city;

    var favoriteFood;

    firstName = "Bob";

    lastName = "Smith";

    age = 45;

    city = "Boston";

    favoriteFood = "Continental";

    var operand1 = 1555;

    var operand2 = 96.255;
```

```
document.write(operand1 +" + "+operand2 +
"=" + (operand1 + operand2));

document.write("<br/>");

document.write(operand1 +" - "+operand2 +
"=" + (operand1 - operand2));

document.write("<br/>");

document.write(operand1 +" x "+operand2 +
"=" + (operand1 * operand2));

document.write("<br/>");

document.write(operand1 +" / "+operand2 +
"=" + (operand1 / operand2));

document.write("<br/>");

document.write("After    increment,    "    +
operand1 + " is now ");

operand1++;

document.write(operand1);

document.write("<br/>");

document.write("After    decrement,    "    +
operand2 + " is now ");

operand2--;

document.write(operand2);

document.write("<br/>");

/* Since there were no instructions to display
the values of the first five variables that were asked
```

to be declared and assigned, they will not be seen in the output */

```
    </script>

</body>

</html>
```

In this chapter we learned about variables, their declaration, initialization, and combined initialization/declaration. You also learned how to output variables.

We also discussed operators, which included the assignment operator and arithmetic operators. You learned that the plus sign (+) can be used as an addition operator or concatenation operator and also learned how to concatenate strings and variables.

Chapter 13. JavaScript Essentials

Since this chapter is quite dense, here's an overview of what you can expect to learn:

- Data types - how JavaScript classifies information. This is important because knowing what type of information you have will also tell you what you can do with that information (e.g., you can't multiply 5 with apples.)

- Comparison Operators - lets you compare certain types of information (e.g., is 5 less than 10?). This is useful when you want to give the computer instructions that relies on certain conditions being met (e.g., allow the user to register only if the age is more than or equal to 18)

- Console.log() - lets you display the output of a single line of code - useful when you want to see how information flows in your program per line of code.

- Flow Control - if-else statements give the computer different instructions to execute depending on which condition is met (e.g., allow the user to enter site if the age is more than 18, otherwise, display an error message)

- Debugging - when your program behaves erratically (e.g., misspelling the user's name or forgetting it completely), then you need to find which part of your code is messing up your program's behavior - this process is called debugging. This can become rather daunting when the code spans more than a thousand lines - knowing where to look will come in handy.

So far, you've played with strings and numbers using JavaScript. In the programming world, these categories of information are referred to as data types.

Data Types

Data types simply tell the computer how your information should be read. For instance, if you type the following into the console:

```
"5" + "5"
```

You'd get "55." This is because by enclosing 5 using quotation marks, you're telling the interpreter that you want 5 to be treated as a string, not a number. The addition operator, then, instead of adding the two numbers, combines the two strings. Now try removing the quotation marks and notice how the output changes to 10. There are different things you can do with different data types, so it's extremely important to know which one to use:

- Strings - Anything you enclose in quotation marks will end up being a string. This can be a combination of letters, spaces, numbers, punctuation marks, and other symbols. Without strings, you wouldn't be able to get the user's name, address, email, and other important details.

- Numbers - Self-explanatory; numbers are the ones you can perform addition, subtraction, multiplication, and division to, among other mathematical operations. Remember not to put quotation marks or you'll turn them into strings!

So far, we now have strings and numbers at our disposal, but remember the console output when you've tried playing with confirmation dialogues? Whenever you press OK, the console returns true, and whenever you press CANCEL, the console returns false. These outputs aren't surrounded by quotation marks, but they surely aren't numbers, so what in the world are they?

- Booleans - booleans are data types that can only be either true or false. This is different from a string or a number, because it helps the computer make decisions based on whether or not certain conditions are met. For example, if you want to prevent minors from registering in your site, you'd have to have some sort of code to separate minors from the adults, like:

```
var age = 17
```

```
age >= 18
```

The console, then, returns false because the age is under 18. Now try the following mathematical expressions out and see what you get:

```
5 > 10
```

```
6 < 12
```

The first line should return false, while the second line should return true.

Comparison Operators

So far, we've talked about three data types (numbers, strings, and booleans), as well as some basic mathematical operators (+, -, *, /). What you've just used to test out booleans, however, are comparison operators (<, >, =), which are extremely important in managing the flow of your program. Here's the complete list and what they can do:

> Greater than

< Less than

>= Greater than or equal to

<= Less than or equal to

== Equal to

!= Not equal to

To test out these operators, replace the '@' symbol with the correct operator in the following statements in order to make the console output true:

```
console.log(5 @ 1);

console.log(1 @ 5);

console.log(5 @ 2);

console.log(1 @ 6);

console.log(5 @ 5);

console.log(10 @ 5);
```

Knowing what the Interpreter is Thinking

Notice how the JavaScript interpreter only gives you the latest output of the commands you type in, so if you've typed in three lines of code that should have different outputs:

```
5 > 10
6 < 12
7 > 14
```

Executing them all at the same time in the console, you'd only get the result of the last line (false).

You can, instead, enter each line of code individually so you can see the output of each command, but this gets especially tedious in larger bits of code. When you get to more complicated stuff, you'll eventually run into more errors and bugs. When this happens, you'll want to know what happens in specific commands you give so that you can pinpoint exactly where things go wrong.

console.log() takes whatever code you put inside and logs its execution to the console. That being said, let's see console.log() in action:

```
console.log(5 > 10)

console.log(6 < 12)

console.log(7 > 14)
```

Now you can see the output of each line of code!

Flow Control

You now know the most basic data types, mathematical operators, comparison operators, and a couple of neat console tricks. In order to make them useful, however, we need to be able to manipulate the flow of commands. For instance, if you wanted to create a user registration form that asks for the user's name, email address, age, and password, you'd first declare the variables as:

```
var name;

var email;

var age;

var password;
```

Now we'd need to store the user's input. For now, we use the prompt function:

```
name = prompt('What's your name?');

email = prompt('What's your email?');

age = prompt('What's your age?');

password = prompt('Please enter your desired password: ');
```

Assuming you've entered the right kind of information in the data fields, the name, email, age, and password variables now have the right type of data to process and store. What if, however, the user leaves the email field blank, or the age field with a letter? We can't just let the program continue if some of the vital fields of information don't have the right kind of data, therefore we use flow control statements. The first one we shall discuss is the if statement.

If Statement

If you've already programmed before, the structure of an if statement in JavaScript should be almost identical to the one you're familiar with:

```
if (<condition>)
{
    <action>
}
```

If you haven't already programmed before, an if-statement basically tells the computer to do whatever is inside the curly brackets ({}) if the if condition is true. If we want to, for instance, prevent the user from entering a blank field, we can do the following:

```
name = prompt('What's your name?');
if (name.length == 0)
{
    name = prompt('You cannot leave this empty. What's your name?');
}
email = prompt('What's your email?');
if (email.length == 0)
```

```
{
    email = prompt('You cannot leave this empty.
What's your email address?');
}
age = prompt('What's your age?');
if (age.length == 0)
{
    age = prompt('You cannot leave this empty.
What's your age?');
}
password = prompt('Please enter your desired
password: ');
if (password.length == 0)
{
    password = prompt('You cannot leave this
empty. Please enter your desired password:');
}
```

The code can seem overwhelming for the first-time programmer, but when you read each line carefully, you'll see that they follow quite a neat and logical structure:

1)   First, since the prompt() function gives you whatever the user types in, you store the string

inside a variable so you can use it later in the program.

2)   The if statements check if the variable is empty by checking if the length is equal to zero or not.

A)   IF THE LENGTH IS EQUAL TO ZERO, IT ASKS FOR INPUT AGAIN.

B)   IF THE LENGTH ISN'T EQUAL TO ZERO, IT DOESN'T ASK FOR INPUT AGAIN.

Take note that this sample code only serves to illustrate how the if statement works. Under no circumstances should you keep using the prompt() function to ask the user for information.

Now, what if you want to do something else in case your first condition isn't met? For instance, what if you want to say "Your name is <name>. Got it!" after the user types in a valid name? Then we add an else condition, followed by a second pair of curly braces that enclose the second set of commands:

```
name = prompt('What's your name?');

if (name.length == 0)

{

    name = prompt('You cannot leave this empty. What's your name?');

}

else
```

```
{
    alert('Your name is ' + name + '. Got it!');
}
email = prompt('What's your email?');
if (email.length == 0)
{
    email = prompt('You cannot leave this empty.
What's your email address?');
}
else
{
    alert('Your email is ' + email + '. Got it!');
}
age = prompt('What's your age?');
if (age.length == 0)
{
    age = prompt('You cannot leave this empty.
What's your age?');
}
else
{
    alert('Your age is ' + age + '. Got it!');
```

```
}

password = prompt('Please enter your desired
password: ');

if (password.length == 0)

{

    password = prompt('You cannot leave this
empty. Please enter your desired password:');

}

else

{

    alert('Your password is ' + password + '. Got
it!');

}
```

Now your code sounds a little more human, as it responds better to user input. Try messing around with the code and see how the interpreter changes the output depending on the conditions met with the if-else statements.

Debugging

So far, you've managed to play around with variables, data types, mathematical operators, comparison operators, user prompts, confirmation dialogues, and alerts, and lastly, if-else statements. Don't worry if you make a couple of mistakes;

computers are intrinsically literal and will not tolerate the tiniest syntactical mistakes. That being said, here are a couple of codes that don't seem to work as intended. Change the following code snippets so that you can produce the appropriate output!

```
var name = "Chris";
alert('Hi ' + 'name' + '! It's nice to meet you.');
```

In this code snippet, the output is supposed to be "Hi Chris! It's nice to meet you." What's the current output and what do you think is wrong with the code? Notice that the console doesn't complain and throw you an error message when you execute this code. This kind of problem is called a 'bug,' because while the JavaScript interpreter sees nothing wrong with this code, it doesn't work as the creator intended.

Now try to correct this code snippet that contains both bugs and errors:

```
var name;
var age;
name = prompt('What's your name?');
if (name.length = 0);
{
    name = prompt('You cannot leave this empty. What's your name?');
```

```
}
else (name.length != 0)
{
    alert('Your name is ' + name + '. Got it!');
}
age = prompt('What's your age?');
if (age.length = 0)
{
    age = prompt('You cannot leave this empty.
What's your age?');
}
else (name.length != 0)
{
    alert('Your age is ' + age + '. Got it!');
}
```

This code is a distorted version of a previous sample code, so you may try to compare the codes and see why this one doesn't work. If you feel stuck, you can check out a program called 'linter,' which is a handy tool that checks your code for errors and tells you which lines have them. It's good exercise to practice your debugging skills now, because when you create more complex programs, debugging becomes almost routine.

What to look for when debugging:

Looking for bugs and errors can be quite overwhelming if you don't know where to look. Here are some of the most common mistakes programmers make when coding:

- Using '=' instead of '==' to compare two values - the '=' sign in programming is used as an assignment operator, which means that if you use this instead of the '==' sign, you end up replacing the value of the variable on the left hand side of the equation with the value on the right hand side of the equation.

- Misplacing the semicolon - just as periods end sentences in the English language, semicolons end statements in JavaScript, as well as other programming languages like C, Java, etc. If, for instance, you've accidentally put a semicolon in the middle of a statement, JavaScript would see the statement as incomplete and produce an error for it.

- Misusing the quotation marks - quotation marks tell the interpreter that you're using a string, so if you enclose a variable or a number in quotation marks, you're effectively turning them into strings. This'll lead to anomalies when you try to perform numerical operations onto numbers that you've accidentally enclosed in quotation marks.

So far, these are only the most common mistakes newbies tend to make, but along the way you should be able to see bugs and errors quite easily as you get more practice making more complex codes.

Recap

We've covered quite a lot of concepts so far, so let's review what we've learned:

- Variables and data types

  ○ *numbers - can be integers or numbers that contain decimals (e.g., 3.14, 5, 100)*

  ○ *strings - anything you enclose in quotation marks (e.g., "5", "I am a JavaScript master", "I love the number 7")*

  ○ *booleans - true or false*

In order to declare a variable, simply type:

```
var <variable name> = <value>;
```

You can also just declare the variable name without the value if you don't have one yet:

```
var <variable name>;
```

JavaScript doesn't care what type of data you put in. If you've programmed in C or Java, you might have been used to declaring the variable's data type (int, float, char, etc.), but in JavaScript, you can put anything in a variable without any problems.

Chapter 5 Pop-up boxes

◦ *alert("Hi There!") - you can pop-up alerts to the user.*

◦ *confirm("Are you sure?") - you can ask for a confirmation from the user.*

◦ *prompt("Type anything here.") - you can ask for input from the user*

- Flow-control

◦ *if-else statement - in a nutshell, if the first condition is met, then do whatever's in the first bracket enclosure and skip the 'else' part. Otherwise, go to the bracket enclosure for the 'else' condition and do whatever's inside it.*

Chapter 14. Regular Expressions

What are regular expressions?

Regular expressions represent a pattern. In JavaScript, regular expressions can be used to perform operations such as searching a pattern, replacing a pattern, checking if a string matches a given pattern or breaking of a string into smaller strings based on a specific pattern. In JavaScript, regular expressions are objects.

Making a regular expression

There are two ways by which you can create regular expressions in JavaScript, which are:

8. Using regular expression literal:

In this method, the pattern is specified within two slashes // followed by the character(s) which are known as modifiers. You will learn about what modifiers are later in this chapter; modifiers are optional.
Syntax:

/pattern/modifiers

/pattern/

If this method is used, then the regular expression is compiled when the script is loaded and thus if the regular expression is constant, this method improves the performance of the program.

- **Using constructor of RegExp object:**

  In this method, we use the 'new' keyword to initialize a new object of RegExp which stands for Regular Expression. The pattern is passed as the first argument to the RegExp constructor and the modifier as the second argument, note that the modifier argument here is optional too.

  Syntax:

new RegExp("pattern", "modifiers");

new RegExp("pattern");

If this method is used, then the regular expression is compiled at runtime, this method is generally used where regular expression is not a constant.

MODIFIERS

A modifier is used to change the way a match of pattern based on regular expression is done. Listed below are the modifiers and the details on how they affect the operation.

- i

  Makes the match case insensitive, by default matching done is with regular expressions is case sensitive.

- m

Makes the match of pattern extend to multiple lines one if there are more than one lines in the string that the match is being performed on.

9. g

By default, the operation stops after finding the first match for the pattern, but if this modifier is used the operations don't stop at the first match and thus performs a 'g'lobal match.

Simple patterns

If you want to match a sequence of character directly, then you can write it in the place of the pattern. For example, the regular expression /test/ will match any string with 'test' in it, so there would be a match for a string like 'this is a test, ' but there would not be any match for string like 'this is a est' because the character 't' is missing from the sequence specified.

Certain characters denotes something special in a regular expression like '*' or '.', if you want to match these characters directly then you need to escape them, i.e., add a backslash before them. So for matching the exact string 'te*st', the regular expression will be /te*st/. You will learn about all the characters with a special significance in regular expressions in the very next section.

Special character(s)

Here is a list of special character(s) that can be used for a regular expression and what they do:

- ^

  If present at the start of the regular expression, this character signifies that the following pattern should be matched from the beginning of the input. If the 'm' modifier is used, then the starting of each line is also tested for the match.

  For example, the regular expression /^test/ will not match anything in the string 'this is a test' as 'test' is not present at the beginning of the string, but the same regular expression will match with the string 'test is going on'.

- $

  If present at the end of the regular expression, this character signifies that the pattern should be matched with the end of the line. If the 'm' modifier is used then the end of each line is tested for the match.

  For example, the regular expression /test$/ will not match anything in the string 'test is going on' as 'test' is not present at the end of the string, but the same regular expression will match the string 'this is a test.'

- *

This character is used to match the expression preceding this character zero or more times.

For example, the regular expression /te*st/ will match 't' followed by zero or more 'e' and that followed by 'st', so the string 'this is a teeeeeest' as well as the string 'this is a tst' will be matched but the string 'this is teees' won't be matched since a 't' is missing from the sequence to be matched.

Chapter 15 +

This character is used to match the expression preceding this character one or more times, i.e., if the preceding expression occurs at-least once.

For example, the regular expression /te*st/ will match the string 'this is a teeeeeest' but won't match the string 'this is a tst' or the string 'this is a tees'.

- ?

This character is used to match the expression preceding this character zero or one time.

For example, the regular expression /te?st/ will match the string 'this is a test' and 'this is a tst' but won't match the string 'this is a teest' or the string 'this is a tes'.

- {x}

This form of expression is used to match exactly x occurrences of the preceding expression, where x is a positive integer.

For example, the regular expression /te{3}st/ will match the string 'this is a teeest' but won't match the string 'this is a test' or the string 'this is a teeeeest'.

3. {x, y}

This form of expression is used to match any number of occurrences between x and y of the preceding expression, where x and y both are positive integers and x is less than or equal to y.

For example, the regular expression /te{3, 6}st/ will match the string 'this is a teeest' and 'this is a teeeeest' but won't match the string 'this is a test' or the string 'this is a teeeeeeest'.

- {x, }

This form of expression is used to match at-least x occurrences of the preceding expression, where x is a positive integer.

For example, the regular expression /te{3,}st/ will match the string 'this is a teeest' but won't match the string 'this is a test' or the string 'this is a teest'.

- .

This character is used to match any character except a newline one.

For example, the regular expression /te.st/ will match the string 'this is a tOst' and 'this is a tZst' but won't match the string 'this is a tst'.

- [abc]

This form of expression is used to match any character or expression that is present between the square brackets.

For example, the regular expression /t[eyz]st/ will match the string 'this is a test' and 'this is a tzst' but won't match the string 'this is a tpst' or the string 'this is a trst'.

You can use ranges like a-z and 0-9 which matches all the character from 'a' to 'z' and '0' to '9' respectively.For example, the regular expression /t[a-z]st/ will match the string 'this is a test' and 'this is a tkst' but won't match the string 'this is a t9st' or the string 'this is a t2st', but the regular expression /t[a-z0-9]st/ will match all the strings mentioned in this particular example.

- [^abc]

  This form of expression is used to match anything EXCEPT the character(s) or expression(s) that is present between the [^ and].

  For example, the regular expression /t[^eyz]st/ will match the string 'this is a tpst' and 'this is a trst' but won't match the string 'this is a test' or the string 'this is a tyst'.

  You can use the ranges, just like in the above-mentioned expression, in this form of expression too.For example, the regular expression /t[^a-z]st/ will match the string 'this is a t9st' and 'this is a t8st' but won't match the string 'this is a test' or the string 'this is a tast'.

  - (abc)

This form of expression is called a capture group. The pattern between the () is matched normally but is stored in memory for later use; you will learn about this expression usage in methods like .exec() later in this chapter.

Meta Characters

These are the special character sequences that are used to match certain characters or range of characters. Some of the most used metacharacters are:

- **\w**

  Matches any word character, i.e., any alphanumeric character including underscore.

  - **\W**

    Matches any non-word character. All the characters that are not matched by \w are matched by this.

  - **\d**

    Matches any digit, i.e., any character from 0 to 9.

  - **\D**

    Matches any non-digit, i.e., any character except from 0 to 9.

  - **\w**

    Matches any whitespace character, i.e., characters like tab, space, line ends etc.

  - **\W**

    Matches any non-whitespace character, i.e., any character except whitespace characters like tab, space, line ends, etc.

Using regular expressions

Now that you have learned about how to make up a regular expression, we can move on to learn about how to put them into action. Listed below are the methods which you can use with a regular expression.

- regexObject.test(string)
  This method tries to match the regular expression with the string passed as the argument, if it is matched, this method returns true else false.
  Examples:

var result1 = /example/.test('this is an example');

var result2 = /example/.test('what is this');

console.log(result1); //prints 'true' on the console screen

cosnole.log(result2);//prints 'false' on the console screen

- regexObject.exec(string)
  This method tries to match the regular expression with the string passed as the argument, if it is matched, this method returns an array filled with information else it returns null. The returned array first item is the matched string and the second is the first capture group present if any and third item is the second capture group present if any and so on.
  Examples:

```
var result1 = /exam(pl)e/.test('this is an example');

var result2 = /example/.test('what is this');

console.log( result1[0] ); //prints 'example' on the
console screen

console.log( result[1] ); //prints 'pl' on the console
screen

cosnole.log( result2 ); //prints 'null' on the console
screen
```

9. string.search(regex)
   This method tries to find a match of the regex passed as the argument. If found, it returns the index(position) of the match else returns -1. Note that the index begins from 0, not from 1. So the first character's index in a string is 0 and the second character's index is 1.
   Examples:

```
var result1 = 'an example'.search(/a.p/);

var result2 = 'an example'.search(/55/);

console.log( result ); //prints '5' on the console
screen

cosnole.log( result2 ); //prints '-1' on the console
screen
```

11. string.replace(regex, replacer)
    This method tries to find a match of regex passed as the first argument if found it

replaces the match with the second argument(replacer).
Example:

```
var original = "this is an example";

//replcaes first s and a with 9

var new = original.replace(/[sa]/, '9');

//replcaes each s and a with 9, since the'g' modifier is used

var new2 = original.replace(/[sa]/g, '9');

console.log(new);//prints 'thi9 is an example' on the console screen

console.log(new2);//prints 'thi9 i9 9n ex9mple' on the console screen
```

We can also use capture groups in the regular expression in this function and then use them in the replacer string. If in the replacer string we use a $ sign followed by a number then that $ sign with the number is replaced by the capture group of that index. For example, $1 gets replaced by the first capture group in the regular expression and $2 by the second one and so on.
Example:

```
var original = "this is an example";

//places _ on both side of each s and a
```

```
var new = original.replace(/([sa])/g, `_$1_');
```

```
console.log(new);//prints    'thi_s_    i_s_    _a_n
ex_a_mple' on the console screen
```

In this chapter, you have learned about regular expressions. I hope you have got a basic idea of regular expressions in JavaScript after reading this chapter.

Hoisting

What is hoisting?

The word hoist means to lift or raise up by means of some mechanical device like a pulley, but in JavaScript, hoisting means that the functions and variable declarations are moved to the top of the scope or context they are declared in, i.e., lifted up as in hoist, thus the word 'hoist'ing.

The declarations aren't really moved to the top, they are just put first into the compiled code.

Variable hoisting

For example the following code:

```
x = 21;
console.log( x );
var x;
```

Really compiles as this:

```
var x;
x = 21;
console.log(x);
```

As you can see the declaration has moved to the top of the current context, this is what hoisting is.

Let's understand this with a more suitable example:

```
console.log( x ); // prints 'undefined' on the console screen

console.log( y ); // throws a ReferenceError saying 'y is not defined'

var x;
```

This happens because 'x' being declared in the current context, though it is below the console.log line, it is moved at the top of the context and as there is no assignment done to 'x', it is set to 'undefined' by default, whereas in case of 'y' it is not available anywhere in current context, therefore, a ReferenceError is thrown.

Note that the assignment operation is not hoisted, only the declaration is.

Example:

```
console.log(x);  //prints 'undefined' on the console screen

var x; // only this statement is hoisted

x = 21; // this is not
```

You must be wondering about, what if we assign the value to variable while declaring it, like 'var x = 21;', though here it seems that you are assigning value to variable while declaring it but in fact internally the variable is first declared and then the value is assigned to it, so it is equivalent to 'var x; x = 21;'.

So if you declare a variable like this below the line where it is being used but in the same context then only declaration part is hoisted.

Example:

```
console.log(x);  //prints 'undefined' on the console screen
var x = 21;
```

This is how the above code is compiled:

```
var x;
console.log(x);  //prints 'undefined' on the console screen
```

x = 21;

Function hoisting

Just as variable hoisting, functions are also hoisted. As a result the functions can be called even before they are declared, given that it is declared in the current context or scope.

Example:

```
test();
function test() {
console.log('This is a test');
}
//prints 'This is a test' on the console screen
```

It is to be noted that function expressions, i.e., functions that are assigned to variables through the assignment operator '=' are not hoisted. The case of hoisting function expression is same as assigning a value a variable, which has been discussed above.

Example:

Just as variable

```
test(); // throws a TypeError saying 'test is not a function'
testRandom(); // throws ReferenceError saying 'testRandom is not defined'
var test = function {
console.log('This is a test');
};
```

In the above example, the difference in types of error is caused due to hoisting. As visible the variable 'test' is declared in the current scope therefore its declaration is moved at top and hence it is declared, though its value is undefined at the point where it is used, so a TypeError is thrown which indicates that the 'test' is defined but is not a function, whereas the function 'testRandom' is not declared anywhere, so a ReferenceError is thrown.

Order of precedence of hoisting

Functions are always hoisted over variable declaration.

Example:

```
function test() {
//function code
}
```

var test;

```
console.log( typeof test ); //prints 'function' on
the console screen
```

Even if the position of the variable line and function line are swapped in the above example, the output will remain the same.

But functions are not hoisted over variable declaration, given the assignment is done above the line where it is being used.

Example:

```
function test() {
//function code
}
    var test = 21; //now assignment is being done
    too
    console.log( typeof test ); //prints 'number' on
    the console screen
```

Even if the position of the variable line and function line are swapped in the above example, the output will remain the same.

As mentioned this is valid as long as the assignment is done above the line where it is being used, when the assignment is done below, then the function is hoisted over the assignment.

Example:

```
function test() {
//function code
```

```
}
```

var test;

console.log(typeof test);//prints 'function' on the console screen

test = 21;

console.log(typeof test);//prints 'number' on the console screen

CONCLUSION

It is always the best practice to declare variables or functions on the top of the scope where they will be used to avoid any confusion, even though due to hoisting variable declaration will be moved to the top of the scope or context automatically.

Chapter 15. Basic Data Types of Variables

Variables have four basic data types. These are numbers, strings, Boolean, and objects. We'll skim through these types, because going in-depth in discussing them will leave us not time in learning your JavaScript basic codes.

- Numbers

In JavaScript, generally, all numbers are considered as 64-bit floating point numbers. When there are no values after the decimal point, the number is presented as a whole number.

Examples:

- 9.000 is presented as 9

- 6.000 is presented as 6

- 2.00 is presented as 2

JavaScript and other computer programming languages are based on the IEEE 754 standard, or the Standard for Floating-Point Arithmetic.

Number literals can be a floating-point number, an integer or a hexadecimal.

Example of floating-point numbers:

- 4.516

- 9.134

- 6.01

- 4.121

Examples of integers:
- 34

- 45

- 21

- 30

Examples of hexadecimal numbers
- **OxFF**

- **-OxCCFF**

Special number values
- 'NAN' AND 'INFINITY' - are JavaScript's two 'error values'

The NaN (Not a Number) error appears when the browser cannot parse the number, or when an operation failed.

On the other hand, Infinity is an error that appears when the number cannot be represented because of its magnitude. The error also appears when you divide a number by zero (0).

- -0 AND +0 – the -0 rarely appears, so don't get confused about these special number values. You can ignore them, for now.

- NULL – these are obtained when the browser cannot return a value.

2. Strings

Strings are data types that are typically enclosed in matching single quotes or double quotes. The elements can be numbers or texts.

- Boolean

These data types represent either 'true' or 'false'. Through the use of Boolean, you can find out whether a JavaScript expression is 'true' or 'false'.

The 'true' returns are generally obtained from expressions with true values, such as number equations and similar expressions.

In contrast, 'false' returns are obtained from expressions without true values.

EXAMPLE 1:

_(3 > 9)_

Of course, this is false because 9 is definitely greater than 3.

Example 2:

(2<3)

Obviously, the statement is 'true'. There's no need for an explanation on that one.

EXAMPLE 3:

(4=9)

A 'ReferenceError' will occurre on the third example. This is because in JavaScript language, and most computer programming language, the equal sign (=) is not a symbol of equality. The equal sign is used in assigning the values or elements of variables.

See next image:

When the correct JavaScript syntax was utilized, the expression returned with a 'false' value because even with the correct sign, 4 is still not equal to 9.

- Objects

Objects encompass all data types in the sense that numbers, Booleans, and strings can be objects. Data, such as arrays, regular expressions, dates and math are objects, as well

Objects contain many values and have properties (name:values pair) and methods (process or action). Thus, they are containers of named values. This name:values pair is called property (name) and property values (values).

They can be a collection of various different data.

EXAMPLES:

- student: "Johnson"
- country: "Sweden"
- street: "Reed Avenue"

EXAMPLE:

var students = {firstName: "Lena", lastName: "Dean"};

SEE IMAGE BELOW:

They are typically expressed in pairs as 'name:value'. Take note of the colon in between the pair, and the commas after each pair. The property values are in quotes, and the entire statement is in brackets.

Chapter 16. The window object

What is the 'window' object?
As the name suggests, this object represents the current window. All major parts of the BOM are the direct children of this object. For example, window.document (The DOM), window.history, etc. Note that each tab on the browser has a unique window object. They don't share the same object! Some properties like window size, which is the same in all tabs, have the same value and technically those properties are shared. The window object contains references to useful properties and functions that may not strictly be related to the window only.

Even though there is no strict standard for the 'window' object, it is supported by all browsers.

The default references to the 'window' object
Since the 'window' object is present on top of hierarchy with no other object present at its level, all references to the window object's methods and properties can be made without writing the starting of the dotted notation part, i.e., the 'window.' part. Example:

WINDOW.ALERT()

alert()// same as above

var x = window.length;

var y = length;

// x will be equal to y since the refer to the same property

All variables declared are actually 'window' object's properties

As stated above, even the variables declared in the program are the direct child of the 'window' object, and are its properties.

Example:

var x = 21;

console.log(window.x); // prints '21' on the console screen

The 'window' object's method references

Here is the list of the 'window' object's major methods and their description:

- .ALERT("MESSAGE")

This method is used to display a dialog box on the screen, a type of pop-up, with a message that is passed as the argument of this function. The dialog box this will open has only one button, which is "OK"

Example:

window.alert(" Hello from JavaScript! ")

OR

alert(" Hello from JavaScript! ")

Both of the above statements are equivalent.

- .CONFIRM("MESSAGE")

This method is used to display a dialog box on the screen, with a message that is passed as the argument of this function, along with two buttons which are "OK" and "Cancel". This method returns a boolean value. It returns true if the "OK" button was clicked and false if the "Cancel" button was clicked.

Example:

var val = confirm(" Do you accept our terms and agreement? ");

if(val == true) console.log("User pressed OK");

else console.log("User pressed Cancel");

- **.prompt("message", "default text")**

This method is used to display a dialog box on the screen, with a message and an input box where the user can enter a value, along with the "OK" and "Cancel" button. This method is used to take an input from the user. The 'default text' parameter is the default value of the input box in the dialog box. This method returns the value entered by the user in the input box if the user presses the "OK" button. If the user presses the "Cancel" button, this method returns 'null'.

Example:

var val = prompt("What is your name?", "Enter your name here");

if(val === null) console.log("User pressed the cancel button");

else console.log("User's name is " + val);

- **.open([URL,] [name,] [specs,] [replace])**

This method is used to open a new window. All the parameters in this method are optional. This method returns the window object of the newly created window. Here is the description of the parameters:

→   URL

This parameter is used to specify the URL of the page to be opened in the new window. The default value of this parameter is 'about:blank' which opens a window with a blank page.

→   NAME

This parameter is used to specify how the URL is opened in the window or the name of the window. The following values are used as this parameter:

❖   **'_blank'**: This is the default value of the 'name' parameter. If this value is used, the URL is loaded in a new window.

❖   **'_parent'**: If this value is used, the URL is loaded in the parent frame.

❖   **'_top'**: If this value is used, the URL replaces any of the framesets that have been loaded previously.

❖   **'_self'**: If this value is used, the URL replaces the current page and is loaded in the current page.

❖   **Any other value**: If any other value is used, it acts as the name of the window. Note that the name of the window is not the same as the title of the window.

→ SPECS

This parameter is a string which contains some attributes, separated by a comma, of the new window to be opened. You can specify things such as width, height etc. of the new window using this parameter.

→ REPLACE

This parameter specifies whether the new URL to be opened will replace the current URL in the history object list or not. It takes boolean values, true or false. If 'true' is passed as the value of this parameter, the new URL replaces the current URL in the history object list. If 'false' is passed, it does not.

Example:

var newWindow = window.open("http://mySite.com", "", "height=210,width=700"); // creates a new window with 210px height and 700px width.

• .CLOSE()

This method is used to close a window.

Example:

var newWindow = window.open("http://mySite.com"); *newWindow.close(); // closes the window as soon as it opens*

• **.scrollTo(xCoords, yCoords)**

This method is used to set the scroll of the window to the specified coordinates in the document.

- **.resizeTo(height, width)**

This method is used to resize the window to a specified height and width. The height and width passed as the parameters in this argument are in pixels(px).

The 'window' object's properties
Here is the list of the 'window' object's major properties and their description:

- .PAGEXOFFSET

This property returns the current horizontal scroll distance in pixels(px). It is basically the **horizontal** distance between the actual left corner of the page and the current window left corner.

- .SCROLLX

Same as the window.pageXOffset property.

- .PAGEYOFFSET

This property returns the current vertical scroll distance in pixels(px). It is basically the **vertical** distance between the actual left corner of the page and the current window left corner.

- .SCROLLY

Same as the window.pageYOffset property.

- .OUTERHEIGHT

This property returns the full height of the window, including the document, the toolbar, and the scrollbar.

- .OUTERWIDTH

This property returns the full width of the window, including the document, the toolbar, and the scrollbar.

- .INNERHEIGHT

This property returns the height of the content area of the window where the HTML document is displayed. It does **not** include the scrollbar or toolbar height.

- .INNERWIDTH

This property returns the width of the content area of the window where the HTML document is displayed. It does **not** include the scrollbar or toolbar height.

- .FRAMES

Returns an array of all the <iframe> element's in the current window if any.

Example:

<body>

```
<iframe src="https://mySite1.com"></iframe>
```

```
    <iframe
src="https://mySite2.com"></iframe>
```

<SCRIPT>

console.log(window.frames.length); // prints '2' on the console screen
</SCRIPT>

</body>

- .CLOSED

Returns a boolean value indicating whether a window has been closed or not. If the returned value is true, the window has been closed. If false, the window has not been closed.

Example:

var newWindow = window.open("http://mySite.com");

function isNewWindowOpen()

{

    if(newWindow.closed == true)return "NO";

    else return "YES";

}

Chapter 17. Maps and Sets

The map class is used to hold a set of key value pairs. The values can be primitive types (like numbers or strings) or object types. The syntax for declaring the map object is shown below.

```
var mapname=new Map();
```

Where 'mapname' is the name of the new map object. To add a key value pair to the Map, you can use the 'set' method as shown below.

mapname.set(key,value)

Where 'key' is the key for the key value pair and 'value' is the subsequent value for the key. To get a value from the map, we can use the 'get' method to get the value for the subsequent key.

Let's look at a way maps can be used through an example.

Example 64: The following program is used to showcase how to use a map class in JavaScript.

The following things need to be noted about the above program:

- We first declare a map object by using the 'new' clause and using the 'map' class.

- Next we set a key/value pair by using the 'set' method.

- Finally we display the value for the key by using the 'get' method.

With this program, the output is as follows:
JavaScript Program

The value for key1 is value1
Let's look at another example of using maps, this time using multiple keys and values.

Example 65: The following program shows how to use a map class with multiple key value pairs.

```html
<!DOCTYPE html>
<html>
<body>

 <h2>JavaScript Program</h2>

  <p id="demo1"></p>

  <p id="demo2"></p>

  <p id="demo3"></p>
<script>

var map=new Map();
map.set("key1","value1");
map.set("key2","value2");
```

```
map.set("key3","value3");

document.getElementById("demo1").innerHTML
= "The value for key1 is "+map.get("key1");

document.getElementById("demo2").innerHTML
= "The value for key2 is "+map.get("key2");

document.getElementById("demo3").innerHTML
= "The value for key3 is "+map.get("key3");

</script>

</body>

</html>
```

With this program, the output is as follows:

JavaScript Program

The value for key1 is value1
The value for key2 is value2
The value for key3 is value3
There are multiple methods available for the map class. Let's look at them in more detail.

Table 3: Map Properties and Methods

Property	Description
size	This is used to display the number of elements in the map

clear	This is used to clear all the elements in the map
delete	This is used to delete an element in the map
has	This is used to check if a map has a particular element or not
keys	This is used to get the keys of the map collection
values	This is used to get the values of the map collection

size Property

The 'size' property is used to display the number of elements in the map. Let's now look at an example of this property.

Example 66: The following program is used to showcase how to use the size property.

```
<!DOCTYPE html>
<html>
<body>

 <h2>JavaScript Program</h2>

  <p id="demo1"></p>
```

```
<script>

var map=new Map();

map.set("key1","value1");

map.set("key2","value2");

map.set("key3","value3");

document.getElementById("demo1").innerHTML
=  "The  number  of  elements  in  the  map
"+map.size;

</script>

</body>

</html>
```

With this program, the output is as follows:
JavaScript Program

The number of elements in the map 3

clear Method

The 'clear' method is used to clear all the elements in the map. Let's now look at an example of this method.

Example 67: The following program is used to showcase how to use the clear method.

```
<!DOCTYPE html>

<html>

<body>
```

```
<h2>JavaScript Program</h2>

<p id="demo1"></p>

<p id="demo2"></p>
<script>

var map=new Map();

map.set("key1","value1");

map.set("key2","value2");

map.set("key3","value3");

document.getElementById("demo1").innerHTML
=  "The  number  of  elements  in  the  map
"+map.size;

map.clear();

document.getElementById("demo2").innerHTML
=  "The  number  of  elements  in  the  map
"+map.size;

</script>

</body>

</html>
```

With this program, the output is as follows:
JavaScript Program

The number of elements in the map 3
The number of elements in the map 0
delete Method

The 'delete' method is used to delete an element in the map. Let's now look at an example of this method.

Example 68: The following program is used to showcase how to use the delete method.

```
<!DOCTYPE html>
<html>
<body>
  <h2>JavaScript Program</h2>
    <p id="demo1"></p>
    <p id="demo2"></p>
<script>
var map=new Map();
map.set("key1","value1");
map.set("key2","value2");
map.set("key3","value3");
document.getElementById("demo1").innerHTML
= "The number of elements in the map
"+map.size;
map.delete("key2");
document.getElementById("demo2").innerHTML
= "The number of elements in the map
"+map.size;
```

```
</script>

</body>

</html>
```

With this program, the output is as follows:

JavaScript Program

The number of elements in the map 3
The number of elements in the map 2

has Method

The 'has' method is used to check if a map has a particular element or not. Let's now look at an example of this method.

Example 69: The following program is used to showcase how to use the has method.

```
<!DOCTYPE html>

<html>

<body>

  <h2>JavaScript Program</h2>

    <p id="demo1"></p>

    <p id="demo2"></p>

<script>

var map=new Map();

map.set("key1","value1");
```

```
map.set("key2","value2");

map.set("key3","value3");

document.getElementById("demo1").innerHTML
= "The number of elements in the map
"+map.size;

document.getElementById("demo2").innerHTML
= "Does the map have the element key2 "
+map.has("key2");

</script>

</body>

</html>
```

With this program, the output is as follows:
JavaScript Program

The number of elements in the map 3
Does the map have the element key2 true

keys Method

The 'keys' method is used to acquire the keys of the map collection. Let's now look at an example of this method.

Example 70: The following program is used to showcase how to use the keys method.

```
<!DOCTYPE html>

<html>

<body>
```

```
    <h2>JavaScript Program</h2>

      <p id="demo1"></p>
<script>

var map=new Map();

map.set("key1","value1");

map.set("key2","value2");

map.set("key3","value3");

var text="";

for (var key of map.keys())

  {

    text+=key;

    text+="</br>";

  }
document.getElementById("demo1").innerHTML
= text;

</script>

</body>

</html>
```

With this program, the output is as follows:

JavaScript Program

key1

key2

key3

values Method

The 'values' method is used to get the values of the map collection. Let's now look at an example of this method.

Example 71: The following program is used to showcase how to use the values method.

```
<!DOCTYPE html>
<html>
<body>
  <h2>JavaScript Program</h2>
    <p id="demo1"></p>
<script>
var map=new Map();
map.set("key1","value1");
map.set("key2","value2");
map.set("key3","value3");
var text="";
for (var value of map.values())
  {
```

```
    text+= value;

    text+="</br>";

 }

document.getElementById("demo1").innerHTML
= text;
```
</script>

</body>

</html>

With this program, the output is as follows:

<u>JavaScript Program</u>

     value1
     value2
     value3

<u>set Class</u>

The 'set' class lets you store unique values of any type. The values can be primitive types, such as numbers and strings, or object types. The syntax for declaring the 'set' object is shown below.

```
var setname=new Set();
```

Where 'setname' is the name of the new set object. To add a value to the set, you can use the 'add' method as shown below.

setname.add(value)

To check whether the set has a value we can use the 'has' method. Let's look at a way sets can be used through an example.

Example 72: The following program is used to showcase how to use a set class in JavaScript.

```html
<!DOCTYPE html>
<html>
<body>

  <h2>JavaScript Program</h2>

    <p id="demo1"></p>
<script>
var set=new Set();
set.add("value1");
set.add("value2");
set.add("value3");
var text="";
document.getElementById("demo1").innerHTML = "Does the set contain value2 "+set.has("value2");
</script>
</body>
</html>
```

With this program, the output is as follows:

Does the set contain value2 true

Table 4: Set Properties and Methods

Property	Description
size	**This is used to display the number of elements in the set**
clear	**This is used to clear all the elements in the map**
delete	**This is used to delete an element in the map**
values	**This is used to get the values of the map collection**

size Property

The 'size' property is used to display the number of elements in the set. Let's look at an example of this property.

Example 73: The following program is used to showcase how to use the size property.

```
<!DOCTYPE html>
<html>
<body>
```

```
<h2>JavaScript Program</h2>

  <p id="demo1"></p>
<script>
var set=new Set();
set.add("value1");
set.add("value2");
set.add("value3");
var text="";
document.getElementById("demo1").innerHTML
= "The number of elements is "+ set.size;
</script>
</body>
</html>
```

With this program, the output is as follows:
JavaScript Program

The number of elements is 3
clear Method

The 'clear' method is used to clear all the elements in the set. Let's now look at an example of this method.

Example 74: The following program is used to showcase how to use the clear method.

```
<!DOCTYPE html>
<html>
<body>

  <h2>JavaScript Program</h2>

    <p id="demo1"></p>

    <p id="demo2"></p>
<script>
var set=new Set();
set.add("value1");
set.add("value2");
set.add("value3");
document.getElementById("demo1").innerHTML
= "The number of elements is "+ set.size;
set.clear();
document.getElementById("demo2").innerHTML
= "The number of elements is "+ set.size;
</script>
</body>
</html>
```

With this program, the output is as follows:
JavaScript Program

The number of elements is 3

The number of elements is 0

9.10 delete Method

The 'delete' method is used to delete an element in the set. Let's now look at an example of this method.

Example 75: The following program is used to showcase how to use the delete method.

```
<!DOCTYPE html>
<html>
<body>
  <h2>JavaScript Program</h2>

    <p id="demo1"></p>

    <p id="demo2"></p>
<script>
var set=new Set();
set.add("value1");
set.add("value2");
set.add("value3");
document.getElementById("demo1").innerHTML
= "The number of elements is "+ set.size;
set.delete("value2");
```

```
document.getElementById("demo2").innerHTML
= "The number of elements is "+ set.size;
</script>
</body>
</html>
```

With this program, the output is as follows:

JavaScript Program

The number of elements is 3

The number of elements is 2

9.11 values Method

The 'values' method is used to get the values of the set collection. Let's quickly look at an example of this method.

Example 76: The following program is used to showcase how to use the values method.

```
<!DOCTYPE html>
<html>
<body>
  <h2>JavaScript Program</h2>
    <p id="demo1"></p>
<script>
var set=new Set();
set.add("value1");
set.add("value2");
```

```
set.add("value3");
var text="";
for (var value of set.values())
  {
    text+=value;
    text+="</br>";
  }
document.getElementById("demo1").innerHTML
= text;
</script>
</body>
</html>
```

With this program, the output is as follows:

JavaScript Program

value1
value2
value3

Conclusion

In this book, I have provided you with the basic knowledge that you will need to start your journey in programming using JavaScript. The different concepts taught here, such as functions, loops, branches, and objects will equip you with the skills that you need to create your first JavaScript project. Also, continue practicing and taking on small projects to start improving your skills. Through the knowledge imparted in this book, coupled with practice, you will be able to work on building your own websites or coding your own projects.

In your further study, I recommend that you learn and take on advanced topics such as troubleshooting in JavaScript, explore different frameworks and libraries, and expand your knowledge in using regular expressions.

I would also strongly recommend that you learn other programming languages, so that you may be able to take your knowledge to the next level, and become a top-class programmer. Because you have gone through this course, you will be astonished to find that learning other languages is easier than expected, for JavaScript has strikingly paved the way for you. I recommend Python or Java as the best languages to learn next.

www.ingramcontent.com/pod-product-compliance
Lightning Source LLC
Chambersburg PA
CBHW051043050326
40690CB00006B/580